THE FAST RIDE

THE FAST RIDE

SPECTACULAR BID AND THE
UNDOING OF A SURE THING

Jack Gilden

UNIVERSITY OF NEBRASKA PRESS   LINCOLN

The University of Nebraska Press is part of a land-grant institution with campuses and programs on the past, present, and future homelands of the Pawnee, Ponca, Otoe-Missouria, Omaha, Dakota, Lakota, Kaw, Cheyenne, and Arapaho Peoples, as well as those of the relocated Ho-Chunk, Sac and Fox, and Iowa Peoples.

Library of Congress Cataloging-in-Publication Data
Names: Gilden, Jack, author.
Title: The fast ride: Spectacular Bid and the undoing of a sure thing / Jack Gilden.
Description: Lincoln: University of Nebraska Press, [2022] | Includes bibliographical references and index.
Identifiers: LCCN 2021036609
ISBN 9781496230508 (hardback)
ISBN 9781496231819 (epub)
ISBN 9781496231826 (pdf)
Subjects: LCSH: Spectacular Bid (Race horse) | Thoroughbred horse—United States—Biography. | Race horses. | Horse racing. | BISAC: SPORTS & RECREATION / Animal Sports / Horse Racing | HISTORY / United States / 20th Century
Classification: LCC SF355.S644 G55 2022 | DDC 798.40092/9—dc23/eng/20211004
LC record available at https://lccn.loc.gov/2021036609

Set in New Baskerville by Laura Buis.
Designed by N. Putens.

For the family who have made me so happy: my son, Max, because I am proud of him, and my courageous and talented daughter, Iliana. And also for Angel and Penny.

My doom has come upon me; let me not then die
ingloriously and without a struggle, but let me first do
some great thing that shall be told among men hereafter.

—HOMER

Contents

Author's Note

The reader may notice that I have chosen to include the full spelling of racial epithets in the story, particularly those aimed at Hispanic people. That was not a gratuitous decision, nor one I took lightly. Those references remain because I felt that they were critical to understanding the uglier aspects of the story and certain key characters that sent the central action careening out of control. For me, those epithets also point to the larger truth of what a serious and long-standing problem anti-Hispanic racism is in the United States. It cannot be, nor should be, covered up, sugar-coated, or censored.

THE FAST RIDE

Introduction

A great deal of light was shining, but it was neither the warm glow of adulation nor the harsh glare of the spotlight. It was the unforgiving noon sun crashing down on a small patch of dirt in East Baltimore and on the weary, unhelmeted head of Ronnie Franklin. Many years earlier Franklin had been an American sensation, emerging from utter anonymity to the front pages of newspapers and magazines all over the United States. After only two years or so of experience around the racetrack, he was already the dominant rider on a horse that won twelve straight stakes victories, set speed records, and won the Kentucky Derby and the Preakness.

But that was all long behind Franklin. Twenty-five years later, while yet another rider and horse were preparing for the Belmont Stakes and a run at the Triple Crown later that week, Ronnie was doing the grunt work, lugging heavy supplies and tools to a worksite where he was breaking up concrete, mixing mortar, and laying bricks and blocks on the site of an old gasoline station. His employer was "improving" the now empty lot by building a few new row houses in a city that already had thousands of them that were crumbling to the ground.

Franklin's unprotected bald head glistened under the assault from the sunbeams, and his eyes, without glasses, squinted in the glare, proof of his burdensome life. He was indistinguishable from any other laborer in America that day except for one thing. A newspaper reporter was there to ask him questions and write a story about how he had squandered his money and opportunities.

The reporter asked Ronnie a series of hard questions. He wanted to know about the former jockey's embarrassing loss in the Belmont Stakes, and he asked him about the cocaine addiction that ruined the rider's once-promising career. After that, the scribe also hunted down Buddy Delp, Franklin's so-called mentor and father figure, who had brought the boy into the racing world when he was but fifteen years old. Buddy had given Franklin a job at his barn, a bed at his house, and a seat on the best goddamned horse in the world.

Franklin earnestly blamed himself for losing the Belmont Stakes. He said he "got too antsy" lagging behind and chased an 85–1 shot, exhausting his horse.

"I probably rushed him," Ronnie confessed.

Franklin also led the reporter to believe that the trauma and "shame" of that bad ride in the biggest race of his life was the reason for his addictions. "[The Belmont] was a big downfall in my life," he said ruefully. "I held on to it."

Buddy Delp corroborated for the reporter that all the blame was Franklin's: "Ronnie rode that day like he was in a hurry to get the race over with," Buddy said for the record, never shy and ever the boss.

But about Ronnie's out-of-control drug use, Delp spoke in the nomenclature of a disappointed dad. He told the writer that he had cautioned the boy: "Ronnie," Buddy had said, "you better settle down because sooner or later there'll be some rainy days."

Finally, Delp mournfully explained how he had in the end fired Franklin for "blowing a $2,300 paycheck on drugs."

It all added up to a great yarn; the only problem was that none of it was true.

I came into the story as Franklin lay in an East Baltimore hospice gasping his last breaths. I was aided and abetted by one of his friends who had decided it was time that the truth came out.

Right away I could see that Spectacular Bid's story was actually two stories. There was the one that everyone knew. That one was about the miraculous horse who lost the biggest race of his career due to the ineptitude of his young, out-of-control rider. That narrative was formed during the Bid's career, and it was so powerful and pervasive that even many people in the horse's inner circle believed it, convinced either by lies or self-deceptions.

In just a few cursory interviews, however, I could see just how wrong it all was. Talking to people in a position to know, people who were closest to both Franklin and Buddy Delp, I could see a far different and more sinister story beginning to appear. The key to understanding Spectacular Bid's greatness and failure was all in the hidden relationship between Buddy Delp and Ronnie Franklin. If the bonds between those two men could be unlocked, the real story would emerge.

While the two principal characters were dead or dying by the time I began my exploration they had nevertheless left behind the spores of their existence, strands of who and what they really had been. I went to see their friends, their family members, and their colleagues. I talked to their competitors and their haters. And I spoke with members of the press from their era. I found people who had briefly but memorably brushed up against them. I went to the physical spaces they had inhabited.

The farther I paddled down the river of the story, into the dense jungles of the truth, the more I realized that nothing was as it had seemed. And every mistaken notion hinged on just one fallacy, and that was the supposed father-son relationship of Delp and Franklin.

Spectacular Bid's story may have been more about the father than any horse story ever written. The only question was: Whose father?

The Bid himself was the son of Bold Bidder and the grandson of Bold Ruler. Both were legendary winners and sires. He was owned by the father-and-son team of Harry and Tom Meyerhoff and Harry's second wife, Teresa.

Harry, then close to fifty, was an extraordinarily successful developer with a huge fortune of self-generated wealth. In Baltimore, Harry was also considered a town father with the strength and wisdom to guide things.

Tom Meyerhoff, then in his early twenties, still felt the sting of a boyhood in which his busy and distracted father was mostly absent, not present physically or emotionally. By the time the Bid came into their lives, Tom was still yearning for a closer relationship with his dad.

And Buddy Delp was the ultimate father figure. He was an iron-skinned man who mastered his career while also handling the burdens and responsibilities of raising two young sons all by himself. Delp was well respected by the press and horse racing fans, who admired him for outlasting crippling reversals and achieving the trappings of a winner.

Buddy was paterfamilias not only to his boys but also to a string of aspiring jockeys whom he generously mentored. The last of these was Ronnie Franklin.

Franklin was written up in the news reports of the day as though he was a Babe Ruth–like orphan, an urchin off the streets of Baltimore. Like Ruth, Franklin had parents, but he was painted as an incorrigible whose defiance of his mother, father, and educators led him to drop out of school at age fifteen for the dismal prospects of a full-time fast-food worker.

But Franklin's fortunes changed in a thunderbolt when a family friend brought him to Pimlico Race Track and presented him as an aspiring hot walker, the lowliest job in a community of low wages. Nevertheless, that's where Ronnie came under Delp's attention. Buddy took him into his home and then took him to the winner's circle at the Kentucky Derby, all in the span of about three years.

To the press of that era, the connection between the boy jockey and the tough-guy trainer was good copy. Reporters wrote cloying stories about Franklin and Delp and often referred to them as a "father-and-son team." Few mentioned, however, that Ronnie had a real father, Tony Franklin, a good man whom he loved and idolized. They usually failed to say he had been brought up in a clean and happy home where his hard-working parents provided him with every comfort that they could.

Even I wasn't immune to all of the talk of fathers and sons. As I wrote this story and immersed myself in it, it affected me in deeply psychological ways. For one thing, I couldn't help but notice that over the course of my work my own son passed through the same progression of ages that Franklin does in the book. My boy was about fifteen when I started researching and writing. When I finished, he had just celebrated his nineteenth birthday.

I tried to imagine the kid I saw in front of me, my son, in the same situations as Ronnie Franklin. When I looked at my fifteen-year-old, I couldn't imagine him out of my grasp and away from my protection. I couldn't fathom watching that boy risking his life to make a living. My son is a smart young man, but I had no idea how he would handle it if he was forced to speak on national television in moments of extreme pressure. I couldn't say for sure what he might do in the face of temptations like women and illicit drugs, especially if others were urging him on.

I tried to give my son the very best upbringing and stressed level-headed thinking to him. I often discussed with him the importance of making sound moral choices and stressed decency over decadence. But at fifteen or sixteen or even nineteen I couldn't say for sure what he would do in the moments when I wasn't looking.

My years-long obsession with these questions and thoughts even resurrected my own father, who visited me twice in incredibly realistic and vibrant dreams. My dad had been dead for a few years—he had had a stroke when he was in his early eighties—and yet there he was right in front of me, looking all of about twenty-seven years old, with perfectly barbered, shiny blue-black hair and a jawline drawn with a T square.

He came two times in the late hours before the Jewish high holiday of Yom Kippur. That was an odd and exalted point of arrival since we were both utterly assimilated. Yet those sacred midnight hours became his gateway to my mind and a symbol of our indestructible bond.

In his first visit, he didn't have anything of great importance to tell me. We only chatted about books for a little while, and then he was suddenly absent. I awakened happy to have seen him for a little while but with a tight and aching throat.

But the night before I wrote the very last page of this book, he visited me again. This time his words were a little more mysterious. He spoke to me about his deep brown eyes, so similar to my own, and he said he had an unusual request for me: "I don't need these anymore," he said, referring to his eyes. "I want you to give them to someone who can use them."

Well, the last I had seen him alive, he was wearing thick bifocals. When he couldn't find the elusive ketchup bottles right in front of his nose in our refrigerator, my mother used to call him "Magoo," like the old cartoon character who wore impossibly thick glasses but couldn't see a thing.

So I teased my old man a little: "Dad," I said with a laugh, "who would want your eyes? They don't work!"

But the next day, reflecting on the wild and imprecise iconography of dreams, I realized that his eyes worked all too well. I suddenly understood exactly what he was trying to tell me, and I am writing these words to fulfill his request.

In this book you will see the elusive true story of Spectacular Bid more clearly, and understand it far better than you ever have before because you will see it through a father's eyes.

As my dad knew, most men live their entire lives in there.

1 *A Steel Spine*

There were no horse trails where Ronald Franklin grew up; there were only highways and alleys. The grass didn't grow high or stretch beyond sight in rolling emerald-green meadows; it was sparse and opportunistic and bristled out of the cracks in the concrete or little openings in the mortar of stone walls. To the extent that it was cultivated at all, it was only in neat little backyards the size of postage stamps or in public parks that were bordered by loud streets buzzing with traffic.

In those days Franklin's hometown was called "Baltimore," but it was in essence two cities, two populations living side by side and separated by a river that rushed between them like a railroad track. On the west shore was the town everyone knew, the place where Edgar Allan Poe had written and died, where Johns Hopkins had built a world-famous hospital and university, and where Francis Scott Key had survived an all-night battle with a foreign invader to write a poem he called "The Star-Spangled Banner." That was the place where lawyers, doctors, bankers, stockbrokers, journalists, and business professionals of every stripe worked and plied their crafts.

On the east side of the river was an obscure place called Dundalk, a harbor and factory town to rival anything found in the sad pages of Charles Dickens. Its wheezing industrial chimneys jutted high into the sky like giant, vertical, unfiltered Marlboros, relentlessly exhaling carcinogenic plumes that floated inexorably upward, into the lofty heights of the atmosphere. Dundalk's perfume was an acrid bouquet that wafted silently and invisibly, infiltrating nostrils and walloping noses like a clenched fist.

In Dundalk the people lived in little houses and worshipped under low-slung steeples. They tirelessly labored in huge buildings and nursed their nights away on tiny little stools. When they worked, which was frequently and exhaustingly, they manned assembly lines or lifted and loaded crates and canisters, and they transported things. They had job titles like "steelworker" and "stevedore," "truck driver," "longshoreman," and "heavy machine operator."

Many Baltimoreans wore neckties to work. But in Dundalk, where the necks were thick and damp, a full Windsor felt like a slipknot in a rope. So the men who worked with their hands wore their collars wide open, and if they put on a jacket for a Friday night dinner out, it likely was a windbreaker with the name and number of a union local printed on the back.

The men and women of Dundalk manufactured automobiles, electronics, and appliances, among many other things, but huge numbers of them disappeared into the same grim and terrifying plant where they posted for long, grueling shifts, working beside hellish fires. They were tempered every bit as much as the steel they manufactured, and because of that, their product won two world wars and shaped America's great bridges and skylines.

This was the world into which Ronald Franklin was born in 1959, just two weeks before the Colts—named to honor the city's long and storied history in horse racing—won their second straight NFL title. He lived in that hard town with his parents, Tony and Marian Franklin, five older siblings, and, later, his nephew, Walter "Tony" Cullum, all shoehorned into a two-bedroom, one-and-a-half-bathroom house in the middle of a row.

Tony Franklin was a small and strong man. In his youth he had entertained thoughts of being a jockey, but the only thing he ever saddled up was the forklift he drove for the American Can Company. Tony was born Anthony Frankoviak in East Baltimore to a Polish father and an Italian mother. He came of age just after World War II, joining the navy straight out of high school and cruising to Korea for the war. Fully grown, he was 5 feet 7 inches, only slightly shorter than average, and athletic. He boxed in the service and remained fighting trim for the rest of his life, with muscles like steel cords in his neck, arms, and back.

Tony's great strength was undoubtedly a product of his life of hard work. In addition to the hours he put in on the forklift, he drove a moonlight shift in a taxicab and on weekends performed odd jobs and small home renovations for his neighbors.

After his stint in Korea, Anthony Frankoviak came home and reinvented himself. He banged away at his surname like a blacksmith, smoothing out the edges and halving the syllables. He shaped the remainder into the distinctly American handle, Franklin. Soon he met and married Ron's mother, Marian, who came from one of East Baltimore's many Italian families.

Marian was a maternal woman but also a coquette. She was wispy at less than 5 feet tall, with a head full of curls. Trim and flirtatious, she had an outsized and vivacious personality. She was a loving mother who kept a spotless, almost immaculate home for her family.

Marian's defining feature was her hot temper, volcanic but short-lived. Everyone who knew her knew she could flame up to a boil in an instant and then simmer down just as quickly. She passed down that flip-a-switch nature to every single one of her six children.

For Tony and Marian, Dundalk's paved, concreted, and asphalted landscape was their Eden, the place where they enjoyed their marriage, made their money, and raised their family. It was the so-called American Century, and it was such for good reason. The United States dominated in war, business, and building. And Dundalk was the steel spine of all three. Its blast furnace was "the largest . . . in the Western Hemisphere"—a point of pride—and it forged the raw material of warships, the essential parts of skyscrapers, and massive bridges.

As the United States prepared for World War I, Dundalk was the recipient of large shipbuilding contracts. Getting ready for the massive job ahead, the steel company bought a thousand acres and developed housing for all the necessary workers it would soon employ. The real building boom, however, didn't occur until World War II, when the workers came flowing in to defeat the Nazis and then take advantage of the opportunities and prosperity that followed.

After the war, between 1950 and 1956, approximately ten thousand new homes were built in Dundalk. The Joseph Meyerhoff Company built more than three thousand dwellings all by itself. Later on, Joseph Meyerhoff's nephew, Harry, would also become a developer and would purchase racehorses with his earnings.

So Dundalk expanded. The town grew to encompass thirteen square miles and 115,000 residents. The steel mill was the combustible engine that drove this rapid growth, employing more than thirty thousand people all by itself.

For many decades and generations, the steel mill provided a reliable, if dangerous, way to make a living. Author Deborah Rudacille grew up in Dundalk in a family of steelworkers, and she saw firsthand how demanding and dangerous life in and around the mill could be. She noted that the employees "worked in two grueling 10- to 14-hour shifts." Every other week, one team was forced to man a twenty-four-hour shift just so the other team could enjoy a day off. "They had two unpaid holidays a year," she wrote, "Christmas and the Fourth of July."

Relentless and exhausting, the work was also dangerous in the extreme. The plant once built a monument to its employees who had died on the job. It included 110 names. Even that scandalous number was an obfuscation, a mere "fraction of the thousands" who had actually been killed or seriously injured at the plant.

And it wasn't just the unfathomable numbers that were so horrifying; it was also the cruel way in which they accrued. "Many workers died gruesome deaths," Rudacille said. "[They were] burned, crushed, gassed, and dismembered. Others experienced a slower, though no less painful, demise from diseases caused by exposure to asbestos, benzene and other toxins."

The disease and loss of life caused by the plant was hardly confined to its campus. The residents and wildlife that lived nearby suffered too. Rudacille and her friends felt hemmed in "by industries that pumped effluent into rivers, streams and creeks." She said that "during the 1960s and '70s, a fine red dust coated [Dundalk]. . . . The local rivers and creeks, which fed into the Chesapeake Bay, became so contaminated with run-off that dead fish often littered the beaches."

The plant may have leeched its toxicity to the people, but it couldn't poison their minds against it. Decades after the well-paying jobs had dried up, former employees still felt a kind of "smoke-stack nostalgia" for the plant and pined for the heyday of production.

"Sometimes I think the danger of those jobs, the brutal heat and the terrible cold were part of what made the work interesting and attractive to people," Rudacille said. "Men have this thing about going to war and that camaraderie with [one's] fellow soldiers and proving [oneself] in this really terrifying and yet exciting experience. . . . I think something of the same thing was true at the [steel mill]."

But Rudacille knew that the allure of the plant went beyond its adventure or even the economic security it offered. The mill gave the steelworker something he or she might otherwise never have had: the dignity of a mission-driven life. "There was . . . the sense that the work they were doing mattered," she explained. "They took enormous pride that the steel they were making was helping to build America."

In Dundalk dangerous work was a crucible that hardened and enno-bled souls. If you survived, your reward was a roof, a car, and a sack of groceries when your cupboards were bare. And the mill was what made you that greatest and most esteemed of all people: a provider. And if you were one of the unlucky ones, one of the many who posted for the job in the morning but never came home, there was a sort of martyrdom in that.

The people of Dundalk represented every American virtue: hard work, duty, and manufacturing power. And yet Americans, and especially other Baltimoreans, did not see or understand Dundalk's pride. They looked on with skepticism at a community in a dirty shirt that reeked with the smell of hard work. To them, the Franklins and their neighbors lived in a white ghetto where the dialect, mores, and jobs had created a culture on the margins. So-called decent people aspired to higher education, a profession, and an expansive suburban life. In Dundalk they were happy to be urban dwellers and physical laborers. This created a class-based divide and a kind of peculiar prejudice.

One Dundalk woman recalled the humiliation she felt when she reported to college at the University of Maryland in the early 1960s. She met her scheduled roommate for the first time, an exciting moment for any two kids going to school. But the experience was ruined when the other student's mother realized that her daughter would be rooming with a girl from Dundalk. She called the school and maneuvered to get the room assignment changed.

Dundalk was not only the Franklins' hard world, but it was also the place that shaped their worldview.

Tony Franklin's Dundalk life wasn't easy. He worked constantly and earned little. He and Marian raised six children plus their grandson Tony Cullum in their small, brick-box of a home. They made it work with bunk beds and retrofits. They remodeled the house, constructing a kitchen in the basement so that the former kitchen space could be utilized as the master bedroom.

Despite these cramped quarters theirs was by and large a happy home. Marian's superb homemaking skills rivaled those of any mother on television. She kept her large family well fed and happy. Tony was at work most of the time, but he was a kindly and respected presence. Their home was a place that relatives and friends felt comfortable enough to filter through for parties, holidays, and other happy occasions.

Marian's sister Dorothy (called Aunt Dottsie by the Franklin children) lived only about a mile away in an almost identical house to Marian's and Tony's. She had her own huge brood, and on the holidays she brought them all over to the Franklins' to celebrate.

With the combined families inside, the small row home just about exploded. There were aunts, uncles, and cousins everywhere, all of them packed in and drawn together by the intoxicating fragrance of mother-made cooking. Marian and Dottsie worked all day on the meals, especially the spaghetti sauce, their signature dish. It was simmering on the stove even before breakfast, and it slow-cooked all day long until dinner. The sisters were creative sauce chefs who added unexpected flourishes to their product, such as pork spare ribs, cooked right in the same pot with all of the other ingredients.

These were all signs of an unquestionably close family. In the summer they all piled into the car and headed to a riverfront house on Sparrows Point, near the steel mill. The place had been passed down to Marian and Tony and provided them their own private beach. They enjoyed idyllic summer days there, swimming, catching crabs, and playing games on the sand. They also drove over the Bay Bridge to the Eastern Shore, where they took extended vacations in the Maryland resort town of Ocean City. Whatever fun the Franklins had, they had it together.

Ronald came late into this happy home. He was Tony and Marian's sixth and final child and was a particular favorite of both. It wasn't hard to understand why. He was an endearing boy with a tousle of sandy brown hair; large, dark brown eyes; and a lot of personality.

Ronald's close connection with his parents was encouraged by his small size, but his tiny frame was also a cause for concern. They expected that he would have a growth spurt, but it never arrived. Because of that he retained a childlike quality much longer than most boys, and his mother and father loved him all the more for this vulnerability.

But they also worried that his stature might hinder his success and happiness or—worse—be the symptom of some serious health problem. They took him to Johns Hopkins and had him examined, but the doctors determined that he was physically normal in every way. He just happened to be small; that was simply who he was. The family accepted that fact and moved on from it.

Ronald was Marian's baby; she cherished him, and in turn he loved her. But he looked up to his father and had a great deal of pride in his dad. The two were particularly close. Tony made the effort. He engaged his son in manly companionship, doing things with his boy that two pals might do together. Tony would fry up hot baloney sandwiches for them, and they'd chomp away while they watched baseball or football on the TV in their basement den.

One of Tony Franklin's few luxuries was a small watercraft he'd bought. He used it to entertain Ronnie and an assortment of his cousins. They spent entire summer days gliding around the tributaries of the Chesapeake, dropping trout lines into the brackish water to harvest bushels of scudding crabs.

Tony was an avid outdoorsman, but for him the real lure of the boat was engaging the boys. It transported them from the urban streets they knew to the flowing currents and tall grasses of the wild. These voyages took them all over the Chesapeake and connected the kids to the place from which they came and to each other as a family. For the rest of their lives the boys remembered these adventures with Tony, his leadership and kind companionship, the joy of discovery, and the appreciation for the outdoors.

Ronald particularly treasured those days with his dad, and he never let them go. Long after he was grown up and his father had passed away, he found comfort on the bay. When he needed solitude and relaxation, he rented or borrowed a boat to get away and catch and steam his own crabs. It was the most natural activity in the world to him, and it relieved the stresses of his life and career.

When his work took him far from the Chesapeake, Ronnie still required a taste of it. He insisted that Maryland crabs be shipped to him wherever he was. It's not hard to imagine the taste and smell of the unique Maryland spices triggering his memories of Tony and the simpler, more innocent days.

Ronnie and his friends also enjoyed a great deal of unsupervised time. The Franklins' Dundalk neighborhood was filled with young parents like Tony and Marian who had large families and brutally hard jobs. So on most days, the kids were left to their own devices to create their own fun and entertainment.

The children with whom Ronnie grew up did pretty much what kids everywhere did. They gathered together at the local playgrounds for games of pickup baseball, football, and basketball. They haunted the shopping mall. And they simply "hung out," doing nothing but enjoying each other's company and whiling the days away.

And of course, from time to time and in varying degrees, they also fell into mischief. Ronnie and some of the others were cited for throwing mud balls and dead fish into neighbors' swimming pools. Sometimes the kids met in the alleys to smoke cigarettes. They started with tobacco, but like kids all over the country they also found and smoked cigarettes they rolled themselves and filled with marijuana.

Everything wasn't easy in Ronnie's world. For one thing, he did not take well to school. He attended Patapsco High, a public institution named for the river that separates Dundalk from Baltimore. But he was academically incurious and impudent with his teachers. When he was bored, which was often, he refused to sit in his chair and upended the classroom.

There was only one place at school where Ronald felt at home, and that was on the baseball diamond. He made the varsity as a tenth grader, supposedly as a reserve outfielder, but his coach, Rich Bartos, had a specific and valuable role for him. Ronnie, listed at only 4 feet 7 inches tall, was used as the team's "designated walker." He was sent to the plate whenever Bartos felt his tiny strike zone could be of service and Patapsco needed a base runner. And Ronnie delivered. In six trips to the batter's box he walked three times. This skill, such as it was, made Ronnie a valuable addition to a team that struggled to score runs.

One of Franklin's teammates, Rich Cooper, was a behemoth. He stood 6 feet 4 inches tall and weighed 220 pounds. The unusual sight of two teammates scraping the extremes was not lost on the editors at the *Baltimore Sun* who photographed the boys together in a shot that deliberately emphasized their comical gap in size.

None of this offended Franklin or affected his self-image in the least. In fact, there was ample evidence that he had a far different view of himself and his ability than what others saw. He knew their view of him was of a shrimpy little kid struggling to keep up. But Franklin didn't see it that way. He believed he could be a useful everyday player, manning the outfield and taking a full complement of at bats. But it was his uniform that told the real story of his self-image. He picked out and wore 44, the same number that adorned the Braves uniform of Hank Aaron.

Franklin's size wasn't always so charming. It created problems for him in other parts of the school and out on the streets. "He was bullied [and] picked on," his sister Carolyn remembered.

Big, mean kids may have traumatized generations of small boys in the school hallways and playgrounds, stealing milk money and administering punches to the heads and stomachs of the small and the weak. But that wasn't for Franklin. "He was bigger than what these other kids thought he was," Carolyn said.

One neighbor learned that the hard way in the sparring ring of a local YMCA karate class. At first he had no particular fear of Franklin; they were long-standing friends. "I knew he'd never hurt me," the kid said. "A friend's a friend, right?"

But to Ronnie, a fight was a fight. He lunged at his buddy and ended the encounter with only one hammer-like punch. "That's all it took," the bruised kid remembered. "He knocked me out."

Ronnie's skill with his mitts kept bullies at bay not only for himself but also for his more average-sized older brother. "Ronald stood up for his brother and chased them all away," Carolyn said. "He never gave up on anything."

Nothing but high school.

The constant fighting and his inability to concentrate in class all took their toll on him. At first, he skipped a few classes. But after a while he stopped going to school altogether. While most of the other kids were in class preparing for their futures, Ronnie was a truant roaming the streets.

Tony and Marian were distressed. They had already seen five children through to their high school diplomas, and they were unsure how to handle their youngest son's brazen rejection of both school and their edicts. Tony was a stern father at times but far from brutal. He never raised his voice or his hand to any of his kids. He believed in physical discipline, although that did not include hitting his kids or whipping them with the belt.

Tony's creative corporal punishment was making a young offender kneel for an hour or more on uncooked rice that had been poured onto the kitchen's cold, hard floor. As the minutes ticked away, the kernels stabbed at the child's knees and dug into the skin. It was a painful if more humane punishment, and the fear of enduring it kept the other Franklin children mostly in line and respectful of their parents' rules.

But Ronnie was different, the exception. He went beyond typical teenage defiance and added his own odd, indomitable will. Rice-kneeling had no effect on him and neither did fear of his father's wrath. Ronnie loved his dad, and he respected him, but he defied him all the same.

Ronnie simply could not be forced to do anything that he did not want to do. And he did not want to go to high school anymore. "He hated school so much and skipped so many classes," Marian said, "we had no choice but to let him quit."

So at fifteen Ronnie got himself a job at the local Roy Rogers fast-food restaurant and officially became a wage-earning man. It didn't take him long to realize, however, that he was as miserable behind the counter as he had ever been in the classroom.

Tony saw this as a key crossroads in his son's life. He saw his boy was going in the wrong direction. There was every reason to believe that was true. Ronnie was officially a high school dropout, and now he was just another minimum wage worker in a city that was full of them. He hadn't gotten much out of the years he had spent in school. And he was still immature, with a huge chip on his shoulder.

Tony had confessed his anxieties about Ronald's situation to his close friend and neighbor, Hank Tiburzi. Hank was an angular, reed-thin fellow of Italian descent who wore a golf-style cap everywhere he went.

Tiburzi and Tony had a lot in common. They were both hard-working Dundalk guys. (Tiburzi was a tile layer who worked for himself.) And they were both married to tiny but tough women. Hank's wife was named Miss Lucy.

When the two men weren't with their families or at work, they spent a great deal of time together. They shared a mutual love for all sports and were fans of Baltimore's Colts and Orioles. But they especially enjoyed horse racing. On any given day Tony and Hank could be found together, hanging out at Pimlico, Timonium, Bowie, Laurel, or even Delaware Park. They liked to watch the ponies and risk some of their hard-earned cash.

The fathers' friendship extended to their kids. Tiburzi's and Miss Lucy's children were close in age to the Franklins' children, and they played and went to school together. Ronnie in particular spent a lot of time with the Tiburzis, and he saw Hank as a trusted friend and mentor. In fact, later on, many people outside the family mistakenly believed that Tiburzi was Ronnie's uncle.

Like any good friend, Hank deeply felt Tony's concern for his son. He thought a lot about Ronnie's predicament, and he ground his own gears thinking about how the boy might turn his life around. Tiburzi had one quality that uniquely suited him for that job, and that was optimism. While most of the people in Ronnie's orbit dimly saw his problems and limitations, Hank focused on the positive.

Everyone else might think Ronnie too small for many careers, but Tiburzi noticed the kid's ant-like strength. Others looked at Franklin and saw an angry kid. Tiburzi recognized a fighting spirit. Countless times throughout the years Hank had looked out his window and had seen Ronnie fearlessly facing down someone twice his size. Hank admired the quality.

Tiburzi contemplated it all and then, suddenly, he had a revelation. Ronnie wasn't an unmolded and unmanageable kid in a greasy fast-food smock. He was, in Tiburzi's imagination, decked out in a brightly colored silken shirt that rustled in the wind. He could see the kid high on a horse with his little clenched fist raised in victory.

When Hank looked at Ronald, he didn't see him falling behind; he saw him elevating. He envisioned the boy high above the concrete streets and the row house roofs, floating beyond the smoke stacks and even high over the cranes of the working harbor. What Hank Tiburzi saw in that tough, little, troubled kid was the raw, unfired ore of a winning jockey.

2 *The Crucible*

Beneath a nearly perfect November night sky in 1964, unseasonably cool with only the hint of a breeze, the workers along Laurel Race Track's backstretch milled about, relaxed, and performed small tasks much as any other night. But at around 9:20 p.m. the stillness and bliss of the evening was shattered as plumes of black smoke billowed into the inky night sky.

Sparks and flames leapt from Barn 21, a calamitous sight since the barn was an old-fashioned wooden structure with sixty stalls and more than fifty horses packed into it. In an instant, everything was pandemonium as a life and death drama played out right before the eyes of the grooms and other workers. Leaping up to meet their duty to their employers and to save the animals, they braved blistering temperatures and the blinding, choking smoke to free the huge horses who were now wild with fear.

But as they frantically labored to save equine lives, the workers set in motion an even more chaotic scene. Set free from their constraints, the terrified 1,200-pound animals reared and ran in utterly random paths. In the darkness of the night they crossed and collided at full speed and found each other in sickening thuds. In trying to save their own lives, many of the horses found death, not by smoke or fire but in the blunt-force trauma of their collisions.

Barn 21 was a crude structure dating back to World War II. In addition to the horses, it housed abundant supplies of hay and straw, natural accelerants, and heat generators, which efficiently fed the fire.

In the cool, breezy night it took less than an hour for the entire structure to be consumed.

But that was far from the worst of it. The next morning, when the smoke had finally cleared, it was apparent that thirty-four horses had lost their lives. Their carcasses still littered the Laurel grounds, polluting the usually bucolic atmosphere with the grim sights and revolting stench of death.

John D. Schapiro, the track president, offered no explanations for what had happened or why. He fumbled, instead, to cover his own ass. He made it clear that he knew nothing about the fire's origins, yet he could assure everyone that he wasn't the one to blame.

Was faulty wiring the cause? An errant cigarette? Or was it the most dreaded possibility of all—arson? No one knew, Schapiro said but added, "All possible precaution was taken *before* the unfortunate fire."

While everyone tried to square Schapiro's assertion with the horrific scene still smoldering all around—including the horrific site of the charred and distorted bodies being dragged away by tractors—there seemed to be a lack of concern for the future safety of the animals and workers. In his rush to exonerate himself, Schapiro didn't mention anything about the corrective measures Laurel planned to take to prevent similar tragedies from unfolding again in the future.

The one thing that seemed clear was also quite curious. The fire had affected one man like no other. The likable young trainer, Grover Delp, then in his early thirties and known to everyone by the friendly moniker "Buddy," owned thirty-two of the thirty-four deceased horses. In those few frightening hours he had lost almost his entire stable.

It was almost as if the fiery finger of God had reached out to smite just one blameless young man while sparing all others. It was an assault from above on one individual that in its vengeful ferocity and precision might have been inscribed in the Book of Job.

But unlike the troubled man from Uz, Buddy wasted no time mourning his dead or bemoaning his fate. Without self-pity or, interestingly, any stated sentiment, sadness, or regret for the fallen animals he'd spent years training, he was back at work in less than a day.

With the poisonous vapors still rising from the earth beneath his feet, Buddy confidently walked away from his past and went to that day's claiming races to begin the long process of replenishing his stock. At a claiming race, all the entrants are for sale, usually at a reasonable price. Many a frugal racing operation had been built on the cheap with "claimers," though the quality of the horses is generally considered low.

Only eighteen hours after the fire Delp purchased two horses, Brummel and C'est Sufie. Within three days, he had claimed nine new horses, and for better or worse he was back in business.

The other trainers lined up to kick him while he was down. Speaking anonymously to the press, they said that Buddy was "moving too fast" and that he was bound to "make a lot of bad claims." But Delp, who had already formed a reputation as a young comer, was at his most brilliant and proved them all wrong. Only a month later three horses he had acquired right after the fire won at Pimlico on the same day. By the end of the season, Buddy boasted ninety victories and, more than that, the overall-victory crown for Maryland trainers in 1964.

It was an unimaginable achievement. There was nothing comparable to it in the annals of American sports. It would be as if an airliner had blown up with an entire big league baseball team aboard, yet the franchise won the World Series anyway with Minor Leaguers filling the big league players' shoes.

In 1965 Delp would have an even more amazing year. Starting virtually from scratch with his new stable of castoffs, he hit the winner's circle ninety-eight times and once again topped the state in victories.

Right before the eyes of the fans and the press, a legend was born.

Buddy Delp knew something about bouncing back from tragedy. He grew up in rural Harford County, Maryland, about forty-five minutes due north of Baltimore. His perfectly healthy young father died when he drowned while swimming at a summertime family party. Buddy was only three years old then. His bereaved mother was suddenly alone, left to raise Buddy and his brother, Richard, all by herself. It would take six years before she would marry again, but when she did, it was to the successful Maryland horse trainer Raymond Archer. Archer was a strictly local guy, but he was well known and respected throughout the state, where he had been a consistent winner over many decades.

In all the years that he was growing up, Buddy had little to do with the horse business. In 1952, after high school, he was drafted into the service. The Korean War was on, but Buddy missed the Asian theater, and went to Italy instead, where he never saw any combat. When he got back home, Buddy enrolled at the University of Maryland and studied business, but only long enough to know that college wasn't for him. So in 1955, while he was still in his early twenties and with nothing else to do, he went to work for Archer.

Although Buddy hadn't really grown up in racing, it was quickly apparent that he had a talent for organization. He was officially listed as Archer's assistant trainer, but it wasn't long before he was in fact running the entire operation while his stepfather relaxed and took it easy. Archer enjoyed that Buddy was handling his affairs so competently. The old man took to coming in only in the afternoons. Eventually, he only showed up one day a week, and that was payday.

Despite Buddy's hard work and aptitude, he soon found himself struggling financially. Driving the horses as well as training them, he took an alarm clock with him on the road so he could sleep on the turnpike shoulder instead of staying in an expensive hotel. His money was so tight that he had to calculate precisely to make sure he could afford a greasy burger and gasoline on the trip.

Buddy soon grew tired of his arrangement with Archer. He went to his stepfather and told Archer that if he was to continue working for him, he needed to earn a little more. Raymond sized him up coldly. "When are you leaving?" he asked Buddy. It was a cruel blow, but the truth was that Buddy was so adept, he didn't need Archer anymore. He knew the best people to hire, and he knew how to run every aspect of the business.

Forced to move on, Buddy started his own operation, which was quickly populated by an expert staff. His payroll included an assistant trainer, a foreman, a traveling foreman, exercise riders, pony people, grooms, hot walkers, and a night watchman. He also had a Rolodex brimming with excellent independent contractors such as jockeys, blacksmiths, veterinarians, equine dentists, and even massage therapists for the horses.

Buddy also displayed an admirable generosity—or nepotism, depending on how you wanted to look at it. He rescued his brother, Dick, from the dead-end job of driving a clanking milk truck and gave him the unearned title of assistant trainer. Dick was quickly his number two man, though at that time the little brother had almost no formal training in horse work.

Young Buddy Delp was about 6 feet tall and self-assured. He was a little portly and preternaturally bald, with a swooping rim of black hair traveling from ear to ear around the sides and dipping into a cul-de-sac at the back of his neck. None of this seemed to bother Buddy very much. He never covered up or combed over a thing. He simply and unashamedly let the world see his fat belly and his denuded, salmon-colored head, as if to say, "I'm still a damn site better than you are." He wore old-fashioned black horn-rimmed eyeglasses—perhaps as a way of showing the world how unaffected and intellectual he was—loud sport coats, shined-up patent leather shoes, and a hound's tooth fedora in the manner of the gruff Alabama football coach Bear Bryant.

Buddy's comical appearance didn't prevent him from projecting power and control. He appeared every inch like the swaggering man in charge that he was. His composure in the face of the catastrophic events at Laurel had earned him the lasting respect of the fans and virtually everyone in the sporting press. And he handled the adulation with a great deal of humility and dignity.

Buddy gave the lion's share of credit for his miraculous comeback to the various horse owners who employed him. They were the heroes, he noted, the ones who believed in him and quickly put up the cash to back his resurrection.

Buddy was by no means self-deprecating, but he was not yet self-aggrandizing either. "My theories on training don't differ from [those of] most other men," he reasonably said. "If a horse is eating well and feeling well he should run well—providing he is in the proper company and not entered over his head."

That statement offered a rare glimpse behind Delp's magic screen.

His terrific success was based in part on a mild deception. As often as he could, he matched his talented horses against inferior competitors. "Surround yourself with people [who have] money and keep your horses in the cheapest company and you'll win a ton of races," Buddy preached in private.

That practice led to a circle of success. Rich owners acquired higher-quality horses. Good horses matched against second-class competitors led to happy owners. And happy owners brought more horses for training.

"Most people in the horse business made their money elsewhere [away from racing]," Buddy's second son, Gerald, remembered. "They got into the horse business because they love[d] the sport. What they wanted to do was win, not necessarily turn a profit."

"I train for people that can afford the game," Buddy said. "But I don't want to train for an SOB that says, 'Here's $10,000; make me some money.' I want him to say, 'Here's $10,000; let's have some fun.'" Gerald, unschooled in everything but the intricacies of the track, said, "Them people with money, they wanted to win, bring their friends out, get their pictures taken. My father knew how to play the game."

There was no doubt about that. Delp was a consistent winner for decades in all kinds of conditions and locations. He was hands on and involved.

Cathy Rosenberger worked for Delp throughout the 1970s. Cathy was petite. She was about 5 feet 6 inches and 115 muscular pounds, fresh-faced with brown hair, green eyes, freckled skin, and a delicately constructed nose. Despite her small stature she was a no-nonsense and highly focused horse professional. Cathy grew up on a small family farm in Rockville, Maryland, just outside of Washington, where she discovered her life's passion when she was only fourteen. That was the year she started riding.

As she became more deeply involved in the profession, she did just about any job a person in the horse industry could do. She participated in horse shows and hunts. She groomed and she galloped, she raced in relays (once as part of an undefeated team), and she judged races. Cathy married a blacksmith, and the two managed their own horse farm. She obtained her first trainer's license in 1968, and she was eventually licensed in four states—Maryland, Delaware, Pennsylvania, and West Virginia.

Cathy's job title with the Delp organization was "pony girl," someone who rode calm, well-trained horses that lead the thoroughbreds out to exercise and, at the races, to the starter's gate. She closely observed Delp over a number of years and saw him as a manager who tended to business well. "If he wasn't out watching the horses himself," she said, "he would always ask us back in the barn, 'How did it go?' He was always trying to get clues as to a horse's energy, enthusiasm, and how tough he was to gallop."

That information guided Buddy, and he used it to best instruct the staff in handling a horse. "[Delp] trained at the barn," Cathy said. "As the horses came around to go out to the track to exercise, he would walk over and maybe pat a horse and then run his hand down its knees and ankles to check for swelling or heat. Then he would tell the rider what to do: 'Gallop one mile [or] gallop two miles or breeze this horse a half mile today.'"

But in Cathy's experience the Delp organization didn't always show sound judgment. Buddy and Dick sometimes overlooked the advice of their staff. In one instance Rosenberger (then in her early thirties) and her pony led a strong young horse named DeBerry's Ticket out to gallop. Normally, she could hardly hold that strong and energetic horse. But on this particular day she noticed that he was sluggish. She practically had to drag him around the racetrack. That was a sign pointing to the probability that the horse was unwell. So when she got back to the barn, she reported her concern to Dick. "There is something really wrong with this horse," she told him.

But Dick Delp, the former milk truck driver, was her boss, and her opinion meant little to him. When she said that she thought the horse was a little off, Dick didn't pick up the phone and call the vet; he argued with her.

"I don't think this horse is well," Cathy repeated.

"Well, he ate up," Dick responded.

"I don't know," she said. "I just know there is something wrong with the horse. His eyes are cloudy, and he's lethargic."

As it turned out, the animal had an inner-ear infection. Because he wasn't treated promptly, the infection traveled into his brain. The horse had to be sent away. He almost died but eventually recovered and was claimed by a different trainer.

In general, Buddy Delp's philosophy was to drive his animals hard. His tough-it-out regimen would be considered imprudent by latter-day trainers, but even in his own unenlightened day, some believed that he pushed his horses too far. "When we got a good horse that was working well, had breeding and lots of background so that the potential was there, Buddy would start overtraining and really push," Rosenberger said. "In some ways he went back to old-school training; think of Seabiscuit. [The trainers] would race [the horses], and then four days later they would race [them] again. Now, if a trainer did that, they would send him to the nuthouse," she said.

This overwork took a physical toll on the horses, of course, but it also preyed on their psychology. The most poignant case was What A Summer, a talented filly from the mid-1970s. She was a fast runner with a knack for victory but a delicate equilibrium. What A Summer was a tightly wound horse, something recognized by both the exercise rider and the pony girl, but minimized by Buddy. He heard them when they said the horse was high strung but didn't really listen. Despite their warnings, he never changed his hard-assed approach.

In fact, instead of catering to What A Summer's quirks, Buddy ratcheted up the pressure on her. "She was a sprint horse, and she was getting crazier by the day," Rosenberger remembered. "But he just kept pushing her and pushing her."

Finally, with the tension increasing daily, What A Summer snapped. One morning during a half-mile breeze, she suddenly bolted across the Laurel track. Exercise rider Lyn Raymond was powerless to control her. The crazed horse galloped to the outside fence and didn't stop until she had rammed the barrier. Raymond was thrown as though she had been vaulted through the windshield in a car wreck. She went over the fence and landed hard in a concrete drainage ditch on the other side.

Rosenberger looked on in horror. She ran over to help her friend and saw her lying lifelessly in the ravine. Cathy thought that Raymond was dead. She wasn't moving, and her eyes had rolled back into her head. Track workers rushed to her aid, found she was breathing, and called an ambulance.

After it was all over, Buddy walked out to examine the scene of the tragedy. He found Lyn's hard protective helmet still lying on the ground. He stooped down, picked it up by the strap, and went back to the barn with it. Inside he walked deliberately to What A Summer's stall and, still holding the helmet by its strap, whipped her over and over with the hard shell.

What A Summer's owner, Milton Polinger, soon passed away, and the horse was put up for auction. It was purchased by Diana Firestone and so moved on from Buddy Delp's stable to the renowned trainer LeRoy Jolley. The change did wonders for her. Under Jolley, What A Summer was named Maryland-Bred Horse of the Year and Champion Older Mare two times.

Delp's view of the horses, no matter how good they were, was unsentimental and simple. They had to win. He understood that they were living beings with the ability to feel pain, but all of that was subordinated by his need to earn a living. Buddy was focused on his own success, and he had no pity for the animals if their problems stood in his way. The pressure for victory was great and led to some cruel and even illegal training methods.

Cathy found this out when "Mo" Hall, Buddy's top groom, approached her and asked her to pick up supplies for him at the local Southern States store. "I need some horse feed," he told her. And then, handing her an extra twenty-dollar bill, he made an unusual request: "Also, I want you to pick up an electric cattle prod for me," he told her.

Cathy didn't know why Mo would want one, but to her it was no big deal. She had seen them in use before, once while watching ranch hands move cattle along. It was a simple instrument, nothing more than a long metal tube with six "C" batteries inside of it for power. When the cattle, with their thick hides, were struck by the prod, they barely reacted to the jolts.

But when Rosenberger brought the device back to Buddy's operation, she was horrified to see Mo use the instrument on the thoroughbreds.

Operating surreptitiously in the privacy of the stalls, he held the horses by their bridles with his right hand and with his left shocked them on their withers.

The horses took it far differently than the cows had. Cathy saw the electrical charges surge through the thoroughbreds. They jumped violently at the jolts and slammed their huge bodies and heads against the walls. The object of the brutal practice was to awaken the horses' senses and make them run faster when they got out on the track.

The practice was more than just cruel; it was highly illegal. If discovered, it would have resulted in a permanent ban for whoever was deemed responsible. Buddy knew this and insulated himself from any potential accusation or consequences. The word around the barn was that he had made a deal with Mo. The groom handled the cattle prod. If he was ever caught and ruled off for the infraction, it was said that Buddy would provide him a solid income for the rest of his life. The main thing was that Mo keep his mouth shut so that the practice was never traced back to Delp.

All of this was invisible to the press and fans. To them, Buddy was a survivor and a winner. He was an admirable figure and good copy. That was all they knew or cared to know.

But the life could be as hard on Buddy as it was on his horses. For one thing, his wife struggled with mental illness and eventually left him and their two young sons, Doug and Gerald, behind. Buddy, like his mother before him, had to deal with the strains and stresses of being a single parent. By all appearances he did a yeoman's job of it. Even without his wife, he kept his family intact and looked after his boys himself. His career success afforded them all a handsome home and a comfortable life. As Buddy became more successful and affluent, he could afford the luxuries. In contrast to the Franklins' home back in Dundalk, where they struggled to find enough bedrooms, his house had ample sleeping space and even a large, well-appointed game room.

Buddy lived in Laurel's best neighborhood, Hillandale, not far from the track, where his neighbors included respectable figures such as Judge Audrey Melbourne and her husband, Pete Melbourne, a real estate broker. The Melbournes owned thoroughbreds that were trained by Delp. The well-known jockey Bill Passmore also lived close by, and the community was filled with many successful professional people.

Despite the outward appearance of a family coping in adverse circumstances, the Delps were an unorthodox unit. Buddy's single-minded zeal for his work made him ill equipped to oversee young boys on a full-time basis. Because his ambitions revolved around the track, his sons inevitably spent most of their time there too. This came at the expense of conventional childhood activities like sports and friendships.

The Delp boys spent their days conversing with jockeys, examining horseflesh, and discussing wagers and long shots. Gerald, the younger and therefore the more impressionable, took on the qualities of a railbird, something one of his fourth-grade classmates noticed.

"How was school today?" the boy's father asked him over the dinner table.

"Good!" he said. "Gerald had a wad of hundred-dollar bills in his pocket."

By the time he was fourteen, Gerald had saved enough of those bills to pay $3,000 for his own racehorse, Cocktail Ange. Gerald's horse had more advantages than most others since it was trained by Buddy and ridden by Chris McCarron. Both were future Hall of Famers.

Gerald's brother, Doug Delp, apparently required more horsepower than Gerald did. He owned a Pontiac Firebird while he was still just a teenager. He used his hotrod to aggravate the grooms and horses. He'd loudly rev his engine in close proximity to the barn and then make swooping circles in the dirt with it—called donuts—near the stable area.

Most kids might have seen the track as a fun diversion from their regular lives (if their parents even allowed them to go there), but for Gerald the excitement and easy cash became an obsession. He eventually lost all interest in other activities, especially school. At age fifteen he simply refused to go to class anymore, and with the knowledge, if not the blessing, of his father, he quit school for good.

Years later Gerald reflected on how Buddy had raised him. "Was it an ideal household? Heeeeellll no," he said, drawling out the answer to his own question. "My father did the best he could with what he had."

Buddy's brand of fatherhood extended beyond his own boys; he eventually, reluctantly, became the mentor to a string of young jockeys. On the surface his impulse to tutor these boys was noble and altruistic. The reporters certainly saw it that way. They presented it as the story of a successful expert at midlife passing on his knowledge and experience to eager young men hungering for opportunity. And yet, without exception, these forays all ended poorly.

For years Delp had claimed that training jockeys wasn't worth his time. "I don't like to make riders," he'd say. "There are always good ones around already made."

But Buddy relaxed that rule for the first time in the late 1960s, when Kitty Moon, a friend of his and the secretary to the stewards at Laurel Race Track, told him all about her girlfriend's son, George Cusimano. He was fifteen years old, she said, and his dream was to be a jockey. Cusimano's father had also been a rider, but the old man wasn't there to show him the ropes. The old man had left the family cold when George was still very young, and he rarely ever came back around.

Delp accepted Cusimano as a protégé, a favor, as he often said, to Kitty. The kid, Buddy said, "knew nothing about riding when he arrived." So for two years George mucked stalls, walked horses, cleaned the tack, and rubbed down the animals. After years of this, Buddy made George an exercise rider. And then, finally, the kid became an apprentice jockey.

When George turned seventeen, Buddy felt that he was ready for real race riding. And he was. George rode his first winner in late December 1967, at Laurel. In 1968 George was the leading apprentice jockey in the United States. That same year he made history at Delaware Park when he rode six winners in a single day. All told, Cusimano won 290 races in 1968 and brought home more purse money than any apprentice in history to that point.

Although Buddy was described as George's "father figure"—a characterization that the trainer embraced—the arrangement wasn't really close to that. The fallacy was borne out by the fact that George and Buddy dated the same woman, Regina. She started out as Cusimano's girlfriend but ended up as the second Mrs. Delp.

It was an era when many young men Cusimano's age were drafted into the service and sent to Vietnam. George was spared that horrifying obligation by the same virtues that made him a successful rider. At nineteen he was only ninety-four pounds. The army gave him a six-month deferment so that he had "time to grow."

Cusimano never went to Vietnam. He continued as a contract rider for Delp and later as an independent jockey. In his early, successful years, he was highly respected, and Delp often praised him liberally. He compared the young rider's hand work to that of highly respected veterans with national reputations like Angel Cordero Jr. and Jorge Velasquez. He also spoke of Cusimano's fearlessness in willing to race on the inside, by the rail, where things got tight. "What I like most about my jockey," Buddy said, "is that he wins so many races by saving ground." It was a tip of the trainer's fedora to his young jockey's courage.

In 1973 the whole world could see how much faith Buddy had in Cusimano. Buddy asked the kid to ride Ecole Etage in the Preakness Stakes. The fine young colt belonged to Robert and Harry Meyerhoff, two of Buddy's most important clients. The Preakness was the biggest race any of them had yet reached.

It looked like a good decision at the first turn. Cusimano and Ecole Etage led the field. But then a horse emerged from the group, kicked into gear, and streaked past them like a blur. It was Secretariat in the midst of his historic Triple Crown. Ecole Etage finished fourth, and whatever fame he earned was in his all too brief proximity to Secretariat.

Cusimano's success didn't prevent him from being Buddy's beast of burden. The paternalistic Delp insisted that the rider, despite his growing reputation, continue to do menial jobs around the barns, as he had when he was younger. Buddy paid Cusimano, a Preakness jockey, the parsimonious sum of $70 per week to do grunt work. Delp explained the unusual arrangement much like a concerned father would. He bragged that the stingy fee he paid George was a character builder. That money was for living expenses, while the money the jockey earned race riding was placed in "sound investments" chosen by Buddy himself.

All of this was very good publicity for Delp, and the press painted him in sympathetic hues. Not only was Buddy a successful breaker of horses; it appeared he was also a stern but loving molder of men.

Buddy had certainly taught the young, uneducated George, a boy with few other paths to opportunity, how to make an outsized living. But did he ever pass on a sense of the career's pitfalls and problems?

By age twenty-six Cusimano was married with a little boy and a baby girl on the way. But his life at home wasn't easy. His wife, June, and his mother did not get along, and in fact, they barely spoke to each other.

George dealt with his many career and personal stresses with drugs. He drank heavily, smoked marijuana liberally, and gulped pills. As his dependency on these habits grew, his career went in the wrong direction. By 1977 he was already overshadowed by ascending young riders such as Vince Bracciale and, especially, Chris McCarron, who was recognized by virtually everyone in racing as a special talent.

While these riders gained national attention, Cusimano slipped far off the radar. He was only the eighth leading jockey in the standings at Delaware Park.

On September 3, 1977, at Delaware, Cusimano continued his downward trend. He rode five horses that dreary day, finishing second on one and completely out of the money on the other four.

After the work was done, George and his agent, Larry Waters, were scheduled to play softball in the "backstretch league," one of many fun diversions track officials organized to keep employees entertained and out of trouble. But before the game Cusimano and Waters met up in the jockeys' parking lot to down a few beers. As they drank, they got out of control, bragging and goading each other into a drag race. Finally, they jumped into their cars, and leaving their friends behind, they drove to a spot behind the grandstand. In their inebriated states they had peered out on the long, smooth stretch of uninterrupted asphalt and saw a motor raceway.

Cusimano wasn't a great driver. He had only recently wrecked his Cadillac, which meant that he was driving June's Opel. A popular model in its era, the Opel was manufactured by General Motors to be a sports car for the masses. GM copywriters bragged that it was a "spirited" vehicle of "uncomplicated excitement."

But George was about to find out otherwise.

He hopped behind the wheel of June's vehicle, revved the engine, and sped off into his impromptu competition. In the heat of the race, he lost control, and in a thunderous collision smashed into a tree beside the road. His small, slick machine no longer resembled a car; it was a grotesquery of twisted steel.

Firemen rushed to the scene, but they were too late. They cut and pried the shell open just so that they could lift out Cusimano's already lifeless body.

Because George had been a popular figure around the Maryland and Delaware tracks, his sad death was reported in Baltimore, Washington, and Wilmington newspapers, and a day of tribute was hastily arranged for him at Bowie Race Track.

If Buddy grieved the death of his protégé, he didn't agonize about it very long. Just one month after the accident he was interviewed for a *Washington Post* article. Sorely lacking in either sentiment or discretion, Delp brutalized the kid's memory. "George . . . had a terrible temper," Buddy said. "I think that is what kept him from making it to the top. If a horse would run bad, or if George got himself in a tough spot during a race, and it happened early on in the program, that would affect his riding the rest of the day."

Delp criticized more than Cusimano's riding skills. He also attacked the rider's character, claiming he was barbaric with the animals. "[George] would get so mad at times," Delp said, "that he'd abuse a horse with his whip."

Buddy also depicted Cusimano as a money grabber, caring more about the pay than the profession. "I don't think George really loved horses, or horse racing," Delp said. "Certainly, he didn't like it the way you have to love it if you want to be great. He liked the money it made for him. But that was about it."

Finally, Delp summed up his former protégé as lazy and unmotivated. George was "content to be ordinary," Buddy said. Over and over Buddy had punctured the boy's dignity and privacy, seemingly throwing in everything and sparing nothing as he cataloged Cusimano's failings. And yet he never mentioned the young rider's drug abuse.

Was it an accidental oversight or, perhaps, a deliberate act of omission? Certainly whatever had gone wrong with Cusimano, whatever he was involved in, Delp would have known about it. Gerald knew of Cusimano's drug use, and so did Buddy's veterinarian, Jimmy Stewart. And Buddy himself, as employer and father figure, was closer to Cusimano than anyone. He had spent years tutoring and nurturing George's career, he had held Cusimano's contract for many years, and he was the only male role model the kid had ever known. So if anyone had molded the kid's character and habits, it was Buddy Delp. What, then, did it say about Delp that he found Cusimano so lacking?

If no one bothered to ask those questions, one thing was for sure: the deceased kid's mother and his eight-months' pregnant widow could read every unflattering word Buddy Delp had said, and they read it all on "George Cusimano Day" at Bowie Race Track.

Cathy Rosenberger knew George Cusimano well, as she did many of the young riders, called "bug boys." She worked with them at the track and rented rooms to some of them in her home. Her place was so close to Laurel Race Track that she could hear the announcer from her backyard. Cathy knew from hard experience that they were prone to all kinds of dangers and grifts.

Working and living with these young men, Cathy had a unique view of their travails. She saw them struggle with boredom, depression, weight maintenance, and relationships with women. She saw them grapple with the pain that was endemic to their careers. Cathy knew they self-medicated because she found the evidence of it in her own laundry room. That's where she would pick up the rolled-up dollar bills, the makeshift straws they used to snort cocaine.

Cathy remembered one jockey who was constantly struggling with his weight. He took an awful spill one day at Bowie Race Track and was immediately helicoptered to Shock Trauma in Baltimore. At the hospital he was started on an IV for nourishment. That slow drip must have been fattening. The young, injured jockey "gained twelve pounds in twenty-four hours," Rosenberger remembered.

Perhaps the most destructive force attacking the riders was their own success. The influx of cash in their inexperienced hands made them easy targets for exploitation. When the money showed up, so did the women that the track workers derisively called "jock chasers." They soothed the young athletes, eased their anxieties, and in the most pleasant way possible relieved them of their cash. "They're happy to help you spend your money," another boyish jockey, Steve Cauthen, said.

A different kind of threat arrived at the barns in shiny shoes. It was the agents who came bearing big smiles and dozens of donuts. They arrived looking for clients, using the sugary treats like worms on a hook. Their job was to protect the young jockeys' interests, yet they could deliver the most long-lasting and devastating damage of all to an emerging rider's life.

The agents' kindness seemed to have no bounds. Many claimed that they would do anything to help a client and protect him. To prove it, an agent would sometimes move a young rider right into his own home. It all appeared so altruistic, an act of extreme generosity. But it was rarely what it seemed. "The [agent] would have a party on the jockey's tab," Rosenberger remembered. She said it wasn't unusual in those days for the agents to introduce their young clients to cocaine, hooking them on the highly addictive drug just as their incomes were soaring. While the good times rolled, the jockey paid for all the drugs in the agent's house, including the coke-and-pill binges for everyone who visited.

Everything was fine as long as the jockey was a winner and a good earner. But early success rarely lasted. Careers stalled as bodies matured and healthy weight was gained. If and when that happened, the kid would be cut loose from his representative, put out of the house, and left with little more than a fat tax bill for money that had long since been inhaled. "The young jockeys had a lot of trouble managing their money and nobody helped them," Rosenberger said.

Buddy Delp was there for a few of them, but only to a point. Despite his protests that training jockeys was not for him, he took on other aspiring riders. The first one after Cusimano was Wayne Berardi, and like George, he was an early winner and popular with race crowds. At Delaware Park the management passed out custom pins that said "Wayne Will Win."

Berardi was a good boy. He was attached to his parents, lived at home, and saved his money. His mother and father were his biggest boosters, coming to all his races and watching him perform his dangerous work. His mother in particular had a hard time viewing it.

"She's at the track every time I ride," the young Berardi said. "She still can't watch the horses break from the starting gate. She says she fears something might happen to me. But once the gate opens she watches me all the way."

When her eyes were open, Mrs. Berardi saw a lot of great moments. Wayne came along on the heels of Chris McCarron's magical ride. McCarron had just been named the nation's top apprentice, and Berardi was showing a great deal of promise too.

On the track McCarron and Berardi were fierce but friendly rivals. They were the same age, with identical ambitions, and often found themselves nose-to-nose in the same races. Though McCarron was clearly a superior talent and already making a big name for himself, on any given day Berardi was capable of beating him. In fact, on one particular day, Berardi beat McCarron twice. Off the track their friendship was cemented by a mutual love for ice hockey, and they skated together in the same league.

But while McCarron's best years were still ahead of him, Berardi's days as a top jockey were severely limited. That became evident at Laurel one late October day in 1974. With his mother in the stands anxiously looking on as usual, Berardi got a leg up for the twelve-horse second race and sat atop Ready 'n Willing. McCarron, then the leading rider in the nation, was aboard Better Bee Great.

Berardi broke well from the gate and at the three-eighth's pole challenged for second place. But just then Ready 'n Willing's leg snapped, throwing Berardi to the ground. He was stunned by the fall, and in his groggy state he sat up. That simple act exposed his head to the rest of the field and, with most of the horses still behind him, put his life in danger.

Swift Wink tripped over the vulnerable Berardi and threw his rider, Danny Wright. Landing on the track, Wright painfully broke his collar bone but, all things considered, got off easy. Berardi, on the other hand, was hit by several horses as they thundered over him. The very last one, Annie Active, kicked him in the head with astonishing force.

Mark Reid, a young groom sitting by the rail and watching the race, ran out onto the track to help Berardi and was instantly sickened by what he found. "[Berardi's] body wasn't moving at all," Reid said. "I thought he was dead. When I got to him out on the track, I could see a large hole in his skull. I could see his brain."

Berardi was flown by helicopter to Baltimore's University of Maryland Hospital, where he fell into a coma. Meanwhile, back at Laurel, Ready 'n Willing was in even worse shape and was humanely destroyed. In almost a footnote to the tragedy, Annie Active won the race. But that was small consolation for her rider, Herbie Hinojosa, who went to the winner's circle with tears flowing from his eyes.

As for Berardi, up till then his life had been one of rapid forward motion. By the time he was twenty years old, he had already surpassed one hundred career victories. But now he was lying motionless in a Baltimore hospital bed with a swollen brain. His life was teetering.

Berardi came through as he always had, courageously outracing death like a homestretch competitor. But the road back to life was a tough one. After his coma he went into a stupor. After that he was finally allowed to go home, where he convalesced under the loving gaze of his parents. They had watched all of his glorious moments, but now they were forced to look on as he relearned the fundamental things they'd taught him as a child: how to feed himself, how to get dressed, and how to bathe. Incredibly, he also learned how to ride again. But he would never be the same jockey or young man.

After the accident and through the long, slow recovery there was quite a bit written about Berardi. The press was fascinated by his accident and especially by his journey back to the irons and competitive racing. Yet quotations from one man were scarce. Buddy Delp had but little to say about Berardi's cheating death and miraculous come back. Buddy had learned a lot of things in racing, but most of all he knew when it was over. Soon he had a new protégé.

Delp had said that he didn't like to "build" his own jockeys, but there was a rational reason for doing it that could be summed up in one word: control. The young riders who were largely uneducated and desperate for financial opportunity did what they were told.

The next one was Richard Duncan.

Much like George Cusimano, Duncan—called "Dicky" by everyone—was referred to Buddy by a family member who was connected to racing and knew the trainer. Dicky had grown up on horse farms and was already an adept rider when he reported to Delp's stables.

Duncan owned his first pony when he was only four years old. On Christmas Day, after all of his presents had been opened, his dad led him outside in his bathrobe and pajamas. They walked across the frozen ground together, holding hands, and went into the barn. There in one of the stalls was a magnificent black pony with a white patch in the shape of the letter "L" on his side and a big red bow attached to his shoulder. It was Dicky's last Christmas present, and at the sight of it he burst into tears of joy. They named the horse Nicky, and the boy and his pony were so inseparable that they came to be known as "Nicky and Dicky," as though they were a single unit.

Years later the mere memory of that Christmas could still reduce Duncan to tears. When he became a professional jockey, it was the fulfillment of the only dream he'd ever had.

Buddy took him on with the intention of bringing him along slowly, but circumstances accelerated the timeline. Dicky was exercising a horse one day when he overheard Delp and his regular jockey, Bobby Woodhouse, in the tack room raising their voices. Eventually they came bursting out of the door, both of them clearly enraged and shouting at each other.

The argument ended with a bang when Woodhouse violently crowded Delp and sputtered in his face, "Fuck you, you baldheaded son of a bitch!" With that, Woodhouse stormed off, and Delp was left standing alone, mopping his face and beet-red bald pate with his handkerchief. Recollecting himself and looking around, he spied Duncan sitting atop one of the colts and ordered him down.

"Get off that fucking horse!" Delp shouted.

"Yes, sir," Dicky said.

"You're riding eight today," Buddy told him.

In other words, Delp assigned him to ride eight horses that afternoon in place of the deposed Woodhouse. And with that Dicky Duncan's career was off and running.

Dicky soon rode winners at Laurel, Bowie, and Pimlico, and Delp and other trainers were feeding him quality horses on a daily basis. But

Duncan's good relationship with Delp didn't last long. For Dicky the first warning sign was that Buddy attempted to become overly familiar with him. In a sociable mood after work one evening, Buddy produced a bag of cocaine "the size of a flour sack." No doubt in Buddy's mind the sheer volume of the coke spoke to his power and success. But to Duncan it said something else. A regular coke user himself, Duncan found Delp reckless and conspicuous about his illegal hobbies. Dicky didn't like being in the presence of that much cocaine. "I was afraid he'd get us all arrested," he said.

But that was nothing compared to what came next. A few days later, Buddy pulled Dicky aside just prior to a long day of racing and, in lieu of instructions, the trainer made a rather forceful demand: "The horse you're riding in the seventh today does not hit the board," Buddy said.

Dicky's horse was the favorite, and from Delp's own stable, but Buddy wanted to ensure that it wouldn't even finish third. The reason was simple. Delp had placed a bet on a different colt. And what was the risk for Buddy? If the jockey was determined to be holding back or cheating, the problem would be all Dicky's.

In that era trainers regularly manipulated races to their advantage. In fact, many of them considered it a necessity of doing business and getting ahead since purses were so small. They might use what they knew about a horse's condition as an advantage at the betting window. It also wasn't unusual to tell a jockey in a claiming race, "Don't abuse him." In other words, don't use the whip too much. The goal was to win if the jockey could win it, but if he couldn't, he was told to hold the horse back so he wouldn't finish second or third. That kept a good animal from getting claimed. Then the next time the horse ran, with expectations for him lowered, the trainer could place an educated bet on that horse, knowing that its record didn't match its ability.

Buddy took these practices a step further by demanding that Duncan throw the race altogether. Dicky did exactly as he was told, and everything worked out smoothly. The horse lost. Buddy won his bet. The rider kept his job. And everyone was happy.

But if there was any relief for Dicky when it was all over, he was sadly mistaken. The successful completion of the mission only begged for more of the same. Soon Buddy was asking him to hold horses on a regular basis. Duncan didn't have much choice but to comply. Defying his powerful boss was tantamount to losing his best patron and perhaps his whole career. So every time Delp asked him to throw a race, he did it.

It happened seven times in all.

But it all came to an ugly end one wet day when the reins were slippery, the surface was muddy, and the horses difficult to control. Again Buddy instructed Duncan to finish out of the money. But under the burdensome riding conditions the neophyte Dicky lost control of the horse and despite himself finished third. Worse than that, he utterly lacked artifice. He fumbled with the reins, making his manipulations and intentions so obvious that at least one experienced observer knew exactly what he was doing and why.

After the race, a highly respected veteran jockey pulled Dicky aside and furtively told him to meet him in the jockeys' room shower. It wasn't an offer of romance; the showers were their funky "Cone of Silence." They stood under the dripping nozzles, fully clothed in their silks and speckled with mud and with no one to listen in on their furtive conversation but the bathroom tiles.

The older jockey looked at Duncan with a careworn face. He didn't waste time pretending. "I know what Bud is asking you to do," he said, "but if you get caught, you'll be the one going to jail for ten years."

The older rider was one of Buddy Delp's long-standing friends, and he had ridden for the trainer many times. He'd also seen other riders arrested for the very same thing he had just witnessed Dicky doing. He promised the young man that he would speak to Buddy that night and tell him to back off.

But the next morning, Delp wasn't contrite; he was livid. Upon first sight of Duncan, Buddy grabbed him and threw him in the tack room. "You're fired!" Buddy boomed. "You're through. You'll never ride another horse for me again."

It was a hard thing for Duncan to hear. He'd dreamed of this career, race riding, since he had gotten his first leg up on his Christmas pony. And he knew that something far worse than losing a job had happened. He'd taken something very innocent and meaningful to him, something sacred and pure inside of him, and he'd allowed Buddy to corrupt and profane it.

All the frustration and self-disgust welled up inside Dicky until he turned to his former mentor with wild eyes and a suddenly unfiltered mouth and vomited his revulsion. "Go fuck yourself, you baldheaded mother fucker," Dicky yelled at Buddy. But it was also a fitting eulogy for his own innocence.

And just like that another young protégé stalked off from Buddy's stable forever. Every one of the young jockeys had come to Buddy Delp looking for the same thing: recognition of talent and confirmation for their feelings of self-worth. They needed a leg up, a chance to earn, and a moment in the sun. All any of them ever wanted was experience. Buddy gave that to them, all right—much more than they had bargained for.

3 *Old Hilltop*

When Ronnie Franklin entered Buddy Delp's world, he was nowhere near adulthood. In fact, at less than 5 feet tall with stick-thin arms and legs and a smooth face, he appeared prepubescent, as though he could still be sitting on the floor at his parents' house playing with toy cars or soldiers.

Instead Hank Tiburzi presented him at Pimlico as an aspiring "hot walker." It was a low-paying job, and it required no previous experience or skill set. The one and only advantage to the job was that it was always available. "All you have to do to start work on the track is to show up at the main gate in the morning," an article in *Practical Horseman* magazine said. That would land you a job for $65 to $75 a week. For that you were expected to "walk six to 10 hot horses a day for four to five hours each morning, seven days a week."

Franklin was barely out of high school, but he was already no stranger to work that was low pay and low prestige. He didn't care about that. For him the key was the easy point of entry to the racing life.

Cathy Rosenberger described the job in its simplest terms. "Turn left,'" she said. "That's all you have to think about: 'Turn left.' Give 'em a sip of water and turn left. And you do that for about five hours every morning." In short it was the perfect job for a sixteen-year-old with a tenth-grade education.

It was Hank Tiburzi's idea for Ronnie to seek a career at the track, and it was Tiburzi who brought him there for the first time and asked the security guard to announce him over the loudspeaker. It just so happened that it was the Delps who needed a hot walker at that moment, so they dispatched Dougie to fetch the kid.

Nobody in the Delp organization initially saw anything in Ronnie that was in the least bit out of the ordinary. "[The boy] had never held a horse or hardly ever seen a horse," Rosenberger said. The first day he arrived at Pimlico, "He didn't know what he was doing at all," she noted.

As an unskilled laborer, young Ronnie Franklin had a grueling day. His morning began around 5:00 a.m., and he worked without break until around 11 a.m. In between he walked horses. Each horse that didn't go to the track had to be walked for twenty minutes. That removed the equine occupant from his stall so that the groom could muck it out and bed it down.

When the horses who did exercise came back from their workouts, Ronnie and the other hot walkers held the animals while the grooms bathed them. Then, depending on the weather, they draped a sheet or blanket over the horse for comfort and warmth. After that, Rosenberger said, "The hot walker took the horse in the barn and turned left."

If the horse had worked out, Ronnie walked it for half an hour just to cool it down. Without that attention the horses were prone to sickness. "The hot walkers are steady, moving the whole time we are training," Rosenberger said. "One after another after another."

Some hot walkers were assigned to come back for the afternoon racing as well. It was a hard day of work, but "turning left" suited Franklin far more than Algebra 1 or having to ask the incessant question: "Would you like fries with that?"

Ronnie was just one of many hot walkers, but he was restless and oddly ambitious. He had enough gumption to walk right up to Cathy, a young woman he barely knew, and tell her, "I want to ride your pony."

The ponies Cathy rode belonged to her, and they represented her livelihood. She had reason to be cautious with them. Even so, she generously allowed Franklin to ride them through the "shed row," around and around, just to give him a feel for the activity. But it was obvious he had no background or skill with horses.

Rosenberger's horses were outfitted in Western-style saddles, and Ronnie mounted them like a matinee tenderfoot; he bounced around in the saddle and clutched the horn just to keep himself from falling off the horse.

The Delps generally didn't approve of Cathy's efforts to teach Ronnie. That became apparent one day when she took over his duties holding horses for the blacksmith while he rode her pony. Dick Delp walked by, saw the reversal of responsibilities, and wasn't pleased.

"What are you doing?" he demanded.

"Oh, Ronnie wanted to ride a little bit," she said.

Dick made it clear that he didn't like what he saw, so she took her horse and went home for the day.

Buddy also wasn't keen on her efforts to teach Franklin. At one point she approached him and said, "I have been giving this kid riding lessons on my pony, and we need to go forward a little bit. How about if I take one of the older horses, tack it up? I'll put Ronnie on the horse and take him out to the track, but I won't let go. We'll just walk and jog a little bit."

"No," Buddy said. "I have plans for Ronnie."

Ronnie wanted to ride; that's why he'd come to the track. He might not have been progressing as quickly as he would have liked, but he appeared for work every day, and that in itself was a small miracle.

The Franklins owned only one vehicle. Tony Franklin had to be at his job early every morning, and now Ronnie had to do the same, only he had to go all the way over to the other side of town. It was a thirty-five-minute car drive from Dundalk to Pimlico, even in light traffic. The only way for both of them to get to work on time was for Tony to usher his son out the front door by 4:30 a.m. He got Ronnie to Pimlico without complaint, and then he backtracked to get to his own job.

But that was Tony Franklin. He was a worker, and long before there was any glory or real money in racing for Ronnie, he was proud that his son was a worker too.

Tony Franklin had the very best of intentions when he dropped his young son off. Pimlico, with its long, storied history and famous brand, represented not only opportunity but also a sense of purpose and dignity.

It was one of the oldest and most legendary sports venues in the United States.

The roots of Pimlico Race Track went all the way back to a Mexican American war hero and Maryland governor named Oden Bowie. In 1868 he was one of the invited guests to an important party at Delmonico's Restaurant in New York thrown by the influential horseman M. H. Sanford. The men were gathered to discuss how to revive the Maryland Jockey Club and southern horse racing in the aftermath of the Civil War.

Bowie grew up on a plantation and was a former slave owner. When he was a child, his life revolved around horses as he foaled, broke, and fast rode his own "unruly colts." From this inherited mantle of wealth, he was an unmistakable member of the ruling class and quickly became a powerful force in Maryland Democratic politics. He rose to the highest offices in the state and attended the Chicago Democratic Presidential Convention of 1864 that nominated General George McClellan to run against Abraham Lincoln.

The talk at the dinner party eventually turned from the revival of racing to the creation of a new stakes race. The guests called it the "Dinner Party Sweepstakes" because they'd given birth to it at the table that night, and initially the entries were to be limited only to the horses owned by the men who were there that evening. It wasn't long, however, before word got out and other sportsmen clamored to get in on the action.

Saratoga made a play for the new race, but Governor Bowie brought it home to Maryland by promising to build a showcase race track for it. Bowie delivered and built his new track in Baltimore, a city on the rise. It was already a major seaport, the Western Hemisphere's leader in railroading, and the world leader in medicine. And it was about to explode as a center of manufacturing muscle too.

To fulfill Governor Bowie's promise, a parcel of land in northwest Baltimore called Pimlico was chosen as the site for the new track. There were many theories as to the roots of the name, but the most plausible one was that it was the brand name of an English beer.

The first Dinner Party Sweepstakes at Pimlico was held in 1870. The winner was a beautiful bay colt named for the small town in New Jersey where he was foaled: Preakness.

Within three years the Dinner Party Sweepstakes was renamed the "Dixie Handicap," a sign of Maryland's unreconstructed and racist core clinging to its past. At the same time, a new stakes race for three-year-olds was established and named in honor of Pimlico's first major race winner: the Preakness Stakes. The inaugural Preakness was run on May 27, 1873, a Tuesday. It was won by a colt named Survivor.

So two years before the first Kentucky Derby, thirty years before the first World Series game, about a half century before Jack Dempsey became king of the heavyweights or Babe Ruth opened Yankee Stadium with a humdinger, and almost a century before the first Super Bowl, Pimlico hosted events that captivated the entire nation.

In 1877 a special race among three horses—Parole, Ten Broeck, and Tom Ochiltree—representing the North, South, and West, was held to decide America's best thoroughbred. Interest for the event was so high that Congress adjourned for the day, and many of its members rode up to Baltimore to watch the race in person.

Despite its early and indelible mark on popular culture, Pimlico was never quite what it seemed. Baltimoreans nicknamed it "Old Hilltop," a charming and evocative moniker, but it actually referred to a nuisance. There was a hump of land in the infield that annoyed fans and obstructed race views. In fact, the track was under near constant criticism and threat. In the late nineteenth century the Preakness was briefly moved to New York, first to Morris Park (a site between Westchester and the Bronx) and then to Gravesend Course at Coney Island. The famous race returned to Pimlico in 1909, but the threat that it would one day move again was persistent and would last more than a century.

In 1938 the directors of the Maryland Jockey Club voted to make one sorely needed major improvement to the track but forgo another. They agreed to pay for a lumpectomy (removing the hill from Old Hilltop), but at the same time they refused to build a new and long-discussed clubhouse. Their willingness to do the one but not the other revealed a serious schism. The directors of the Jockey Club ran the races at Pimlico, but they didn't own the track. Pimlico was the possession of a trust. The Jockey Club only leased and operated it.

William R. Hammond, a grain dealer from Baltimore, had purchased the property at auction in 1904 for $70,000. A little later he acquired the clubhouse too, for an additional $40,000. When he died in 1917, he established a trust to run the property for the benefit of his daughter, who no longer even lived in Baltimore. Like one of the swells in *The Great Gatsby*, she had married well and split her time between New York and Connecticut.

Hammond's decision to keep Pimlico for his daughter was a brilliant one. His original $110,000 investment earned her $80,000 per year in rent from the Jockey Club, as well as $90,000 to $100,000 annually in maintenance and improvements. All that, and the Jockey Club paid Pimlico's tax bills too.

It was a sweetheart of a deal—for the trust. But for the Jockey Club the lease was a straitjacket.

Meanwhile, after years of use, major aspects of the track had worn out, and the costs for renovation were astronomical. A new grandstand was desperately needed, and it would require more than a million dollars to build it. The bill, of course, would go to the Jockey Club, while the improvement, once completed, would belong to the trust.

Good fortune didn't keep the trust from exhibiting obnoxious behavior. With time running out on the old lease, it gave the Jockey Club only two days to decide whether it wanted to renew under the same old oppressive terms or purchase the property for $1.3 million.

The Jockey Club directors were both strapped and affronted. Their first thought, naturally, was to bolt. They planned to build their own track, somewhere in the Baltimore area, though the precise location was an unrevealed mystery. These plans, however, were stymied by a myriad of complexities. Horse racing was regulated by the state, and any attempt to leave Pimlico to race elsewhere was a serious political and legal issue that required the blessing of the governor and legislators.

Sensing that the shoe was finally on the other foot, the trust stepped up to protect its interests. It opposed the Jockey Club in Annapolis, the state capital, and worked against a bill that would have allowed the club to purchase and operate its own track.

It seemed that the trust had all of the leverage. Even politicians who were sympathetic to the Jockey Club's dilemma had few options in helping it. Maryland state law did not license organizations for racing; it licensed sites. This was a key distinction that made it nearly impossible for the Jockey Club to simply leave and build its own track.

But the Jockey Club was run by extraordinarily rich and powerful men, and they didn't give up easily. They lobbied to have the law changed so that the Racing Commission could issue a license to any qualified party. And they didn't stop there. In the legislation they favored, the Jockey Club directors also proposed a provision to block anyone else from racing at Pimlico in the event that they left the property.

With all parties aggrieved, angry, and pointing guns at each other, a compromise was struck, and the Jockey Club came out stronger than ever. It finally purchased Pimlico under agreeable terms and acquired two other Maryland tracks, Laurel and Timonium, to operate under its auspice. The most interesting feature of the deal was that it brought "Old Hilltop" under the control of a venerable American family called Vanderbilt.

Alfred Gwynne Vanderbilt Jr. dominated the Maryland Jockey Club as its major stakeholder, and by extension that made him a major mover and shaker in American horse racing. His name might've evoked more urbane locales, such as Manhattan or Newport, Rhode Island, but Alfred Vanderbilt was as Baltimore as they came. His maternal grandfather was Captain Isaac Emerson, a Baltimore druggist and inventor who created and manufactured Bromo Seltzer, a headache remedy that was in fact the go-to cure for hangovers. Needless to say, it was an enormously popular product in the highly intoxicated states of America, pre-Prohibition.

Emerson was a master marketer at the very beginning of a century that would be defined by branding. He pioneered techniques such as multimedia advertising, promoting Bromo Seltzer in newspapers and radio and packaging it in distinctive blue bottles that stood out on store shelves.

Even Emerson's manufacturing plant was a marketing opportunity. He built a factory that was a reproduction of the Palazzo Vecchio in Florence, Italy, including a 289-foot tower. The Emerson Building—or Bromo Tower as it was more commonly called—was completed in 1911. Just as Captain Emerson hoped, it immediately drew attention. First of all, it was the tallest building in the city with a four-face clock that beckoned in any direction. The most distinctive feature of all was the building's cap: a thirty-ton spinning electric-blue Bromo Seltzer bottle. On clear nights its azure glow could be seen clear across the bay on the Eastern Shore of Maryland. "All Baltimoreans may be divided into two classes," the famously cranky newspaperman H. L. Mencken once wrote, "those who think that the Emerson Tower is beautiful, and those who know better."

Many years later Bromo Seltzer lost its luster and went out of business when it was discovered that the brand Captain Emerson touted was far different from the reality. The product contained a number of toxic ingredients. Nevertheless, Bromo Seltzer had highly beneficial effects on one vital organ—the Emerson family bank book.

That was Vanderbilt's maternal family. His father, Alfred G. Vanderbilt Sr., was the number one heir to a railroad fortune valued at more than $800 million. Even so, he wasn't destined for a long, happy life. He died on the *Lusitania*, the civilian luxury liner torpedoed by a German U-boat. He was on board only so that he could acquire high-quality English fox-hunting horses. Vanderbilt's body was never recovered, but back in Baltimore, his namesake, Alfred Jr., inherited two things—much of his father's vast wealth and the old man's love of horses.

Since the first day he walked into Pimlico as a young boy, Alfred Jr. had no other ambition but to be a horseman. Going to the track was "the most exciting thing I ever experienced," he recalled years later. "It was what I wanted to do all the time."

The centerpiece of Vanderbilt's equine empire was Sagamore Farms, a brilliant swath of rolling green meadows in the Baltimore County countryside, framed in crisply painted white wooden fences that traveled over hill and over dale and seemed to stretch on into infinity. The property had been assembled by Captain Emerson and presented to young Alfred as a twenty-first-birthday gift—a far grander gesture than giving him a car or pen and pencil set. Sagamore included a ninety-stall barn that at times housed and trained many of the twentieth century's greatest racers. But it was most well known as "the Home of Native Dancer."

This man of comfort and privilege, Alfred Vanderbilt Jr., headed the

Jockey Club and by extension also ran Pimlico. And under his direction, Old Hilltop occupied a preeminent role in its sport.

Alfred was the man who finally brought Seabiscuit and War Admiral together on the same track, which of course was Pimlico. Their challenge race in 1938 was one of the most compelling sporting events in American history. President Roosevelt interrupted a cabinet meeting, where he was only discussing how to end the Great Depression and avoid entering World War II, to tune in the match race on his radio. Not until the undefeated gladiators Muhammad Ali and Joe Frazier met in a boxing ring three decades later would any sporting spectacle match the anticipation and intrigue surrounding Seabiscuit and War Admiral. The early Super Bowls didn't even come close.

But for all of its excitement and venerability, Pimlico also had its share of scandals and sketchy characters. Beyond the sterling brand, there was a seamy side to the track, and it was obvious early on that it was a place that could be contentious, brutal, and corrupt. One unlikely hero came to clean it all up, and yet in doing so, he opened a box of furies that would have wide-ranging negative implications for the entire country that would last well into the twenty-first century.

His name was George P. Mahoney, and his career in public life began with a short, stormy tenure as the Maryland state racing commissioner. Born in 1901, Mahoney was the eleventh child of an Irish cop. Like many an American success story, he achieved material wealth without the virtue of an education. He quit school in the seventh grade.

Mahoney was to amass a great fortune in Baltimore, but he began as humbly as possible. He started his working life in New York City, first as a doorman and then later as one of the laborers digging the Holland Tunnel. An ambitious young man, he capped off an exhausting workday in a night school classroom where he studied business all evening.

He returned to Baltimore in 1921 and discovered a world of opportunity. He founded his own business, Mahoney Brothers, a hauling and paving company. He entered that field but without a high probability of success. In the late 1930s a four-company consortium had a stranglehold on the city's paving contracts, making it nearly impossible for anyone else to break through and flourish. But Mahoney succeeded through a kind of frugal cunning. His first office was in the basement of his parents' small row house. His vehicles and equipment were low-cost army surplus purchases.

With his overhead fixed and low, Mahoney devised a foolproof plan for defeating the consortium and winning city business. He bid projects so low that he was losing money on each one. But those deficit deals allowed him to force his way into the club of companies paving Baltimore. And anyway, he didn't lose money for long. By the end of the decade Mahoney Brothers was making more than a million dollars per year.

Mahoney became so wealthy, in fact, that he lived like a Vanderbilt. He bought a 325-acre horse farm just minutes from Sagamore Farms, and with that he entered the privileged world of thoroughbred owners. He was still only a horse novice when Governor Herbert O'Conor, a buddy from his old East Baltimore neighborhood, appointed him to the racing commission. It wasn't long before Mahoney was its chairman.

Mahoney came to power as part of a good old boy network, but with his new money he had all the earmarks of an outsider. He had absolutely no qualms about sticking it to the fat cats, and in fact, he seemed to take a certain delight in it.

As head of the Racing Commission, Mahoney rocked the boat hard. He was a zealous investigator who found corruption under every stone and pebble. Decades before Ronnie Franklin or even Buddy Delp had ever come through Pimlico's gates, Mahoney uncovered fixed races and doped horses there. In late 1945 he administered saliva tests to the animals, looking for trace amounts of drugs. It was one of the first such efforts in the United States, and it bore plenty of fruit.

Five tests returned positive for "narcotic drugs."

The stables that owned the tainted horses and their trainers were suspended from Maryland racing. At Mahoney's request, federal drug agents raided the barns at Pimlico. Drugs weren't his only target. His policies also put two horsemen behind bars for using ringers.

Mahoney saw himself in messianic terms, claiming that his efforts gave horse racing "a new lease on life." "Racing could not have continued as long as drugging or doping went undetected," he said. "Soon or late, dishonesty would bring about its collapse."

Mahoney's crusading hardly endeared him to the members of the state's horse racing fraternity. They labeled him a grandstander and felt he was out to embarrass them all by dragging the industry's private matters before the press and public.

The entrenched power structure didn't take it lying down. The president of the Maryland Horseman's Protective Association threatened to advise his 550 members to leave Maryland until Mahoney was "out of the saddle." The Jockey Club's directors were particularly incensed. One of their group, Vaughn Flannery, a noted artist and publisher of a weekly newspaper in Harford County, Maryland, lampooned Mahoney as "Silk Hat George." In an editorial cartoon Mahoney was depicted kicking out horse racing experts in favor of meddling politicians.

In fact, Mahoney's progressive ideas were a demonstrable improvement. With corruption cleaned up and a fairer game in place, requests for stall space at Maryland tracks increased to record levels. And while Maryland tracks faced stiff competition from neighboring states, both attendance and betting remained strong in Maryland. Because of these accomplishments, the *Baltimore Sun* wrote that the state could not "afford to lose Mahoney . . . in these critical times."

And yet the powers that be were aligned against him. When Mahoney's old pal Governor O'Conor resigned, his replacement, William Preston Lane, gave into the pleas of the wealthy horse racing interests and fired Mahoney. Instead of crushing Mahoney politically, however, firing him made him something of a national folk hero. "Like all fighters for the little people, [Mahoney] stepped on some important peoples' toes and is being attacked for it," one New York scribe sympathetically wrote in his column.

The Association of State Racing Commissioners, an important and prestigious governing board, rebuked Maryland's governor by adopting one of Mahoney's key reform recommendations and by electing him third vice president of its organization, a fast track to its presidency, even though he was, in fact, no longer a state racing commissioner. It should have all added up to a graceful and satisfying exit from the public scene for Mahoney—except for a couple of things. Mahoney had acquired a taste for populism, and he was out for revenge. He would soon transition from corruption crusader to the symbol of the very worst impulses in American life.

In 1950 Mahoney challenged Governor Lane in the state's Democratic primary, utilizing a resentment-based campaign that featured the tag line "You're the Boss." Many Maryland citizens liked it. Mahoney gathered fifteen thousand more votes than Governor Lane. But he lost the election anyway owing to a complicated primary structure that was later ruled unconstitutional.

Mahoney nevertheless accomplished what he'd set out to do. He weakened Lane so much that the Democratic governor lost the general election to his Republican opponent. Mahoney couldn't quite win, but he had proven that he had the power to burn it all down if he wanted to. And from that point on, he would be a thorn in the side of his own party and a boon to its enemies.

Mahoney reached his nadir in 1966, when he ran for governor yet again. A great racial reckoning was under way in Maryland, as it was in the rest of the country, and policies and customs that had segregated neighborhoods by race and religion for most of the century were under fire.

For Mahoney the righteous movement toward equality was merely something to oppose for political purposes. He had found out a long time ago that defiance gathered a crowd. This time Mahoney's tag line was "Your home is your castle; protect it." It was an unambiguously racist statement that aligned him, and the state of Maryland, with Alabama governor George C. Wallace, the intellectual leader of the segregationist movement.

In the short term, Mahoney's message created deep divisions and raised levels of hate in his state. And yet, his tenor reverberated for decades and utterly changed American political behavior. First, although he was a Democrat, he opened the door for significant Republican victories, including for his own opponent in the Maryland governor's race, Baltimore County executive Spiro T. Agnew.

Many Maryland Democrats were so aghast at Mahoney's abusive and nakedly racist rhetoric that they left their own party and flocked to the polls in support of Agnew. Agnew played along, masquerading as a moderate. He contrasted himself with Mahoney and pledged his support to a limited open occupancy law. It was the first law of its kind south of the Mason-Dixon Line, and it was a small but significant step in ending neighborhood segregation forever. He also overturned an old Maryland anti-miscegenation law that banned marriage between whites and Blacks.

But all of that was only window dressing. Once Agnew was safely in office, he showed that he was far from a racial moderate. "He wasn't who the voters thought he was," said Michael Olesker, for many years a top columnist and television commentator in Baltimore. "He fooled everybody." That became apparent when Agnew refused to meet student protestors at historically Black Bowie State College; the students were merely asking for better facilities at their school. Not to be denied, two hundred of them came to Annapolis for a sit-in protest there. Rather than ignore them again, Agnew had them all arrested.

Agnew picked a poor time to exacerbate racial tensions. Martin Luther King Jr. was assassinated just a few hours after the students were arrested. And then everything snapped. Baltimore, a city more combustible than most, blew up. Riots and raging fires broke out, and then it was Agnew calling for a meeting with the city's Black leaders.

At first, Agnew said he needed their help in ending the calamity. But instead he ambushed them. Grandstanding for political gain, Agnew bizarrely accused the Black leaders of not speaking out against "Negro racism." With their dignity strained, the Black leaders walked out of the governor's meeting, saying they would not return until Agnew was ready to speak to them as "ladies and gentlemen."

The absurdity and indecency of the moment was not lost on national Republican Party leaders, who looked at chaotic Maryland and liked what they saw. They nominated Agnew for vice president on the same ticket with Richard M. Nixon. Together, Nixon and Agnew turned the party of Lincoln into the new party of the segregationist South. The bitter racial divide they created would go on for many decades more.

People had long forgotten that so much national corruption began with the corruption at Pimlico. They didn't remember that Baltimore's famous race track had a large enough platform to elevate the profile of a humble man, with limited education, and make him a prominent national figure and newsmaker. And yet George Mahoney's very fine work at Pimlico was the catalyst for so many calamitous American ills. Even after Mahoney left the State Racing Commission, Pimlico remained a place of bare-knuckle brawling between monied and political interests.

Governor Lane named Stuart Janney Jr., a legendary steeplechase jockey and old-line lawyer, to replace Mahoney. In a sense it was a restoration of order, a return to aristocratic rule. Janney was a graduate of the prestigious Gilman School, Princeton University, and Harvard Law School. He was also a respected barrister with the old-line Venable, Baetjer, and Howard firm. Janney was no barbarian from the lower rungs of new money like Mahoney was; he was solidly establishment, and the Jockey Club saw him as one of their own.

And indeed Janney was on board with the Jockey Club's agenda to break out of Old Hilltop; shut it down; and move lock, stock, and barrel to Laurel. Because Governor Lane also backed the move, everything appeared to be in place to end racing at the historic venue.

It was a sad moment for traditionalists, but the truth was that Pimlico had always had its limitations. For one thing, it sat on but 115 acres, shoehorned between residential neighborhoods, large country residences for the wealthy on the east side of the track and humble row houses and storefronts on the west. Laurel, by contrast, was in an expansive pasture with a luxurious 325 acres under its control.

More to the point, Baltimore was just beginning a slow and painful postwar decline. As its manufacturing base eroded, high-paying blue-collar jobs were slipping away while white middle-class residents were abandoning the city and moving to the suburbs. Laurel, on the other hand, was suburban. It was the type of place where white people were moving. Laurel wasn't in suburban Baltimore. It was a Washington-oriented town, and many of the residents had stable, high-paying government jobs.

Still, Pimlico had charm and history on its side. The track's "Old Clubhouse," a post–Civil War structure built in 1870, had the bearing and appearance of an antebellum plantation house. The patina that had settled over the rest of Pimlico did not apply to the Old Clubhouse. It was one of the most elegant architectural elements associated with any sports venue in the United States. The building looked like an iced gingerbread cake that had been baked in three layers of magnificent beauty. The building had loomed over the races at Pimlico since Preakness, the horse, had won the first stakes race. It was a moment so ancient that the fans on the porch that day had worn black armbands in respect of Robert E. Lee, the Confederate general who had just passed.

The Old Clubhouse was renovated and lovingly restored to its original opulence in the mid-1950s, and every little touch was a reminder that horse racing was a toy of the rich and elite. The walls were covered in Waterman Collection wallpapers. Georgian chandeliers hung from the ceilings. And imported Victorian drapes framed the windows. In the Old Clubhouse's dining rooms headwaiters wore tuxedoes, the gentlemen were attired in jackets and ties, and the ladies were canvases for the finest fashion designers.

The Old Clubhouse was also home to the greatest memories in racing. Pimlico had assembled a museum-quality collection of racing memorabilia and a Jockeys' Hall of Fame, much like Cooperstown, New York, had done for baseball. There were hand-painted master works of each of the Hall of Fame members framed and hanging on the walls. Eddie Arcaro, the winning rider on two of the first eight Triple Crown winners, was one of the first inductees. George Woolf, the winning jockey in the Seabiscuit–War Admiral challenge race, had his crimson-and-white silks on display there.

These collections, galleries, and the Hall of Fame were not only Pimlico's gift to the racing community; they were also a sign of Baltimore's place at the heart of it all. The potential shuttering of Pimlico was not only a rebuke of the facility but also a sign of Baltimore's declining influence and fortunes. But for the gentlemen of the Jockey Club, and the governor too, it seemed to be only about money. The mania to move was like the lifting of a veil; everyone could see that history and tradition meant nothing to racing's stewards. All they cared about was cultivating more bettors.

The directors of the Jockey Club believed that moving to Laurel was a sure thing, but they never considered the one and only thing that could derail them—political cowardice. Governor Lane was solidly in their corner until Baltimore legislators convinced him at the last moment that he was angering voters and endangering his reelection possibilities. That was all he needed to hear. He folded his hand and withdrew his support. Instead, at 10:30 p.m., under the cover of night, he pushed through a compromise solution that gave the Laurel and Bowie race courses ten additional racing dates each year but that also preserved racing in Baltimore.

So it was pusillanimity that saved Pimlico.

But fate accomplished what politics could not one calamitous night in June 1966, when one hundred years of elegance and history were consumed by fire. A blaze sprang to life in the front portion of the Old Clubhouse at around 11 p.m., and by 1:00 a.m. it was an eight-alarm catastrophe.

Like everything else about the building its destruction was spectacular. The flames leapt high into the night, stretching forty to fifty feet beyond the roofline. The flickering light could be seen many blocks away, and the heat was so intense that wooden ladders hanging on the sides of the fire trucks blistered and smoked. By 2:00 a.m. the entire building had burned to the ground. The only things that had survived the blaze were a brick chimney and the horse-and-rider weather vane that sat high atop the ornate cupola.

It was a tremendous blow to Baltimore's ego and self-image. Even worse, it was a suspected though unproved arson. The flames that danced across the Old Clubhouse's balconies, kitchens, libraries, and art galleries consumed more than a building. They destroyed the words, images, and objects connected to racing's past and its glory, its noble animals and human heroes. The flames had wiped clean the institutional memory of the entire enterprise.

Pimlico bounced back to have many more great racing moments. In 1973 Secretariat bolted his way to victory at the Preakness and then the Triple Crown. A few years after that Seattle Slew and Affirmed, in 1977 and 1978 respectively, both won the Preakness and the Triple Crown.

And yet with the death of the Old Clubhouse and the bonfire of its memories, racing was never quite the same again. As an enterprise, racing had always toddled the thin, unsavory line between sport and gambling venue. After the fire, that line all but disappeared.

So it was a very different Pimlico than the one of lore that Ronald Franklin came to in the mid-1970s. There was no more genteel Old Clubhouse or paternalistic Vanderbilts, no more beautifully attired women or four-star meals.

Even the neighborhoods surrounding Old Hilltop had changed. The once well-kept houses and stores around the west side of the track were crumbling under the weight of predatory landlords and impoverished residents. And a host of urban ills struck, especially the rise of the drug culture, both inside and outside the track gates.

This was Ronald Franklin's Pimlico, the place he came to live in the mid-1970s, when he was only a teenager freshly moved out of his parents' home. By then, "Ronald" was "Ronnie," close to the Delp family and in particular to Gerald, Buddy's young son, who was also a teenage hot walker.

In Gerald, Ronnie found a soul mate. They were close in age and had a similar outlook on life. They both had dropped out of school and yet had retained a certain exuberance. Gerald was an easygoing and companionable young man with a good sense of humor.

Before long Ronnie and Gerald were not only best friends, but they were also roommates at the track, living in one of the apartments above the stables on the backstretch. It was a place made for guys like them—hot walkers and grooms, the working poor.

The living quarters were spartan, basically an empty room. The resident of the moment furnished it, usually with little more than a hideaway bed. There were no closets, and garments were usually kept in a bag or simply strewn on the floor. An enterprising and fastidious tenant might drive a nail or two into the wall to hang things up.

There were no kitchens in those rooms, and hotplates were strictly forbidden. Bathrooms and showers were in the stable area. To prevent even the allegation of sexual assault, women were banned after dark. The male residents, despite their low status and lack of financial assets, were known to be industrious and nonthreatening. "A lot of the grooms were Black men who came up from Virginia or North Carolina," Cathy Rosenberger remembered. "They were generally very kind, gentle people. In fact, many of them asked me to pick up necessities for them, such as toothpaste, because they were afraid to leave the confines of the track due to the crime they heard about in northern cities like Baltimore."

But not all of the worries were outside the gates. There were many unhealthy lures right on the grounds. Willie Brown, an exercise rider similar in age to Ronnie, knew all about the delightful dangers and temptations. "Anything was available inside or just outside the gates of Pimlico," Brown said. "Heroin, coke, pot, pills [ups and downs], whatever you wanted."

Brown was introduced to drugs at Pimlico, and ultimately that led him to many decades of substance addiction. But Ronnie Franklin was different, Brown said; he resisted the urge to experiment. "At that time Ronnie was focused on chasing his dream," Brown remembered. "He didn't want to get ruled off. He was more focused on getting his jockey's license than anything else."

That dedication paid off. Although Cathy Rosenberger couldn't convince the Delps that Ronnie had the qualities of a rider, Gerald did. He talked to his father quite a bit about his new friend. "Dad," Gerald said, "Ronnie looks like a jockey; he's strong as an ox."

Buddy noticed when Gerald told him. One day after work he called Ronnie into his office and told the kid that he was sending him to Middleburg, Virginia, for jockey training.

For Franklin it was the realization of a dream. At the beginning of the year he had been nothing more than a fast food worker. Just a few weeks earlier he was still sneaking rides and clutching the saddle to keep from falling off. But now, thanks to Buddy Delp, he was going to one of the top horse-training facilities in the world to ride honest-to-God racehorses and to learn the finer points of being a jockey.

His life was in full gallop.

4 *The Beard*

O'Henry's was a bar in midtown Baltimore with a charming façade that bravely peeked out on North Charles Street, the literal heart of the city. It was easy to assume it was a simple Irish pub but, in fact, the owner was an older Jewish man named Henry Segal. He gave his place its jaunty Irish moniker believing that the neighborhood's drinkers would prefer to tip their glasses in a place more evocative of a cozy Dublin pub than, say, a Russian shtetl. The name was a small deception but a deception all the same.

One of the crowd who became a recognizable regular was a cheerful guy in a sport coat and tie named Harry Meyerhoff. By the late 1970s Harry was slightly past midlife and transitioning physically and emotionally. A great athlete in his youth, he had thickened out only a little bit with the years. He'd lost most of his hair, and the scraps that were left over were mostly colorless. But with Harry's undeniable advancement of age came something else. He cultivated an impressive gray beard that didn't merely grow but seemed to flow from him in waves, enhancing his Semitic features and adding an air of Old Testament wisdom to his already formidable visage.

Just a few years earlier Harry had awakened to the idea that he was unhappy and restless. He'd been married to his wife, Marilyn, for a long time, and it was a generally happy marriage. The only tension between them that their children could easily see was when they prepared to go out. Marilyn took an inordinate amount of time to get ready, changing makeup or outfits multiple times. Harry liked to be prompt, so Marilyn's delays annoyed him and sometimes provoked uncharacteristic bickering. But that was minor stuff, and Harry eventually learned how to play the piano to peacefully occupy his time while he waited for his wife.

All told, Harry was married to Marilyn for about twenty-five years. The first twenty-two had been mostly happy, but the last three had not. Suddenly they were not getting along so well. At about the same time, Harry and his brother, who had always been close, were also struggling. The two situations were not unrelated.

Like many middle-aged men, Harry took steps to stave off decline or depression or death anxiety, and he detached from his wife and his work. Harry vowed to enjoy his life with more fervor than he ever had before. And O'Henry's was one of the places he found his escape. He felt comfortable at O'Henry's. It was his favorite bar, a place to have a few laughs and a few drinks and unwind from his stresses and anxieties. But most of all it was the place where he could see a single beautiful face that he greatly admired. It belonged to a struggling but attractive young waitress and bartender named Teresa Riberdy Murdick.

Harry and Teresa enjoyed each other's company, but they came from entirely different worlds. Harry was Jewish; Teresa, Roman Catholic. He was rich; she was a student and a low-income worker. He had been raised in Baltimore, the son of a wealthy and successful land developer; she was born at home in a small town called Half Moon, New York. Teresa was the youngest of seven children. Her father, a dairy farmer, assisted in her delivery.

Harry was at a place in his life where he was putting the past behind him; Teresa was still struggling to ensure her future. He had graduated college at the dawn of the 1950s, and after an abbreviated but brilliant career he was on the cusp of retiring. Teresa was still at Antioch College, studying psychology and working on her feet.

The only thing Teresa really knew about Harry, other than his name, was that he was a good bit older than she was. When they met, he was forty-four, and she was only twenty-five. But with his bald head and long gray beard he presented as much older.

It wasn't hard to see why he was attracted to her. She was an ingenue with long blond hair, a flawless face, and the trim and alluring body of a woman who was still a half-decade away from her thirtieth birthday. Despite her youth, she was intelligent, a passionate conversationalist, and a woman with strongly held opinions. She also had a social conscience; through the years Teresa had marched for a variety of causes that she felt would make the country better and more fair.

At first, Teresa merely found Harry charming. He was a nice guy with a ready smile and a few self-deprecating jokes. He had a sense of humor about his baldness, and he could even poke fun of his own heritage. He joked about being cheap, though she found that he was in fact generous and tipped well.

One thing that they did not have in common was their marital statuses. Teresa was free of her husband, a man she found abusive, while Harry was still married and living with his wife, a piece of information he did not readily disclose to his new girlfriend. Harry eventually admitted to Teresa that he was married, and she continued their romance anyway with her eyes wide open.

It didn't take Harry long after meeting Teresa to leave Marilyn. It was almost immediate. There was a great deal of risk for Harry in his behavior, with its implicit dishonesty and betrayal. Of all the things he stood to lose, at the top of the list was the affection of his adult children. They might have felt righteous rage on behalf of their jilted mother.

Instead the affair and dissolution of the traditional family structure actually brought the children closer to their dad. He was visibly happier, less tense, and more approachable. He moved from the suburban Baltimore home he'd shared with Marilyn and bought a palatial old farm on Maryland's Eastern Shore, 340 acres and a river view, called Hawksworth. That would be his home with his new wife, Teresa.

Hawksworth was a kind of Eden for the Meyerhoff offspring. It brought so much pleasure to the kids that one of them wondered aloud, a little resentfully, why their dad had never purchased a place like that when they were younger.

The relaxed atmosphere on the new farm was a perfect reflection of the new man. To the outside world he might still be a fearsome figure with the power to literally change the landscape, but to his family he was a different guy. He was in love. He was mellow. He smiled a lot. Most of all he spent more time with his kids and got to know them better than he ever had before.

The Meyerhoff children didn't mourn the end of their parents' marriage as much as they felt a sense of pleasure and relief that they were finally getting to spend time with their father. All the years they were growing up they had been starved for his presence, attention, and affection.

While Harry's business might have been somewhat behind him, there was one arena in which he continued to stoke his competitive fires, and that was horse racing. He and his brother, Robert, had been co-owners of their own stable since the early 1960s. But much like Harry had ended his marriage to Marilyn and ceased his active business partnership with Robert, he had also ended the brothers' horse racing arrangement.

Both brothers continued racing, and at extraordinarily high levels, but they did so apart. Robert worked with "Dicky" Small, an excellent trainer, and owned Fitzhugh Farm in Harford County, Maryland. His stable included Broad Brush, a horse that had earned more than $3 million, and Concern, a winner of the Breeders' Cup Classic.

After deposing Robert, Harry made Teresa and his son, Tom, his new racing partners. The idea was to make a more cohesive family unit. One of the first tests for Harry's new team was in Lexington, Kentucky, where the Meyerhoffs and trainer Buddy Delp were all due to attend the Keeneland Fall Yearling Sale to choose colts for their new stable.

Some of the best one-year-old thoroughbreds in the world were for sale at Keeneland. Buddy's influence at the auction, interestingly considering his vast knowledge, was relatively small. Harry, an expert businessman but a racing outsider, was the one who scoured the catalog looking for the right bloodlines and who determined which colts deserved his money and how much of it.

Buddy basically came along to have a look at the horseflesh in person that Meyerhoff had picked out in print. He wasn't a veterinarian, but he judged the soundness of Harry's choices. In fact, Buddy was so inconsequential to the process that he'd actually missed his flight to Kentucky and had to meet the Meyerhoffs there the next morning. Harry wasn't exercised about it since he felt perfectly capable of buying thoroughbreds without his trainer's assistance.

That year, 1977, there were more than 1,500 yearlings in the fall catalog. The Meyerhoffs and Buddy examined more than two hundred of them. But Harry had come all the way there with just one colt on his mind, a charcoal gray identified in the catalog as "Hip No. 532." He gave himself a budget of $60,000 to acquire Hip No. 532, but he wanted the horse so badly that he secretly vowed that if push came to shove, he would pay even more to get him. But it never came to that.

Harry valued the steel gray far more than any other potential suitor at the auction. When the gavel banged, he found himself with the horse he wanted at a price he had never expected. He paid "only" $37,000 for Hip No. 532, the most he surrendered for the six horses that he bought that weekend, but not by very much. Half of his new purchases were $30,000 or more. Persian Emperor, the most expensive horse at the auction, sold for $200,000.

Meyerhoff's enthusiasm for his new gray horse was mostly a matter of bloodlines. The horse was the son of Bold Bidder and the grandson of Bold Ruler, one of the twentieth century's most productive sires. As Buddy Delp noted, the Meyerhoffs had a long-standing interest in "Bold Ruler blood." So did many other owners. The only reason the charcoal gray did not garner more interest or sell for more was because his mother, Spectacular, had a less compelling lineage. She had but one notable horse in her family tree, and the best days for that one stretched back to the Jazz Age.

Harry not only picked out the new colt, but he named it too. Being an avid card player, he initially came up with "Seven No Trump." It was a bridge term called out by a player who believed he possessed an unbeatable hand. But the Jockey Club refused to approve it since the name was already associated with another horse. Meyerhoff went back to the drawing board and cleverly combined the names of the colt's parents—the mare, Spectacular, and the sire, Bold Bidder. He officially named his new horse Spectacular Bid.

To anyone who knew Harry Meyerhoff it was no surprise that he was the driving force in finding and choosing a great horse or that he was clever enough to provide it with an unforgettable and marketable moniker or that his managerial skills ensured that it would receive the best care and training. Harry was successful at virtually everything he did.

Understanding Meyerhoff meant also understanding his family and city. Harry had been born into wealth, but his hard work, bright mind, and sharp focus assured that he would have his own string of successes and build his own fortune. He grew up on Ocala Avenue in the heart of the city's northwest side. He studied at Baltimore Polytechnic Institute (or "Poly," as it was known locally), a public high school with a special emphasis on engineering. (Poly was a prestigious early example of a "magnet" school with a big reputation, though one of the teachers at rival City College liked to point out, "They say they are training engineers over there [at Poly], but most of them end up reading meters for the Gas and Electric Company.") After high school Harry followed in his brother Robert's footsteps and moved on to Bethlehem, Pennsylvania, where he attended the elite eastern university Lehigh.

If Ronnie Franklin's Dundalk provided the industrial revolution its brawn, Lehigh provided its brains. Among Lehigh's many virtues was that it was welcoming to Jewish students like Harry in an era when many top universities, including Johns Hopkins back home in Baltimore, limited the number of Jews they admitted with anti-Semitic quotas.

Lehigh opened its doors for Harry and others like him and in fact harbored a thriving Jewish community. Harry was only one of several high-achieving Lehigh students from Baltimore's Jewish community. His classmates included Morton Lapidus, a future soft-drink industry titan; Morton Cohen, whose parents, ironically, owned Pimlico Race Track, and Joseph R. L. Sterne, who would be the *Baltimore Sun*'s editorial page editor for forty years. Lehigh's Jewish students were a close-knit group, and many of them, including Harry, belonged to the same fraternity, Pi Lambda Phi. The group was housed off campus on the town's north side.

Harry the college student was a handsome young fellow with a lanky, muscular frame and a tousle of wavy and unruly dark hair. He was a magnificent athlete, a prolific scorer in lacrosse who once netted seven goals in a single game against archrival Lafayette. In 1948 he was named to the All-American team.

But one of Meyerhoff's fraternity brothers, Theodore Madfis, remembered him less than fondly. "You knew he had money," Madfis said. "He made a lot of noise when he spoke. But I don't think anyone was really close to him in the fraternity house. He wasn't someone I wanted to spend time with."

Madfis found Harry to be the least impressive of the Baltimore crowd. "There were several who were much more interesting, more impressive [than Harry]. . . . People liked them better. People didn't take to Harry." The Pi Lambda Phi fraternity brothers "dated the girls from Cedar Crest College, Allentown, Bethlehem," he said. "But I never saw [Meyerhoff] with a date," he said.

When Harry graduated from Lehigh in 1950, he returned home to Maryland to partner with his father and brother in a new real estate development company they called "Jack Meyerhoff and Sons." Family venture or not, it was an exciting business opportunity. In the euphoria following World War II the United States was enjoying a population explosion and a burgeoning economy. Meanwhile, the nation was in the throes of a serious housing shortage. In 1944, with World War II still raging and many potential home buyers away fighting, home starts in the United States had dipped down to only 114,000. Even before the war most builders were small-time operators who put up less than five houses per year.

At the dawn of the Eisenhower age, however, farmland just outside the major cities was inexpensive and ripe for acquisition. To the uneducated eye those acres were still seen as remote and irrelevant. But forward thinkers like the Meyerhoffs saw opportunity. They knew that automobile improvements and a growing network of paved highways were making the suburbs more accessible and valuable than ever before.

Bedroom communities also offered a solution to a growing problem that then vexed many white Americans. Integration of both neighborhoods and schools was coming to the cities, where Black and white people lived. The suburbs were a place for whites to run away, a place where there were fewer Blacks with whom to integrate. The affluence it took to make that move, they thought, would assure that Blacks would not arrive on their doorsteps again for decades to come.

In 1950, just as Harry returned to Baltimore from Lehigh, U.S. home starts exploded to 1.7 million. William Levitt, a revolutionary developer in the greater New York City area, learned to meet that demand in innovative ways. He applied the principals of a well-functioning automobile assembly plant to home building. He broke down the process into twenty-seven component parts. With his greater efficiencies, houses were begun and delivered in a fraction of the time it had taken previous builders. And he sold them at a far more attractive price.

Despite his breakthroughs Levitt didn't have anything on the Meyerhoffs, who, as a family, had already been building suburban homes and commercial properties for decades.

The Meyerhoff business legend is a classic American story of one family rising from the lowest depths to achieve great wealth. As East European Jews, the Meyerhoffs could not have started life in Baltimore from a more disadvantageous position. The East European Jewish refugees who migrated to America were considered by the majority culture to be lacking in education, social graces, and even hygiene.

In the early twentieth century H. L. Mencken, then still a young reporter, went into one of the city's Jewish ghettos and saw Russian and Polish Jews right off the boat working in and around one of the sweatshops. He recorded his revulsion, especially of the small Jewish children: "I . . . was appalled by what I saw," he recalled. "No one seemed to mind that dirty urchins played in the garbage, constructing a chain of potato peelings." Mencken's well-respected biographer, Marian Elizabeth Rodgers, wrote that "the sight convinced [Mencken] that the bulk of Russian Jews lived in filth."

Mencken's family, of German extraction, had only been in the United States a few decades longer than the Meyerhoffs, but it was a more precise fit for mainstream American mores. The Menckens owned a cigar factory in Baltimore, two prestigious homes, and a stake in the Washington baseball club.

Like many Americans of that era, Mencken was an unabashed anti-Semite. He was not in favor of the mass extermination of European Jews, but his plan for saving them from the atrocities of the Holocaust demonstrated the wide difference that he and others saw in Jews from Western and Eastern Europe. Those from the western part of the continent were considered better, of a higher class, than those from the eastern part. Mencken advocated absorbing German Jews into the United States but felt that East Europeans were not ready for life in an advanced society and should be removed to the Soviet Union.

The Meyerhoffs had to work around such irrational biases to have any hope of success in America. And it didn't come fast or easily. The family patriarch was a butcher with a small shop on the north side of town. It was a simple enterprise, but it gave the family enough money and standing to gain a foothold in their new country.

The true origin story of the family's business success, however, started in the early 1920s with one of Harry's uncles, Joseph Meyerhoff. Joseph worked all day at his father's meat market and then spent his nights in a classroom studying law, a subject for which he had no enthusiasm. Meanwhile Joseph's brother, Morris, started a small home-building business and asked Joseph to join him in the venture. Joseph accepted and began by handling his brother's legal matters and working as a laborer on the construction sites.

Joseph started his own building business in 1921 but continued doing his brother's legal work, a job that included endorsing promissory notes. Morris ran into serious financial problems in 1924 and declared bankruptcy. Joseph, because of the endorsements he had signed, was caught in the same financial web. Instead of also declaring bankruptcy, however, Joseph paid back all of the creditors. It took him ten long, painful years to pay the debts, but when all was said and done, his reputation as a man of his word was assured and his business took off in earnest.

Joseph started by building and selling the most ubiquitous thing in Baltimore: row houses. As his fortunes grew, he moved into constructing luxury homes for incredibly opulent Baltimore neighborhoods such as Guilford, Stoneleigh, Homeland, and Roland Park. These communities set the standard for gracious living and helped create the suburb phenomenon nationwide.

All in all, over the course of his long career, Joseph Meyerhoff built more than fifteen thousand homes, seventeen thousand apartments, and nineteen shopping centers. He amassed a fortune that was estimated at more than $100 million. His partner in some of these pursuits was another one of his brothers, Jacob "Jack" Meyerhoff. The brothers had joined forces to form the Property Sales Company. When they split up in 1951 and liquidated that blandly named but highly successful firm, they were both still young enough to start anew but experienced enough to achieve much more than they ever had before.

Jack headed up an important ready-mix concrete supply firm that he built into a valuable commodity before selling it. After that, of course, came his business venture with his boys. The sons' connection to their father's name and reputation was a significant business asset, and so was the old man's knowledge. Jack was considered an expert in retail development, a professional who understood how to construct and operate commercial structures as well as anyone in the country. His reputation was assured with projects such as Edmondson Village Shopping Center in suburban West Baltimore. It was one of the first shopping centers in the United States oriented around the automobile.

Built promptly after World War II, Edmondson Village's Tudor architecture affected the look of a nineteenth-century English lane. Its twenty-nine shops sold everything from auto supplies to ice cream. But instead of seamlessly meshing with the local houses and pubs, it was surrounded by a five-hundred-car parking lot. Edmondson Village was a harbinger of the motorized United States to come, a place in which consumers no longer walked to the corner store down the street but drove from their far-flung homes. For all its fanfare and fine touches, Edmondson Village was basically a strip mall, a pioneer in American blight and sprawl. Similar projects would mar American suburbs for the next fifty years.

Jack's expertise in this area led him to form yet another business, this time with a then little-known mortgage banker. Their new venture, the Community Research and Development Company, was specifically formed to build and operate shopping centers. Jack was named chairman of the board while his partner, James W. Rouse, became president.

This business eventually gained public acclaim under its new name, the Rouse Company. The firm gained national prominence for reviving downtown shopping corridors in America's great but crumbling cities, including Faneuil Hall in Boston, South Street Sea Port in New York, Underground in Atlanta, and the Riverwalk Center in New Orleans. The most famous of these projects was Baltimore's Harborplace.

All of these ventures were hailed for their courage and innovation. James Rouse and Jack Meyerhoff invested heavily in downtowns when others were fleeing them. They made their shopping centers attractions and entertainment centers by filling them with quirkier retailers and restauranteurs.

Harborplace was an especially significant case in point. Baltimore had been hit by many sad reversals after World War II, including steadily declining job opportunities, the sale or relocation of headquartered banks and businesses, the flight of the white middle-class tax base, and the rise of heroin in the city's ever-expanding Black ghettos. The riots after the murder of Martin Luther King Jr. in 1968 rapidly accelerated the decline and highlighted the inequities and violent tensions between white and Black Americans.

With all of these negative trends, retail shopping in Baltimore proper had all but vanished. The city's traditional retail corridor was Howard Street, a main downtown artery where large department stores competed with each other from huge, architecturally beautiful structures. It was Baltimore's version of New York's Fifth Avenue. But the great structures that had housed those once grand stores were abandoned and shuttered with no new tenants to ever arrive. And the marvelous architecture sat fallow and rotting.

Harborplace not only brought shopping back to downtown Baltimore, but it also showcased the natural beauty of a once glorious waterway that had long been ceded to commerce. Out went the rotting old piers and warehouses, and in came two new, gleaming "galleries" of restaurants and shopping.

But the Rouse Company's most startling project and significant achievement was not reviving old cities but inventing a new one. The company bought twelve thousand rural acres between Baltimore and Washington and then planned and built the city of Columbia, Maryland.

More than just a spectacularly audacious development project, it was also touted as a bold social experiment. Columbia's founders claimed to harmonize architecture with nature, retail with residential, and culture with culture.

In Columbia, a synonym for America, everything that Jack Meyerhoff knew about developing land supposedly coalesced and meshed with James Rouse's humanistic views. Black, white, and brown people were to live side by side. Jews, Christians, and Muslims all worshipped at the same "interfaith centers." Wealthy homeowners and aspiring apartment dwellers bridged the social-class gap and coexisted seamlessly.

But some questioned if Columbia was really a city at all or just a well-branded suburb. Its center of commerce wasn't a collection of "downtown" buildings and skyscrapers but a shopping mall also owned by the Rouse Company. Ultimately Columbia included many of the hallmarks of a city, including a concert venue, a hospital, and a community college. A downtown lake offered fishing and "natural" beauty, though it was as faux as the town itself, made not by God but by human hands.

Columbia's aesthetic was highly controlled. Its design standards mandated inconspicuous commercial signage. Green spaces and wooded areas were zoned into existence to preserve a sense of organic beauty. But all of this merely hid the true nature of the project. Columbia wasn't as green as the developers pretended; it was all about the combustible engine. The town looked like the nucleus of an atom with an endless network of high-speed beltways, highways, and interstates encircling it, cutting through it, and zipping around it.

There were other deceptions as well.

Diversity was supposed to be prized in Columbia, yet it was a flavorless town, a beige and bland place that reeked of homogenization and conformity. Worse: it accelerated the exodus of middle-class white families from urban environments in nearby Washington and Baltimore that were legitimately diverse. Columbia helped erode and collapse the tax bases in those cities and further encouraged the so-called white flight that expanded inner-city poverty and the ghettoization of American Blacks.

One prominent Baltimore politician admitted to his son that Baltimore had lost the war to retain white residents a long time ago. "There's nothing left to do now," he told the boy, "but build a fence around the place to keep the jigs in."

Despite all the pieties about "green space" and "organic architecture," Columbia was built on a wide swath of former farmland, woodlands, and open space that the developers had largely bulldozed, ploughed under, paved over, and tamed. No one, however, could take away from the significant business achievement. Jack Meyerhoff and his partners at the Rouse Company walked away with incredible riches and something more valuable than money. They had created a hard-to-refute image of themselves as altruistic intellectuals and social reformers. It was a conflation once known in a more literate era as Babbitry.

Harry and Robert were less audacious in their business pursuits than their father had been in his, but they were highly successful too. Without attempting to reinvent anything, they built houses and garden apartment communities all around the Baltimore beltway. Like their father and their uncles, they were brothers pooling their talents and efforts to generate wealth and prestige for the family name.

A big part of the Meyerhoff mystique was grounded in philanthropy. The family gave away its money and valuables almost as prolifically as it earned them. Joseph Meyerhoff singlehandedly saved the Baltimore Symphony Orchestra and then gave it $10 million to fund a first-class music venue. It was christened, not unreasonably, the Joseph Meyerhoff Symphony Hall.

As a Jew who had personally fled persecution and poverty in Europe, Joseph was particularly interested in supporting self-determination for his people. He estimated that he had written about $5 million in checks for a variety of projects in Israel, including funding five different libraries, a college, and various pavilions.

Robert and Harry Meyerhoff continued the family's philanthropic tradition. Harry threw his support behind Center Stage, an important Baltimore group dedicated to producing excellent theater. Robert and his wife, Jane, cultivated a modern art collection that included works by canonic masters such as Jasper Johns, Jackson Pollack, Roy Lichenstein, Robert Rauchenberg, and Frank Stella (among others). After spending years collecting, they donated their masterpieces to the National Gallery of Art in Washington DC—a gift that was worth about $300 million. It was a highly significant donation. "[This gift] doesn't fit into [our collection]," the modern art curator said. "It defines it."

The Meyerhoffs embodied a muscular Americanism. They had come to the United States with nothing but a legacy of ethnic prejudice aimed against them, and yet through hard work and education they rose to high levels of wealth, respect, and power.

But the Meyerhoffs also had another quality; a thinly veiled greed. Patriarch Joseph, a slender, bald man who favored a pencil-thin mustache and fine tailoring, amassed powerful friends like so many dollar bills. But he paid a steep price to fit in.

Much like his colleagues in the development industry, Joseph built neighborhoods that utilized protective covenants that kept Blacks and, incredibly, Jews out of his homes. That prohibition was especially astonishing since it meant that even he and his family could not live in the neighborhoods that he had built. "It is a plain and proven fact," he said, falsely, "that it is not within my power . . . to alter what has always been a deep-rooted pattern of housing in the Baltimore area." It was his cluttered way of saying that he hadn't invented racism and there was nothing he could do about it.

Joseph's position was shockingly mercenary and out of touch. Already wealthy, he could have manfully absorbed the repercussions of doing "the right thing" like few others could. But the sad fact was he simply wasn't interested in being a leader for any cause that might limit his business interests.

This mercenary attitude rubbed off on Joseph's nephew Harry Meyerhoff. Harry also engaged in questionable activities to enhance his success and wealth.

By the 1960s Maryland had a well-earned reputation as one of the most politically corrupt states in the United States. Much of that misconduct revolved around real estate development. There were two obvious reasons for this. First, there was a lot of money to be made in real estate, and second, making that money relied on the good will of politicians and political bureaucrats.

One powerful man all too eager to take advantage of this situation was

Spiro T. Agnew, the son of a Greek immigrant restaurant owner. Agnew was a tall, dark-haired man with a fleshy nose and a studied, meticulous appearance. He idolized his father but ran from his roots and went by the Anglicized nickname "Ted" rather than the Mediterranean "Spiro."

Ted began as a small-time lawyer with an interest in politics who rose through the ranks with astonishing speed. He went from the Baltimore County Executive Office to vice president of the United States in only about six years.

Agnew spoke a great deal about law and order during his tenure in government, but he was secretly a highly persistent criminal. He was accused of a multitude of crimes, including being offered bribes without reporting them, engaging in inappropriate business deals, using inside information for land purchases near planned public improvements, and taking substantial cash payments in exchange for favors, such as the granting of public roads contracts.

In short, Agnew set up a business in which his favors were for sale. When he became vice president, he relocated that lucrative enterprise to Washington.

Projects that were awarded as a result of secret payments to Agnew included the Chesapeake Bay Bridge project, the Harbor Tunnel in Baltimore, a large bond for a tunnel and bridge, and the master plan for a federal building. His corruption always seemed to be connected to real estate development.

Agnew's misbehavior led to a great deal of scrutiny on Maryland politicians by law enforcement and the press. That was especially true for Agnew's successors in the Baltimore County Executive's Office and the Maryland governor's mansion.

In 1968, when Agnew resigned the governorship to accept the vice presidency, another young lawyer, Marvin Mandel, succeeded him. Mandel was considered an adept, even talented, public servant who was hailed for ushering in many state improvements. But he was also caught taking cash for political favors just like Agnew.

Mandel's political rise was aided by a childhood friend named Irvin Kovens. They had grown up together in the same northwest Baltimore neighborhood. Mandel became governor, but his power paled in comparison to that of Kovens, who was ostensibly a discount furniture storeowner in a low-income African American neighborhood of Baltimore.

In fact, Kovens was an old-fashioned political boss who could raise incredible sums of money for any candidate he favored by prying open a rusty old locked file box in his office that contained the names and numbers of thousands of people who owed him favors. He could make a king simply by picking up his phone. He operated in the shadows, but many argued that his actions were for the betterment of the city and state. Kovens not only backed Mandel in Annapolis, but he also put William Donald Schaefer in City Hall as surely as if he had lifted him up and tucked him into the mayor's big chair himself. Schaefer and Mandel were respected nationally and considered among the best in the country at their respective jobs.

So Maryland's boss system was considered flawed but effective. And indeed, it worked well enough until a woman younger and blonder than Mandel's wife undid everything. The governor's long, torturous personal and professional unraveling began, as it did for many middle-aged men, with an adulterous affair. It ended, however, like that of a doomed jockey—on the low turf of a racecourse. Mandel's case highlighted for everyone the unholy intersection of high-stakes politics, horse racing, and real estate development that drove the state.

One of the worst-kept secrets in Maryland was the fact that Mandel was stepping out on his wife, Barbra (called "Bootsie" by everyone who knew her). Bootsie was from Mandel's world. She had grown up with him in Baltimore's Jewish community. Mandel's mistress, Jeanne Blackistone Dorsey, was almost twenty years younger and two inches taller than he was. She had the fresh face of a debutante and the pedigree of a thoroughbred. Her familial roots went all the way back to the very founding of the Maryland colony.

One night, on his way back from trysting with Jeanne in southern Maryland, Mandel was involved in a fatal accident. The driver of the other vehicle was killed. Mandel survived, but he was bloodied.

Suddenly a harsh spotlight shone down on the governor.

The *Washington Post*, smelling the corpuscles, sent one of its rising star reporters, Richard Cohen, to the governor's mansion. The editors wanted this young man to ask the governor a terribly uncomfortable question: Had the governor been visiting his mistress?

Incredibly, Mandel agreed to see Cohen. Upon arriving at the mansion, the reporter was ushered into the great man's bedroom, where he lay in his pajamas, with the bloody gashes of his trauma still unhealed and fully visible like scarlet letters.

The governor's press secretary, sensing the young reporter's discomfort, enhanced it by goading him forward. "Go ahead," the aide meanly said. "Ask him."

Cohen swallowed hard and then choked out his cringe-worthy question. He point blank asked the most powerful man in the state if he had been visiting his mistress before the wreck.

The governor heavily sighed at the intrusive question he was surely anticipating. He glared at Cohen and then responded with one simple word.

"No," the governor said.

"Now get out!" the press secretary bellowed. And out young Cohen went.

But Bootsie was made of far stronger stuff than that. She made it clear she wasn't going anywhere. She refused to grant Mandel a divorce or even vacate the governor's mansion unless and until he met a list of her demands.

She wanted money, of course, and a lot of it. The problem was that the governor didn't have much. Though he lived in a mansion and traveled by limousine and yacht, Mandel made a working man's salary of only about $25,000 per year.

One thing was clear: it wouldn't be easy to give Bootsie the boot. It meant not only coming up with the huge amount she wanted but also paying astronomical legal fees. The governor had no choice but to turn to his friends for help. And he got it. They gave him enough money to deal with his divorce and a few extras like some snazzy suits and a little cash.

All that was well and good except that his friends, led by Kovens, quickly asked for a favor in return. They demanded that Mandel veto a bill that added racing dates to a dilapidated old junker of a race track called Marlboro. Their goal was to make the value of the track plummet in order to scuttle a deal that someone else had made to purchase it. After the veto Mandel's friends, shielding their identities, swooped in and bought Marlboro at an artificially depressed price. After the deal was finalized, Mandel did indeed sign a bill increasing Marlboro's racing dates, and the property's value skyrocketed again. The governor's buddies had made a pretty good bet. They flipped the track and walked away with a handsome profit.

Thanks to this scheme a few esteemed people, including Mandel and Kovens, went to jail. Years later the verdict was overturned, but Mandel's political career, once so justifiably bright and promising, was irretrievably lost.

Back in Baltimore County a similar scandal found Robert and Harry Meyerhoff. Their man in power was Dale Anderson, a former developer out of their own ranks and now the Baltimore County executive.

In 1974 a federal jury convicted Anderson on thirty-four counts of conspiracy, extortion, and tax evasion. It seemed that Anderson had been charging his old developer buddies a "fee" in order to "expedite" their permit requests. This was accomplished through a system of color-coded index cards. Yellow file cards and folders were assigned to applicants who were put on a fast track.

It is not surprising that major builders were among Anderson's biggest financial backers. And for good reason. Speedy permits were more than a mere convenience; they were a highly valuable business commodity. They allowed builders to plan their projects around labor deadlines and seasonal shifts in the weather, and they also provided substantial savings on project-related interest payments.

Much of the evidence for the color-codes had been destroyed before journalists could investigate. But one yellow file remained. It approved all the permits for a Baltimore-area garden apartment complex and did it in just eight days. For a company less privileged the process would have taken six to eight weeks. That lone yellow file belonged to the Robert and Harry Meyerhoff Building Company.

The man who expedited the paperwork was George J. Mueller. Mueller had only recently become a bureaucrat. Before that he had been an employee at Dale Anderson's development company. Mueller followed his boss into government and did quite well, doubling his initial county salary and getting reimbursed for expenses at a rate double that of anyone else working at the county.

As the investigations intensified, Mueller abruptly left his job serving the citizens and went to back to what he knew; he found work in real estate development at none other than the Robert and Harry Meyerhoff Building Company.

Dale Anderson left his job too, but in his case it was to go to jail. The Meyerhoffs, on the other hand, skated away with very little or no damage done to themselves or their business. After all, the next day a brand new newspaper rolled off the presses, and the reporters and the public were on to new things.

No ink could smear or stain the Meyerhoff name. It was as sparkling clean and as solid as it ever had been. Harry went on to his affair with Teresa and then his happy life with her on Hawksworth Farm. But even on the Eastern Shore he wasn't exactly what he seemed. Without work to occupy him, he became an all-day drinker, starting early in the morning with beer and then, later in the day, switching to vodka. He supplemented his drinking by liberally smoking pot. After years in a jacket and tie and as one of the most respected businessmen in the state, he was, in fact, unconventional.

There was a valuable lesson to be learned in all that for anyone who was paying attention, and almost no one was. There can be quite a wide gulf between a man and the public's perception of him.

In some cases, a great reputation, or even respectability, can be nothing more than a beard.

5 *Middleburg*

Tony Franklin's Ford Gran Torino was just like the one Starsky and Hutch tooled around in on ABC TV every Saturday night, the one they used to chase down pimps and drug dealers. Tony's car was the color gold, and it was strictly for the good guys. He used it to escort Marian to the food market or to chauffeur his kids to their friends' houses and jobs. The Gran Torino was just a ride, but it was also pure Tony Franklin—American-made and as solid as they come. But it was a little badass too.

In the spring of 1977 Tony wheeled the car around front, and Ronnie came out of the house. He opened the trunk, tossed in his grip, and then slammed himself into the back seat. Marian rode shotgun. Father, mother, and son pulled out of their narrow Dundalk street and lit out for the broad highway. They were barreling down the road and headed for the ancient town of Middleburg, Virginia, only about two and a half hours from their front door and yet a world away.

It was a journey that would take them from the cold, hard concrete streets of their industrial hometown to a privileged world of stone fences and rolling green meadows. Middleburg was an old town still clinging to eighteenth-century agrarian values and a stringent caste system, a place where the rich and poor often came together in the horse industry.

The Franklins weren't going there looking for bygone charm. They were hurtling through time and space hoping to find Ronnie's future and, with any luck at all, the origin story of what they hoped would be his legend.

Middleburg, like Dundalk, had plenty of hard-working poor folks, but it was dominated at various times by celebrated American families like the Mellons, the DuPonts, and the Kennedys. They were the ones who gave the small, charming place its edge, its opulence, and its aura.

Middleburg was established before the Revolutionary War, but it was *of* the Civil War. Located in the heart of the Confederacy, it once saw huge armies of boys, not much older than Ronnie, come thundering through on horseback, rifles slung over their shoulders and sabers glinting by their sides. The kids were goaded to clash and spill their blood all for the sake of old men and their financial interests.

The boys wound up on the ground—a feast for buzzing flies, scavenger birds, and foraging dogs—while the powerful old men whose ideals had killed them were sculpted in bronze and bolted to marble slabs. It was an honor, supposedly, but the old men's names faded as quickly as their dreams, and the statues became public toilets for crows and pigeons.

Tony Franklin, as always, was there for his son. To him it was a pleasure to drive his boy to a more meaningful life. But going to Middleburg was also something of a sad ending for the Franklins. It marked the discontinuation of their parental control over him and his ascendancy to adulthood. Success in Middleburg, if Ronald could find it, meant not only a more independent life for him but also a far different life than that of his parents.

Tony and Marian dropped Ronnie off and then returned to the row houses of their neighborhood, comfortable and confident that their son was in good hands. They left him at the prestigious training facility founded by Paul Mellon himself, an heir to a great banking fortune and one of the ten richest men in America.

Tony may have done the driving, but everyone in the car knew it was Buddy Delp who was driving the process. The Franklins were grateful to Ronnie's famous and powerful benefactor. It seemed to them that Buddy alone had the ability to give the boy a real future.

Delp's plan was to have Ronnie tutored in the fine art of race riding by Barbara Graham. Buddy knew Barbara well. She was his go-to source for training and breaking his early-stage horses. Shopping sprees in Kentucky by Delp or his clients ended with Buddy shipping the new stock to Barbara in Middleburg.

Breaking colts was one line of the horse business that held no intrigue at all for Delp. He was more than happy to let Barbara handle that, and why not? To the press and public Buddy got the credit for making racers out of the horses, and he was the one who enjoyed whatever real financial reward there was to be gained out of a horse's success. By the same token, training race-riding jockeys wasn't really in Barbara's wheelhouse. She was known far and wide as a superb rider and early-stage trainer. She even tutored young riders of various sorts from time to time. But rarely, if ever, had she trained a jockey. It wasn't a job that she relished.

Barbara accepted Buddy's request to teach Ronnie, but only because he twisted her arm to do it. In fact, she owed a great deal of her business success to Delp and his unwavering commitment to her organization. Buddy was one of her biggest, most important, and most consistent clients. In a large sense she was financially successful because he fed her work. It was something she could count on year after year. "She didn't just, by the grace of her heart, say, 'Oh, yeah, I'd love to train a jockey and let him ride my horses and fall off,'" one of Graham's employees remembered. She took on Ronnie as a pupil because Delp expected her to do it and he enjoyed the leverage to make it happen.

Tucked away in rural Virginia, Barbara was something of a secret to the wider world, but she was an eminence in Middleburg. She was known and respected by virtually everyone in her hometown as a successful businesswoman. In addition to her humming horse operation, she also ran a profitable farm only about twenty minutes away from Middleburg.

Male admiration for Barbara went beyond the workplace. She was a great beauty, highly athletic at about 5 feet 5 inches and 120 pounds, and possessed of pleasing curves. She had dark eyes and a creamy complexion, but her trademark was her windswept brown hair, proof that she was an outdoorswoman and a professional too serious and self-confident to bother with her appearance.

Barbara sometimes enthusiastically returned the male attention that she got. She was a vivacious spirit, a coquette who openly flirted with men she liked despite the serious and burdensome responsibilities that were constantly on her shoulders. She had more than one great romance in her lifetime.

In her horse obsession, youth, brown hair, ruddy complexion, and painfully beautiful face, the young Barbara bore a striking resemblance to Elizabeth Taylor in *National Velvet*. And like the main character of that film Barbara had a savant's understanding of thoroughbreds.

Barbara's many positive qualities made her attractive to important women too. Jacqueline Kennedy, a rider since her privileged childhood, built a home for herself and her young husband, President John F. Kennedy, in Middleburg's hunt country. She intended it as a getaway from the White House for her husband and a place where she could spend more time on horseback. The Kennedys' estate, called Wexford after the Irish county where the president's forbears had originated, was a Brady Bunch banal rancher, but it held a lot of promise for Mrs. Kennedy, who imagined a family retreat there and a home base for her serious riding.

The one person whose company Mrs. Kennedy sought in Middleburg was Barbara Graham's. The two women enjoyed a close and enduring friendship, and they rode together for many decades, despite the fact that Wexford was sold soon after President Kennedy was assassinated in 1963. They were still riding together thirty years later, until the last year of Jackie's life.

Before Barbara raised and trained horses, she had been raised side by side with them. Her father, Sam Graham, was a farmer and a thoroughbred breeder. His farm in Purcellville was young Barbara's classroom and laboratory. She broke her first yearlings there while she was still only a young girl.

As an adult and a professional, Barbara took her natural talent to another level. One of her clients, Preston Burch, a Hall of Fame trainer with a long resume of stakes victories, paid her to keep his horses in her barns. During his daily visits to check in on his stock he also provided her a free education. Burch taught Barbara his methods for horse care, regaled her with stories from his career, and indulged her endless stream of questions. "I should be paying [Burch]," Barbara said, "rather than accepting money for his horses."

Burch's advice might have been free, but it was valuable to Barbara, who listened to everything the experienced horseman told her and amalgamated it into her own distinct methods. In short, her education about horse care, management, and training was as impeccable as it could be. She knew as much about horses as there was to know.

Graham was ambitious and built an enviable operation at the training center that was her headquarters, dominating Barn 1, the largest structure among the many stables. Her stock also spilled over into about half of Barn 3. She filled her stalls with dozens of thoroughbreds, each one coming to her as little more than a baby but leaving her care after about six months—tame, calm, and ready to fulfill its function at the race track for its permanent trainer.

Working for Barbara was hard but fun. Women, especially in the exercise-rider ranks, dominated her operation. Each December the ladies adorned their protective helmets with reindeer antlers; in the spring, they donned bunny ears. It was a highly cohesive, mostly happy, and totally satisfying professional environment with a familial feel. The only drawback was that no one, except maybe Barbara, got rich working there. Nevertheless, her largely female staff was a model of feminine empowerment in a less than progressive era. Though it was admirable, it was hardly a political statement. "Barbara hired us because she could get us cheaper," her close friend and employee Sharon Maloney remembered with a laugh.

In truth, it was brutal work. After laboring all day for Barbara at the training center, in the late afternoon the ladies hustled over to her farm in Purcellville, where they put in another partial workday. They'd catch the wild horses on her land and break them in her stalls. "It was an all-day thing," Maloney wistfully remembered, "and I got $75 a week for doing it."

If Barbara was a little tight with a buck (her father was rumored to be even cheaper), she was at least as parsimonious with herself as she was with the help. That was never more evident than when she suffered a terrifying mishap. She was exercising a horse they all knew to be difficult when the animal suddenly went rogue and darted for the inside rail. In a frantic instant Barbara was jerked from her saddle and plunged to the hard ground. In the violence of the moment, both of her wrists were broken.

Barbara was in immense pain, but she scraped herself off the ground, hobbled to her car, and drove home to rest for the remainder of the day. The next morning she was back at Barn 1 bright and early and without complaint. She never bothered going to the doctor. That cost money. Cheap and tough, that was Barbara.

Her personality featured some other trying aspects. She was a perfectionist, and when she was in a foul mood, she could be short with her people. If she observed a job being handled poorly, she would quickly eject the errant employee from both the task and her barn. "You do it my way or you get up out of here," she'd say. And then she'd expertly complete the task herself.

Barbara demanded that everyone, regardless of title or primary function, have an expert's knowledge of every task, no matter how difficult or menial. And if you worked for Barbara Graham, you'd better love the job because the days were long and unforgiving. The lights in the barn went on at around 4:30 a.m. The training began at dawn, which meant taking the horses out and galloping them. That would go on roughly until lunchtime, when the animals were cooled down and fed. After a break for the workers to eat and rest up a little, everyone came back to the barn around 3:00 p.m. to pick out the stalls and, eventually, to feed the horses their dinner.

Barbara's workers typically went home around 4 p.m. In addition to her horse-breaking business, however, she also trained horses of racing age. On the days when her horses raced, a Graham employee's "work day" could stretch far into the night. On racing days they traveled to tracks in West Virginia, Maryland, Delaware, or New Jersey to compete, and they rarely came home until midnight or even far beyond.

That schedule was more or less adhered to seven days a week, 365 days a year. "The horses don't know anything about weekends or holidays," John Dale "J.D." Thomas, another Middleburg trainer, said.

While Barbara was universally respected by her staff, there were moments when she was egotistical and even grating. She was known, when the mood struck her, to walk through the barn loudly proclaiming her accomplishments, as though she alone had brought them all off. The word "I" especially stung the ears of her colleagues, but none more than those of her assistant trainer, Horace Marlow Jr. "'Remember when I did this!' she'd shout," Horace said. "'Remember when I did that!'" Horace was sometimes called by his nickname, "Junior," but he was so cool and casual that even his nickname had a nickname, and he usually went by "Junie."

Like Barbara, Junie was born in Middleburg in what was then the apartheid state of Virginia. He was African American and attended segregated schools. His father was a chauffeur and a butler on the large domestic staff of John S. Pettibone, a wealthy land and horse owner.

Junie attended Frederick Douglass High School in nearby Leesburg. It was the very first public high school in the area ever built for African American students, and it wasn't even constructed until 1941. Junie was an easygoing and good-natured man and was mostly untroubled by the oppressive racial mores he encountered throughout his life. "Junie," his old dad told him when he was only a boy, "you ain't no better than nobody else, but there ain't a damned soul better than you."

Junie lived by those words. "I didn't believe in the Martin Luther King turn-the-other-cheek bullshit," he said. "If you hit me, I'm gonna hit you right back. If you cuss me, I'm gonna cuss you back. If you was too big, I was going to find the biggest thing I could find and knock hell out of you."

Despite Junie's eye-for-an-eye credo, rural Virginia in the Jim Crow era was a little kinder to Junie and his family than it was to others like them. When he was a child, Marlow and his siblings had played with white children from a neighboring family. The two sets of kids, raised together, were extremely close, so much so that Billy, the oldest of the white kids, became highly protective of Junie and his siblings. "If some white kid said something to us that we didn't like, Billy would kill us if we tried to go after [that other kid]," Junie remembered. "He'd say, 'Y'all, get back; I've got this.' He'd take care of it. His parents also would take care of my mother and father in the same way."

Junie was grateful for that protection; it saved him from having to do a hard and dangerous job himself. But he didn't believe for a second that it came from any sort of racial progressiveness. It was just familiar affection, an odd aspect of southern life that bound the families so tightly together. "I guess [that family] loved us," Junie said. "If 'John' down the road was Black, they'd treat him like a Black person, but for us it was different."

Despite his tough talk, Junie wasn't a bruiser. He was just average sized and more predisposed to humor than rage. He had suffered with asthma since boyhood, and that had kept him out of sports and, later, the army. After high school, with his vocational options limited by racial inequities, a modest education, and location, he picked up work with a horse trainer and learned the trade.

Eventually he was "discovered" by Barbara, who taught him her incomparable training methods.

By the time Junie reached his forties, he was an exuberant middle-aged man and in full command of his profession. He was the head of Barbara's core business, the horse-breaking operation. If he had weaknesses, they were for whiskey and women. Junie had a passion for both, and both got him into steep trouble from time to time. Nevertheless, Marlow had Barbara's full confidence, and he was her key man at Middleburg in the spring of 1977, when Buddy Delp's protégé, Ronnie Franklin, made his appearance for his jockey training.

After his mom and dad dropped him off, Franklin moved into a bedroom in Barbara's farmhouse, and the Bid was given a straw bed in one of the many stalls in Barn 3. Ronnie was personally tutored in race riding by Barbara, but he also spent much of his time taking orders from the young staff of female exercise riders and from Junie. That didn't sit well with him, especially in the beginning.

Alix White, an exercise rider who personally helped oversee Franklin, experienced firsthand his displeasure at being controlled by anyone or anything. Especially a woman. "Barbara said, 'Teach him everything,'" White remembered. But that wasn't easy. Ronnie rebelled against her instructions. "He was very much a Baltimore boy," White said, and it wasn't a compliment.

Graham wanted Ronnie to learn a lot more than just riding. She wanted him to understand everything about horses, from the ground up, and there were no better teachers than the six young women who attended to the thoroughbreds in her operation. But Ronnie, an impatient and impudent kid, was focused solely on being a jockey. He couldn't understand why he had to waste his time listening to anyone else but Barbara about anything else other than riding. "He was a little wise ass," Alix White said. And her riding colleague, Paula Parsons, knew just what she meant. "He was a kid, a brat," Paula said.

Ronnie did his best to confirm that assessment. If they said something to him, tried to teach something to him, he took it as a personal insult and fired back. "I don't need to know that," Ronnie shouted at Alix. She responded to his babyish protests with ration and reason: "You need to know the basics of how a horse works," she calmly told him. Instead of accepting the instruction, Ronnie protested, pleaded, and complained. "He . . . irritated all of us," Paula Parsons admitted.

Even though Ronnie was young and the women were mature, the give and take of male versus female played a role in their interactions. "You can't tell me nothing; you a girl," Ronnie screamed at his "bosses."

The young ladies felt it too. "It's a pain in the rear when you have [to teach someone] who can't ride and they are at that cocky male age," Paula said. But Franklin's outsized swagger, coupled with his tiny frame, also amused her. She almost saw him as a rooster. "Those little guys are so cocky," Paula said, laughing. "It's the little man complex."

Alix and the other exercise riders took no real offense in Franklin's impudence. And anyway, they knew how to put him in his place. "We knocked him down every day," Alix said. Like any novice, Ronnie was started on sweet-natured horses. "Knocking him down" meant putting him on animals that were, according to Alix, "just pure evil, [animals] that will hurt you." So when Ronnie acted up, the girls put him on something that would buck him right off. And it was a long way down.

Franklin's attitude also earned him Junie Marlow's tough love. "He was a prick, and I could've slapped his ass a couple of times," Junie said. "He was sassy. If you asked him to do something, his answer was, 'I'll do it in the morning.' He was a brat, that's all, a know-it-all."

Ronnie had maturity issues at Middleburg, but no one saw them as evidence of drug issues. Everyone who knew him at the training center was adamant about that. "That kid wasn't on no drugs and wasn't no drunk," Junie Marlow said. "Believe me; I would know." Alix White agreed. "There was no hint whatsoever that Ronnie had any kind of drug problem when he was here," she said.

The teenage rider was sober but difficult. He was a trying kid, but to the professionals at Middleburg that made him all the more qualified to be a winner. "Ronnie Franklin was kind of arrogant," Junie said, "so we knew right away he was gonna be a good race rider. Nice boys, I don't think too many of 'em make good riders."

And nobody at Middleburg doubted for a second that Ronnie had the swagger and the fight and the growing skill set of a successful race rider. "He had good balance on a horse; there was no doubt about that," Alix White said. "He had natural ability."

After a while Ronnie matured on the job, put the bad attitude behind him, and hunkered down in earnest to learn. Barbara's people could see him working harder, and he was finally absorbing their lessons.

As they say in Middleburg, a rider had to know "when to go and when to whoa." So Ronnie learned to ride fast and to pull a horse up. He was taught to warm up the horses and to gallop them. And he developed a natural clock in his head for breezing the animals.

Barbara stood beside the exercise track and watched his progress. She required him to understand the profession's nomenclature. For instance, he had to understand the poles and be able to distinguish the quarter pole from the sixteenth poles. "Go from the quarter pole!" Barbara might scream out to him. When he reached the quarter pole, he had to recognize the marker and kick into high gear when he got there.

Overall, Franklin proved he was an adept student of racing and showed that he could quickly absorb everything he needed to know. He did as well with the subtle physical skills the job required. He learned everything, and he learned it all with the one skill prized above all others in horse racing: speed.

"He learned things in days that took others weeks to learn," Alix White said. "He had a natural seat. He knew how to sit on a horse just right, relaxed, with nice quiet hands." "He had good hands," Junie

Marlow agreed. "He could hold a horse in his hands. We showed him everything. And you knew that this punk was going to be a race rider."

While he was in Middleburg growing and progressing, Ronnie missed his family back in Baltimore. His loneliness was alleviated by occasional visits from his parents and his little nephew, Tony Cullum.

Buddy also made the scene from time to time, but he was a disruptive presence. Barbara was highly respected in Middleburg, but when Buddy was there he spoke to her in condescending tones and without respect. He dominated Barbara and made unreasonable demands of her. On one visit to Middleburg he brought his girlfriend, Regina. Buddy insisted that Barbara find a "lead pony" for Regina to ride. Barbara didn't even own one, but to appease Delp she rounded one up.

A tragicomedy unfolded. "Buddy insisted that his girlfriend wanted to ride [the pony]," Sharon Maloney said, "but we didn't think she wanted even a little bit to do with it." The pony, sensing the tentativeness of the rider, took off with her aboard. Regina was terrified as the horse circled the track twice with her bouncing around on its back, helpless to control it. Barbara shouted, "Oh, no!" as she chased them around the track.

Ronnie had much better luck on one of the first horses he got to ride. It was the steel gray colt that belonged to Harry Meyerhoff, the one that was called Spectacular Bid.

At first no one on the staff saw anything special or unusual about the Bid. Barbara took in about thirty yearlings every single year. They all came from excellent bloodlines, and every single one had high hopes attached to it. Of course, very few were special. Spectacular Bid didn't arrive with shafts of light beaming down on him or a chorus exulting behind him. In fact, much like Ronnie, the young Bid didn't even make a great first impression. "Yeah, he was just another horse to us," Alix White admitted, just another long face in a sea of them.

If the Bid stood out at all, it was for negative reasons. "He was a lazy little piglet," White said. "You had to kick and beat him to make him go. At first, the riders didn't like riding him very much. They considered him slow and lethargic. They took turns on him so that no one would be stuck with him all of the time."

The Bid was "broken" in the same small incremental steps as every other young horse that Barbara trained. He was taken to a small fenced-in pen and "lunged," which simply meant that he was walked in circles. After that, he was outfitted with tack and then lunged some more. After he was used to the equipment, a small man or woman would lie across his back, without a saddle, just to give him the feeling of human contact. Finally, a saddle was added with a rider sitting atop when the staff was sure the Bid would take it well.

These small, slow steps were necessary before rapid movement could begin. And even then everything was incremental and deliberate. The horses were taught to jog before they cantered. They cantered before they galloped. They galloped for one mile before they were driven two miles. They walked through the starting gate before they were taught to bust out of it. After all of these steps, a horse was finally breezed or, in horse vernacular, asked to run.

Bid didn't do anything differently than any of the other horses, and no one noticed anything exceptional in him. But in his steel gray coat he was kind of like Clark Kent stuffed into a conservative business suit that made him appear ordinary or meek. But looking closely enough, one could see the complex network of sinews, bones, and arteries, the machinery of a savage fighter and a winner.

The Bid was in fact physically ideal for a racer. He was a little larger than average but neither too big nor too small for speed. What really stood out were his powerful hindquarters. The Bid's haunches rose high above his shoulders, where his thick thighs culminated in his muscular rump, like a monstrous jackrabbit.

Staff members noticed the Bid's joy in completing all of the tasks of an aspiring racer. They noticed that he was a quick learner and performed without complaint, sensing his comfort in galloping and especially in how he found his rhythm. At the turns he effortlessly changed leads, switching from the right foreleg to the left or vice versa, a vitally important component of a successful racer.

While most fans and bettors would later examine the Bid's physical characteristics, Junie's educated eyes saw something special in his intellect and disposition. "He was one of the smartest, kindest horses," Junie said. "He was a stud horse who never did anything wrong. He never bucked.

A horse like that will nip at you a little bit, bite at you a little bit because he's a stud. Spectacular Bid never did nothing like that. He was a kind horse, easy to break. He was a sweet horse. He was just a smart animal."

Because Barbara's primary responsibility was breaking horses, the young thoroughbreds in her care were never really asked to run at top speed for her. That came later, when they were with their permanent trainers. At Middleburg the primary task was to develop muscle and bone. In fact, the goal was to remodel bone and make it appropriate for a racing animal. They saw a danger in asking a horse to run too fast, too early, believing it could create permanent damage.

Barbara's staff rarely had knowledge of a racer's ultimate, mature speed. But with the Bid, it was different. Junie had a hunch, and he wanted to get a glimpse of exactly what the horse was capable of doing. Early one morning, under an orange-yellow dawn sky he went to the exercise track with three riders and three horses. One of them was the Bid. His instructions were simple: "Make them gallop," Junie said. "Let 'em go."

Marlow, the lifelong horseman, could scarcely believe his eyes. The steel gray immediately leapt out in front. The other two horses, both elite thoroughbreds, were moving as fast as they could, yet their legs looked leaden. They were plodding, barely moving, it seemed, and soon they weren't even in Junie's line of sight. Marlow's eyes were fixed on the Bid, and almost out of the gate he was well beyond his competitors. "[The Bid] whistled Dixie," Junie said. "He took off and left the other two in the dust."

Junie Marlow was the first to know. He saw and recognized that one special horse every horseman waits a lifetime to see. With the help of his watch and his own two eyes, Junie knew that horse had arrived. It was the Bid.

Meanwhile, the world's next great sensation in the saddle was ready to take a ride of his own. Ronnie Franklin was ready to depart. He had grown immensely in Middleburg, appearing on the scene as a petulant little boy, a source of amusement to his handlers and teachers. But in two short years he'd grown disciplined, passed from indolent to industrious, and earned the respect of his skeptical co-workers.

In fact, though, Franklin was still a boy. He was slated to stay in Middleburg until late December, but as the end of November approached, he was homesick. Thanksgiving was coming, and he desperately wanted to be back in Dundalk for the holiday with his mother and father and the rest of his family. So the night before the big day Ronnie called his dad and asked the old man if he wouldn't mind coming to get him.

Tony had expected to take it easy and watch football. Thanksgiving was one of the few holidays Tony allowed himself rest from his grueling schedule. But when Ronnie's call came in, there was never any doubt about what he would do. The next morning, he was up and out the door and in his car by 5:00 a.m. He drove all the way to Middleburg, picked up Ronnie, and then drove all the way back to Dundalk. He spent about five and a half hours in his car that day just to bring his boy home.

By dinnertime Ronnie was seated comfortably at the table, surrounded by all of the people who loved him. He was about to become a professional jockey, and he was the star of the family. All they wanted to talk about was horse racing and his new life high atop the fast and powerful animals. Ronnie knew all about it, but the greatest ride he had had in the last two years was the one earlier that day, going home in Tony Franklin's Gran Torino.

6 *And They're Off*

In his pink silks and with a face still boyish and bare, Ronnie Franklin looked like a baby swaddled in the wrong blanket. But the world was about to find out that if child he was, he was no ordinary boy.

Less than two years after he had first arrived at Pimlico as a teenage French fries server and an aspiring hot walker, Franklin was at Bowie Race Track in the dead of winter for his first-ever race as an American professional athlete, a jockey. It was an astonishing ascendance.

For his protégé's first ride, Buddy Delp had picked out Pioneer Patty, a filly with talent but a complex psychology. She could be so violent at night, kicking and climbing the walls, that Buddy had a soft rubber material installed in her stall to protect her from herself. She wasn't easy on the track either. Most of the jockeys and exercise riders Delp put aboard Patty had difficulty handling her. But Ronnie was different. She was calm underneath him, and for reasons that everybody noticed but no one understood, he brought her an elevated sense of focus.

Gerald Delp believed that Pioneer Patty's improved behavior and performance under Franklin was no accident. "Ronnie was naturally blessed with the ability to get along with horses," Gerald said.

Race day was excruciatingly cold. Temperatures struggled to reach 30 degrees, and the threat of snow loomed. The warm breath of men and horses billowed out of their mouths and nostrils into the frosty air, creating small apparitions that hung momentarily motionless and then floated away. Most people didn't believe Ronnie had much of a chance. It was highly unusual for a rider to win his debut and, in Franklin's case, even less likely since he was aboard Patty, a long shot. Nevertheless, as a show of support, all of the Delps put down small bets on their horse and rider. And Franklin, highly confident, laid down $50 on himself.

Bowie was just the right starting spot for Ronnie. It was a mecca for beginning riders, who came there from all over the country. It lacked the historical gravity of Pimlico or the stakes race austerity of Laurel. It was an unpretentious and working-class track, ideal for a young rider learning the craft before moving on to bigger and better things. Chris McCarron had started at Bowie only a few years earlier, and now he was about to pack up and leave Maryland with the hope of striking gold in the Hollywood hills.

Bowie was not only a showcase for young riders, but it was also a platform for some of horse racing's worst behaviors and addictions. Built in the shadow of Oden Bowie's old southern plantation and constructed mostly of the scrub pine that grew wild right on the site, Bowie Race Track had opened in 1914, the same year that Babe Ruth made his professional baseball debut in a Baltimore bandbox.

Because it was a winter track, Bowie catered to a clientele of highly motivated bettors, and weird things happened there. In the early 1950s, a fully armed U.S. fighter jet exploded in midair right over the track. The wreckage landed in the nearby woods. On another occasion a Cabin Cruiser was found floating in the middle of the infield lake; how it got there no one knew.

One racing day in the late 1950s, with twenty thousand fans packed into the stands, a long and persistent snowfall began. While everyone focused on the action, the snow piled up in the parking lots until the cars were more or less locked in. The large crowd was stranded, and after the ninth race the fans had no choice but to hunker down in the clubhouse for a sleepover.

The place buzzed with boozy chatter as petty thieves worked the crowd and "found" wallets in other peoples' pants pockets. The gamblers, at least, were content. They organized impromptu games of craps, cards, and quarter toss and had a great time winning and losing petty cash.

And then a public health crisis ensued. There were diabetics in the crowd, some without their medicine, who had seizures right on the spot. Others suffered heart attacks. Both groups were in serious trouble since there were no qualified medical professionals on the premises to help them. Incredibly that wasn't even the worst medical disaster in Bowie history. On a 15-degree day in 1961, a train packed with Philadelphians derailed about a mile from the race track. Six people died in the accident, and more than two hundred were injured. The survivors, undeterred, demonstrated the hypnotic power of their addictions. Panicked that they might miss laying down their bets, they trudged through the icy mud, many with blood still streaking down their faces, just to get to the windows. Almost all of them refused medical attention until they could see the results of the Daily Double.

Gambling wasn't only a fan addiction; it could infect the riders too. On Valentine's Day 1975, just about three years before Ronnie Franklin's maiden ride at Bowie, a group of seven jockeys sitting around a poker table hatched a plot to throw Bowie's ninth race. Unfortunately, the caper went awry. Authorities could easily see the plot. All the jockeys' bets were placed by one person, who took them all to the same window. One of the jockey's efforts to deliberately slow his horse were so graceless and obvious he literally stood up in the irons and pulled on the reins right out of the gate.

As their web unraveled, the jockeys quickly lawyered up. One of them hired Peter Angelos, a lawyer with a growing reputation as a wizard and the future owner of the Baltimore Orioles, to represent him. But nothing helped. Four of the seven conspiratorial jockeys went to jail. Even worse, Eric Walsh, the most successful rider among them, was so humiliated by his part in the foolish plot, and by his fears of jail, that he committed suicide. He was only thirty-six.

Bowie also had a long tradition of substance abuse—and not only by the lower social classes.

In 1952 a former baseball executive named Larry MacPhail made a substantial investment in Bowie. MacPhail had a reputation as an eccentric genius, brilliant but crazy, depending on whether he was sober or liquored up. He graduated law school at age twenty. By twenty-five he was practicing law and running two thriving businesses, a tool company and a department store.

MacPhail's service in World War I began his reputation as an unmanageable genius. He joined the service and went overseas. Typical of his style, he had organized his own regiment and rose through the ranks, quickly moving from private to captain. To him, war was an adventure. He cheated death twice and survived both a battle wound and a poison gas attack.

MacPhail also got involved in a weird crusade when he and a handful of men drove from Paris to the Netherlands to kidnap Kaiser Wilhelm in an unauthorized maneuver. They came awfully close to succeeding anyway, making it all the way to Wilhelm's living room in a Dutch castle, where he was squatting. They could even hear the Kaiser in the next room. They were dissuaded from snatching him, however, by Dutch troops in the house and instead absconded with the Kaiser's ashtray. It made a hell of a story, but MacPhail's superior officers weren't amused and he ended up in front of a military court.

When he got back home, MacPhail briefly settled in Columbus, Ohio, and turned his attentions from war to baseball. He purchased the Minor League Columbus Senators for $100,000 and then quickly flipped that team, for a nice profit, to Branch Rickey of the St. Louis Cardinals organization. Rickey recognized MacPhail as a talented executive and retained him to lead the Columbus operation, a decision Rickey would soon find to be both brilliant and regrettable.

MacPhail not only set about a series of bold moves to make the Columbus franchise a winner, but he also quickly transformed, modernized, and improved baseball itself. He started with a colossal failure. He built a beautiful new stadium to attract fans, but it didn't work. Considering the problem, he correctly reasoned that his prospective fans simply weren't available to watch baseball during the sunshine hours; they were too busy manning their jobs. So MacPhail devised a bold plan to fix the problem. He had lights installed at his gleaming new park and started playing games at night. Just as he suspected, the fans came out in droves.

From that experience MacPhail learned to open up new and overlooked sources of revenue and succeeded in targeting groups most others had ignored. He created a ladies' group with reduced seat prices for women. He introduced children's clubs and filled up more ballpark seats with kids.

Under MacPhail's direction the Columbus turnstiles literally clicked day and night. Rickey should have been thrilled with MacPhail's performance, but the truth was he couldn't stand him. MacPhail was almost as innovative about irritating his boss as he was in improving his club. He became territorial about *his* players, refusing to send them to St. Louis to help the parent club. And he upstaged Rickey. The Minor League Senators outdrew the Cardinals by more than thirty thousand fans for the season. Rickey was technically the winner in this arrangement; after all he had bought a victorious club that produced good players and prospered at the gate, yet his dealings with MacPhail exhausted and embittered him.

When MacPhail left Columbus, he moved on to a string of jobs with big league teams. Everywhere he went, he dramatically improved his own club and the business of baseball. But he also usually imploded, unable to control his drinking.

His first stop was with the Cincinnati Reds, baseball's oldest team, yet failing on the field and in bankruptcy. Very quickly, MacPhail installed lights at Crosley Field and oversaw the first night game in big league history. His team traveled by air while his competitors were still in choo-choos. And he enthusiastically embraced broadcasting while his archaic colleagues feared that radio would ruin their gate.

MacPhail recognized the vast promotional benefits of broadcasting and hired young Red Barber, a master storyteller, to describe his games. Instead of harming business interests, baseball translated beautifully through the airwaves and whetted fans' appetites for the ballpark.

MacPhail left the Reds in 1937, but the machine he had built soon went to two straight World Series and won it all in 1940. He moved on to Brooklyn, where the Dodgers were suffering many of the same maladies as the Reds. They were in deep financial distress, and they hadn't won the National League pennant in more than twenty years.

The great executive's innovations transformed that second-class borough and harkened in the "Boys of Summer" era, when the Dodgers were one of the most rabidly followed, beloved, and gloriously profitable teams in the game. It was MacPhail who had created the franchise that would be rhapsodized and then lamented for decades to come.

After another stint in the service for World War II, MacPhail divested himself of his Dodgers holdings, opening the door for Rickey to take over. Meanwhile, MacPhail headed a syndicate that bought the New York Yankees. In his wizard-like way he wrested control of the marquee franchise in professional sports with only $200,000 of his own money. It wasn't much more than he'd paid for the Minor League Columbus franchise just a few years earlier, and now he was president and general manager of the legendary pinstripes.

MacPhail was no easier to work with in the Bronx than he had been anywhere else. In only his first season at the helm he fired two different managers. Yet he was as brilliant as ever.

In year two under MacPhail, the Yankees won the American League pennant and, most satisfying of all, defeated Rickey's Dodgers in a thrilling seven-game World Series. It should have been a moment of triumph, but MacPhail's joy led to a day of ballpark drinking. After the final out he made the grave mistake of stumbling his way over to greet Rickey and console him. In a sloppy show of inebriated sportsmanship, he draped his arms around the Dodgers' leader, who didn't take it well. Rickey was both puritanical and a sore loser; disgusted by MacPhail's condition, he berated him right on the spot. Enraged by Rickey and still highly intoxicated, MacPhail went berserk in the Yankees' clubhouse. He sprayed invective in every direction, and he fired respected employees right there in the winning clubhouse. He even hauled off and clocked a man.

That night, as he sobered up, MacPhail realized that he had embarrassed himself so thoroughly in front of news professionals from all over the country that he had no choice but to resign. He'd just won the World Series, making everyone in his orbit a little richer and a lot happier, and yet his abdication was enthusiastically accepted. And it was all for the want of a few drinks.

Despite it all, MacPhail left the Yankees with his head held high. His fellow owners paid him $2 million for the same shares in the team that he'd purchased for a mere $200,000 a couple of years before.

But something much more valuable than money had been lost. MacPhail was done in baseball. Nevertheless, he was flush with cash, still relatively young and energetic, and overflowing with creative energy. All of that brought him to horse racing. First, he bought a farm for thoroughbreds in Harford County, Maryland, and then he purchased Bowie Race Track. It was quintessential MacPhail at his messianic best. Bowie was failing, and he would save it.

Like almost all of the endeavors in which MacPhail became involved, Bowie Race Track was a tarnished brand when he found it. His vision was to make it a first-class facility that surpassed its competitors. His first step was implementing a $2 million renovation package to improve the physical plant.

But opening day was just another bad day with the bottle for MacPhail. He literally drank in the moment, and as the day wore on, he became highly intoxicated and brutally abusive. He loudly and profanely berated members of the Horsemen's Benevolent Association who were seated near him, incensing them, of course. But the worst was yet to come.

Later in the day, as patrons filed out of the track and took to the roads, MacPhail encountered a state trooper directing traffic. In his stupor MacPhail perceived the officer as slow and incompetent, and he quickly lost his composure. He became physical with the policeman and was arrested. Within the week, MacPhail was officially banned from entering his own race track. All it took, all it ever took to destroy him and undo all the massive good he had accomplished, was a few drinks.

But as bad as things were for MacPhail, the real damage was done to Bowie. The man was embarrassed and hurt, but he could salve his wounds on his rolling horse farm as he merely returned to his life of wealth and privilege. But for that struggling race track, permanently deprived of the guidance and services of perhaps the ablest and most visionary sports executive in the country, potential was squandered and hope was lost. Instead of enjoying a renaissance under MacPhail, Bowie regressed and never became the great venue that only he could have envisioned and produced.

MacPhail died in 1975, but in an interesting example of the past and present intersecting, the former Bowie chief executive was inducted into the baseball Hall of Fame the same week that Ronnie Franklin rode his first race at Bowie. As Ronnie stepped into the irons, many were still recounting MacPhail's brilliance and how it had been squandered by addiction.

In front of a large, cold crowd on February 4, 1978, Delp gave Ronnie a leg up on Pioneer Patty for the fourth race. No one knew what to expect from Franklin. Despite his nearly two years of training with Barbara Graham and his perfect jockey's build, he seemed to many unsuitable, a city kid with limited knowledge and experience with horses. The great jockeys, they reasoned, grew up in the irons.

Certainly no one could have predicted what did happen. Before the race, he brimmed with so much confidence he didn't even bother taking instruction from Delp. Instead he told the trainer exactly how he planned to ride the horse.

Pioneer Patty was slow out of the gate and content to lag behind for two-thirds of the race. She was still three lengths back near the top of the home stretch when the patient Franklin kicked her into gear. Coming from the outside, he rushed the front runners, hesitating only briefly to press in on and crowd the horse Despedida. But Franklin didn't waste any more time. He moved back to the clear and took the lead.

The crowd beheld the smooth maneuvers of the eighteen-year-old and roared its approval. And it was to the chorus of those cheers and in the warmth of that adulation that Franklin and Pioneer Patty crossed the wire, the other horses and riders behind them.

Ronnie finished first in his next race too, and the superlatives started to flow in. "He is further along than any rider I've ever brought around," Buddy said. "I wouldn't hesitate now to put him on anything in the barn."

The *Baltimore Sun* compared Ronnie to Chris McCarron and anointed him the successor to the still young and successful future Hall of Famer who was about to depart for California. And McCarron, himself endorsed Franklin too. "He's got a good head and obviously a lot of natural ability," Chris said. "He's going to win a lot of races."

As the days passed, every kind word uttered about Franklin only seemed to be an understatement. He progressed at a torrid pace, and by the third week of April 1978, he was the hottest apprentice jockey in the nation. After just three months in the saddle he had already taken the reins of 142 mounts and finished in the money an astonishing ninety-one times. On thirty-four different occasions he posed in the winner's circle. His 27 percent winning percentage was the best of any rider at Pimlico.

Franklin's agent, Chickie Lang, revved up the hype machine. "He is the hottest Franklin since Ben," Chickie said.

It is interesting that Ronnie's early successes were all achieved without virtue of the best horse in Delp's stable. While Franklin made a name for himself at the track, Spectacular Bid was still in the stall, untried and unknown to both press and public. The Bid had come to Baltimore from Barbara Graham's farm even less heralded than Ronnie had been. In Buddy's operation of top horse professionals only Gerald, still in his early teens, had a sneaking suspicion about just how special Spectacular Bid was.

"Dad, watch that gray," Gerald said. "I'm telling you he's gonna be a good one."

But Buddy was unconvinced. "I've got Tired Castle in the barn," he told Gerald. "I've got stakes winners here; why're you talking about this young horse?"

Indeed Buddy showed no recognition of what Gerald saw. The trainer chose a mediocre team to look after the Bid, a sign that the horse wasn't viewed as anything special. Instead of assigning the steel gray to his top groom, Mo Hall, Buddy picked out an old hand named Tots. Experienced but elderly, Tots was known primarily for his vices. He liked to drink and smoke, even around the barns, and he was known to snooze on the job, staking out some hidden corner to close his eyes and let it all float away.

These habits were combustible when combined, and they had almost tragic consequences for Spectacular Bid. One day Tots was tipsy and tired when he reclined into an impromptu bed of straw on the other side of the wall from the Bid's stall. Tots lit up a smoke and then nodded off to sleep. Soon, his cigarette gently fell from his lips, and while he quietly snored, the straw beneath him smoldered. And then a trickle of smoke arose from the bed to the air in a winding upward path. As an unimaginable tragedy was about to unfold, another worker smelled the smoke, ran over, and roused Tots. The flame was extinguished while it was still in its baby stages.

Ronnie was chosen to ride the Bid, and this was another sign that Buddy and his team had no idea what they had in the horse. Although Ronnie and the Bid had known each other since Middleburg, Ronnie was still just a beginner—eighteen years old and extraordinarily unlikely to ride anyone's Triple Crown contender.

All of this was not to say that Buddy's team could not see Spectacular Bid's obvious talent and raw speed. It was evident during exercise sessions. But nobody knew how that would translate to race conditions. Many a horse was a morning hero, a stud at the exercise track, racing against just one opponent and in the privacy of an empty grandstand. But in the afternoon, when a roaring crowd was present and there were seven or eight horses in the race, no one knew what an even evidently fast horse might do.

On June 30, 1978, they found out.

Spectacular Bid left his home stall at Pimlico to race for the very first time on Old Hilltop's track. Although it was the Bid's first start, it was no throwaway. The Bid was far from the favorite. There were some good choices in the field, including Strike Your Colors, a fine horse that finished in the money in eight out of nine races in 1978, including three first-place finishes.

Strike Your Colors was an eventual stakes winner but not the favorite that day. That distinction went to the well-regarded filly Instant Love.

Scheduled for the third race, Spectacular Bid walked out in front of the Pimlico crowd for the first time as though he was ready for battle. His steel gray coat glistened in the early summer sunshine like armor. Ronnie was up, in his black-and-blue silks, young and perfect and perched high atop the Bid like a knight.

It wasn't an easy race, though the result was never in doubt. Approaching the homestretch, the Bid was in the lead, though Strike Your Colors was in hot pursuit. And then, right there in his first race, Spectacular Bid revealed something about himself, about his character, that he would demonstrate again and again throughout the rest of his career. At the quarter pole, he became a different horse. When the race was on the line, he became a killer. He hit his stride, quickened his pace, and blew away the field.

The Bid and his young rider won, but what's more, they came within two-fifths of a second of breaking the track record. Ronnie was an even bigger story than his horse. He rode three winners at Pimlico that day, bringing his total at that venerable track up to an even one hundred. He too engaged in behavior that revealed character and that would become a pattern. He was disqualified from one of the races for interference and almost came to blows with the other horse's jockey.

By the third week of July Ronnie was the leading rider at Pimlico with almost forty more victories than his closest competitor. On July 22 he rode the Bid again at Pimlico. Franklin could sense something special happening. In the home stretch he whipped the Bid hard, over and over with his left hand. This time the two of them tied the track record. The success of both the baby-faced jockey and especially the two-year-old horse with the eye-popping speed had everyone in the industry talking about Buddy Delp and his magic touch. The story took on another dimension, however, when the press and public learned that Ronnie not only raced for Delp but that he was also living in the trainer's home.

When Ronnie returned from Middleburg at the tail end of 1977, the decision of where he should live was not an easy one. His last two residences, his parents' house in Dundalk and the small, bare room above the stable at Pimlico, were out of the question. Both were too far from Buddy's home base in Laurel.

Ronnie might have taken up residence on the Laurel backstretch, like George Cusimano once had, but Gerald Delp wouldn't hear of it. He and Ronnie had become the best of friends, and they wanted to spend more time together hanging out. Gerald went to his father and asked him if the young jockey could simply live at their house. To everyone's astonishment, Buddy said yes.

Delp's house in suburban Laurel couldn't have been more different from Tony Franklin's little breadbox row house back in Dundalk. With nothing but men living in it, it felt more like a clubhouse than a family home. Ronnie slept on a rollaway in Gerald's room, and sharing that space, the two boys became more like brothers than buddies. They'd become inseparable, hanging out together all day at the track and all night at the house. For them, Buddy's home was a sanctuary where they enjoyed their off hours and blew off steam in Buddy's subterranean game room, fully outfitted with a pool table and a color television.

To the public the arrangement looked like a wholesome one. It was charming: the wise old trainer and the eager young protégé under the same roof had the feel of the wizard Merlin teaching metaphysics to the future king, Arthur, in some out-of-the-way castle.

But the truth was almost opposite to how the press presented it to the gullible public. The scribes painted portraits of Buddy as a Vince Lombardi for four-legged athletes—a brash, bold, and tough miracle worker. To them he was both a winner and a wit. He was articulate and funny in a world where those things were in short supply. Buddy's charming qualities led reporters to misrepresent his relationship with Ronnie. Instead of referring to Delp as Franklin's employer, they started to call him a "father figure," and Franklin was sometimes described as Delp's "surrogate son."

In fact, it wasn't easy spending so much time with Buddy. At work he could be foul-mouthed and abusive if Ronnie did something out on the track that he didn't like. He communicated in a highly intimidating way, looming over the jockey and leaning his imposing body into his protégé to make a point. At times, he would even threaten to kick the boy out of his house.

In fact, many young men in racing felt intimidated by Buddy, and they didn't have to live with him. One aspiring trainer, Scott Regan, found that out the hard way. Regan was building his own stable in precisely the same way as Delp had once done it—by claiming horses. Regan particularly admired Buddy's operation and, for a while, claimed a string of Delp's racers.

Buddy wasn't flattered. He took notice of Regan's pattern of claims and was soon highly annoyed by it. After yet another race at Delaware Park, where Regan hoped to take home one more Delp horse, Buddy exploded. He followed the young trainer into the secretary's office where claims were filed and came face to face with Regan. He wasn't there to exchange pleasantries. Buddy stuck his thick finger within inches of the young man's nose and eyes and then sputtered at him: "If you claim one more of my horses," Delp said, "I will shut your whole God-damn stable down."

Put a little more plainly, Buddy had just threatened to claim every single one of Regan's horses. That would have effectively ended the kid's emerging business. Regan, knowing that Buddy had both the money and vindictive nature to follow through on the threat, took Buddy at his word. Needless to say, the message was delivered. No more Delp horses were claimed by Scott Regan.

Another young trainer, Ronnie Alfano, a clean-cut kid and Vietnam war veteran, had an almost identical experience. He too claimed a few Delp horses, only to find himself personally confronted. Buddy had just deposited $300,000 into his own account for claiming purposes. In a moment of rage and retaliation Delp told Alfano: "I ought to just give [the entire $300,000] to you. Because I'm going to take every fucking horse you run."

"Buddy is brutal," Alfano confided to his friend, Mark Reid. "He's scary."

But Reid had no fear of him. One summer at Delaware Park, he also claimed a bunch of Delp horses but had a pretty good feeling that Buddy wouldn't say a word to him. Reid, who was then only about twenty-nine, was nicknamed "Heavy." It was an allusion to his athletic 6-foot-2-inch, 240-pound frame. Reid had been a college wrestling champion just a few years before. "Delp was a bully," Reid said. "But he wouldn't have said 'boo' to me. He would've gotten hurt."

Anyway, Reid understood Buddy, and the code that he and all the old guys lived by. Reid's first boss, Richard Dutrow, had made it all clear to him early on. "Don't make friends at the track," Dutrow had warned. "Every time another trainer wins, that's the food being taken from your kids' mouths. Give no quarter and expect no quarter to be given. This isn't a game for sissies."

That was Buddy's credo too.

If Buddy was someone for a young man to fear at work, he was downright scary when he attempted to be a father. One night, after dinner at a nice restaurant near Pimlico, Ronnie and Buddy's sons all piled into the old man's Lincoln Continental for the ride home. In those close and happy quarters, Buddy took the opportunity, as a lot of father's might, to lecture his three teenage passengers about drug use. "I know you all smoke a little weed," Buddy told them. "I read what you kids are doing today. But there's a lot of bad shit out there, and you don't know what you're getting."

With that he departed from conventional norms and reached into his sport coat and pulled out a large marijuana joint. He lit it up, unleashing the pungent odor, and took a drag from it right there. The boys were flabbergasted. Gerald, then only about sixteen, couldn't believe his eyes. "What the fuck?" he muttered to himself.

"If you are gonna smoke," Buddy continued, "I like to know that you're getting the good stuff. I like to know that it's not laced with anything bad." So, apparently in the best interests of the kids' well-being, Buddy passed around the pot, and he and the kids took turns in the cloudy car all the way home.

It was the first time any of them had ever seen Buddy use drugs.

Cathy Rosenberger didn't know what Buddy and the boys did in their spare time, but she could see that the boss wasn't running a tight ship. As an organized and utterly reliable member of his organization, she was tasked with getting Ronnie to work in the morning. She was supposed to pick him up at Buddy's house twice a week at 5:00 a.m. and take him to the barns at Laurel. But on many days when she arrived, it was hard to get anyone to answer the door. She would ring and pound for a while before Buddy himself would finally appear in the doorway, disheveled and attired in nothing more than boxer shorts and a "wife-beater" undershirt. Still groggy, Delp would tell her, "I can't get Ronnie up." Then he would make her wait in the kitchen while he roused the young rider out of bed and pushed him outside.

It wasn't Rosenberger's place to question why Ronnie wasn't ready in the mornings. But the truth was that Buddy's place was the setting for occasional parties in the evenings. The boys and their friends, usually other race track people, got together to play pool and poker, to drink, and to listen to music or watch TV. Sometimes Buddy's girlfriend slept over.

Much of the fun was harmless, a way of passing time and blowing off steam. But some of it was very much at odds with a family-like atmosphere. That was especially apparent one evening when Buddy and the boys were all shooting pool in the playroom with a few of their friends from the track.

In between shots, Buddy asked Ronnie to run upstairs and get him a beer out of the refrigerator. Ronnie did as he was told, but when he came back downstairs, the scene had changed. No one was playing pool anymore. Instead the table had become a makeshift green felt surface for small sheets of glass. Everyone in the room was bent over the table and inhaling lines of white powder through rolled-up dollar bills. Even Buddy. Ronnie was stunned, but he slowly continued down the steps.

He looked at Buddy, the man who had saved him from the streets and taught him a profession, the man who was his employer and his landlord. As everyone good-naturedly exhorted Ronnie to join the fun, he accepted a rolled-up bill, leaned over the table, and did the same as everyone else—right beside the man the newspapers called his father figure.

It all began for Ronnie at Bowie that winter. He won his first-ever race there, and just a few weeks later he purchased his first bag of cocaine from another jockey there. He'd been hailed as the next great rider, but the seeds of his painful ending had already been planted.

7 *Rough Riders*

When the spring meeting at Pimlico ended in 1978, Buddy Delp split his stable. As he always did, Buddy sent a large contingent of his horses and staff on to Delaware Park to continue racing. But this time he stayed behind in Baltimore with the remainder of his stable so that he could keep a constant eye on his rising star, Spectacular Bid.

After the Bid won his first two races at Pimlico, in nearly record-breaking fashion, Buddy had changed. For years he'd been known as a great trainer and yet primarily a trainer of claimers. Now he had a once-in-a-lifetime horse on his hands. In public he developed a confident persona, even braggadocios. And he seemed well suited to the spotlight. He was charming, smiled for the cameras, and in his own folksy way was highly articulate and eager to talk. In a moment reminiscent of Muhammad Ali, he branded Spectacular Bid "the greatest horse to ever look through a bridle," even though Secretariat was still alive and well and living on a Kentucky breeding farm having more fun than any other male on the planet.

In private it was a different story. Buddy suffered bouts of anxiety and paranoia. The pressures came as easily as the pleasures, and it started to show. Suddenly Buddy was a far more hands-on trainer, at least where the Bid was concerned. He usually relaxed in the barn while his horses exercised, but for the Bid he personally oversaw all of the workouts.

He even moved the valuable horse's stall so that it was immediately adjacent to his office.

Buddy had a hard time hiding his increased tension. One day he lost his composure just watching a low-level man perform a routine chore. He was in his office working when he heard the sound of a groom raking the shed row, a highly routine activity that maintains the neat and organized appearance of a well-run organization. The sound of it, along with the whinnying of the horses, is the ambient noise of a horse barn. Yet on this particular day, with the pressures rising, Buddy apparently didn't feel the Zen of the rake. In fact, he found it to be an intolerable racket. He was sure that somehow the noise was damaging his prize horse. So he leapt out of his chair and profanely chastised the low-wage worker, screaming at him and berating him for supposedly disturbing the horse.

Ronnie Franklin had barely started his career, but good fortune and fame were already having negative consequences for him too, though he didn't know it yet.

As the principal rider for Delp's operation, he took the mount of competitive horses every single day, and when he was in the irons on Spectacular Bid, he was moving about as fast as a man could on horseback. But along with the winning, the easy money, and the showers of adulation, there was one other thing, and that was resentment. The other young riders were jealous of Franklin's meteoric rise, and the more experienced jockeys were simply incredulous that it was possible.

But perhaps the most offended of all were the Latino riders, who were then in the midst of asserting themselves as racing's dominant force. One of them was Edwin Canino, like Ronnie a young apprentice with a burning desire to succeed in racing and better himself. But Edwin saw his journey as a rough one, especially in contrast to the magic carpet ride he believed Ronnie was on. Edwin had immigrated to the mainland from San Juan, where he'd started his career. He found the island confining and with limited opportunities. There was only one race track there, and without success he didn't even have the respect of his parents, who called him "a bum." The States weren't easy for him either. He found that the paths to opportunity were more plentiful but still difficult to enter with gatekeepers everywhere. While he struggled, grappling for his meals, he noticed Franklin's relatively easy rise. Keeping up with Franklin's success became something of an obsession for him.

To Edwin, Ronnie represented everything that kept him down and held him back. Franklin, in Canino's eyes, was a figure of the white-gringo establishment. For a young white man with a name like Franklin, the breaks came easy and the success was assured.

There was a lot of resentment there, but also some truth. Ronnie ran at the better venues, crossing the finish lines in front of big crowds at Laurel, Bowie, Pimlico, and Delaware. Meanwhile, Canino schlepped along in the woods of Charlestown, West Virginia.

Canino believed that Ronnie had found work as an apprentice jockey easily, while he had had to learn on the job and endure deep humiliations along the path. He had begun as an exercise rider who couldn't control his horses. It wasn't unusual for one to take off underneath him while he bounced around on its back, powerless to control it. More than once, an outrider had to chase him down and "save" him.

While Ronnie slept in the comfort of Delp's plush home, Canino endured his first American winter with no more possessions than the clothes and shoes he was wearing. As befitting an insider, Ronnie had excellent representation. His agent, Chickie Lang, was the son of Pimlico's esteemed general manager Chick Lang. Edwin's agent was a guy named Dave Posey, who'd only recently been a real estate agent.

Edwin viewed his own life through a lens of comparison to Franklin's, and a great resentment welled up inside him. He so often told his young, white girlfriend, Shirley Campbell, about his distaste for Franklin that she came to believe that he actually hated Ronnie.

Shirley was a petite, brown-haired teenager with hazel eyes and a prematurely voluptuous build. She wasn't quite sixteen years old then, but she had already been hanging out at the race track for years. Her father had introduced her to the horses and the betting windows when she was still just a little girl. Her dad had wandered to Baltimore from his home in rural Virginia with only a sixth-grade education. He came north looking for work in Baltimore's job-rich east side, and he found it as a dues-paying ironworker in one of the shipyards. His hard profession offered him a stable life, but he paid for it in excruciating aches and pains in his joints while he was still a relatively young man.

Shirley's dad was well proportioned, a 6-footer who carried only 190 lean pounds on his work-hardened frame. He favored loud shirts with bright colors and dizzying patterns. By the time Shirley was in high school, his hair was long and snow white, and a white stubble beard bristled from his face.

Shirley knew her father's secret: he cared more about the track than his trade. He loved to gamble, and though he often won, he rarely came home a winner. His hot streaks were inevitably parlayed again and again until all his money was lost, including his original stake.

The horses weren't his only gambling interests. He was also a bookie and a card player, with a talent for cheating. He passed on that roguish skill to his daughter, who was grateful for the training. Shirley wasn't as successful learning in the classroom. She did so poorly in school that she gave up after the ninth grade. She had ditched her classes so often and was so far behind that there was no point in ever going back.

So while her friends boarded the school bus, Shirley hopped on the city bus and headed across town to Pimlico. At first, she went to watch the horses like any fan, but eventually she saw an opportunity at the track and picked up odd jobs. She worked concessions, sold corn on the cob at the gates, and hawked White Owls and El Productos in the grandstands. And like so many other low-skilled people, she also found paying work on the backstretch, where she was a hot walker and then, later, a groom.

Shirley's parents didn't really mind that she had quit school. In fact, her dad was thrilled when she told him that she was going to the track. He especially loved hearing that she was betting and winning with a method of her own. But she eventually came to realize that she had a gambling addiction, just like her father. She spent her days laying down bets at Pimlico and then zoomed her car up Highway 83 North to Penn National, near Harrisburg, where she gambled all evening as well.

If Shirley was in fact an addict, she didn't see it as a destructive vice, at least not in herself. Unlike her dad, she knew how to win and walk away. She never tried to run the table; she simply folded her money into her wallet and then ran home and tucked herself into bed.

In love, she wasn't so lucky or rational. Shirley had deep feelings for Canino but wasn't satisfied that he returned her affections appropriately. On her sixteenth birthday he let her down in the most painful way possible. As a surprise, he took her to a motel room with two of their friends, one of hers and one of his. But Canino didn't have a party in mind; he had a suggestion. He wanted to get into bed with her friend, he said, and he told her that he didn't mind if she coupled up with his buddy.

The mere suggestion of such an arrangement from a man she loved shattered the young girl, and she ran for the motel's third-floor balcony and jumped off it. She crash-landed on the ground, and the impact of the fall snapped her pelvis and caused her to chomp a hole in her tongue. But her aches and pains were nothing compared to the sense of humiliation and outrage she felt. Weeks later she was still incensed about it. At about the same time, Donald Teague, a valet and a friend of hers, told her all about his new workmate, a young, winning jockey named Ronnie Franklin. "You've got to meet Ronnie," Teague told her. "He's going to be a star."

Shirley, of course, already knew all about Franklin since he was the leading man in Canino's tirades. And then it struck her. The perfect revenge against Canino, she thought, would be for her to sleep with Franklin. Teague assisted her in this plan and set up a small gathering at his house in Laurel and invited Shirley and Ronnie as guests.

When Shirley finally saw Ronnie in person, she was immediately attracted to him. But he was so painfully shy that they barely spoke to each other. At the end of the night she still didn't really know anything about him, but she took the initiative anyway. "Call me," Shirley said as she handed him a slip of paper with her number on it, and then she quickly walked out the door. It wasn't long before Ronnie dialed her up. There wasn't much to their conversation other than arranging a midday tryst at a nice motel in suburban Pikesville, only about ten minutes from Pimlico.

Ronnie paid for the room, and it was clean and nice with two large beds in it. Shirley and Ronnie took up residence in the first one. In the second bed, all by himself, was Gerald Delp. Gerald was a tall, slim young man with a shaggy head of brown hair and an irrepressible smile on his face. He came along to the hotel at Ronnie's invitation. Shirley didn't object, but she had one caveat: Gerald was to be a spectator only.

Despite its lurid qualities, it was a mostly forgettable encounter. It is not surprising that the teenage jockey was built for speed. When it was over, all three of them simply left the room with no further encounters planned or desired by any of them. In the end, they were just three lost teenagers with too little supervision and too much time and money on their hands. They had come together for all of the wrong reasons and motivations.

For Shirley it was a particularly transactional encounter. She had gotten what she wanted, which was the ability to tell Canino all about it. Edwin had wanted her to sleep with another man, and now she had. She had gone to bed with Ronnie Franklin, Canino's nemesis, the one man who stoked his jealousies like no other.

Ronnie's unwitting role in humiliating Canino was only his first unpleasant encounter with a Latin jockey, but it would be far from his last.

By the 1970s Latinos were arriving and rising in all aspects of American life. Although they had always shared the North American continent and the Western Hemisphere with "los Americanos," the people of the United States, they were never quite seen as equals in the land of the free. Hispanics were treated as more alien than most East and West Europeans, even though they were from neighboring countries. Many Americans pointedly saw them as something less than white.

Even so, at one time Hispanics were courted and welcomed into the United States. They were invited with open arms for their willingness to work in the fields and aid the nation's powerful farming and agribusiness enterprises. Eventually, however, there was a racist backlash, and they were turned back. In the 1950s one program, literally called "Operation Wetback," used military-style tactics to round up Hispanics, primarily Mexicans, and return them to Mexico. Some of those rounded up and deported were actually American citizens.

American views of the Spanish-speaking peoples were heavily influenced by the motion picture and television industries, which usually depicted Latino characters in a variety of unflattering ways. They were the *banditos* who murdered a deranged Humphrey Bogart in the *Treasure of the Sierra Madre*, an artistic study of the darkness of the human soul.

In the 1950s the male lead in the most popular show on television was a Cuban bandleader named Desi Arnaz. The show became one of the most popular in American history, but when it was first pitched to network executives, they rejected it. They said that Americans would find it implausible that a creamy-complected Anglo beauty like Lucille Ball would marry a swarthy man like Desi. "Well, I have been married to him for ten years now," Lucy said.

The very idea of such a show was offensive in a nation that still had and enforced anti-miscegenation laws. Eventually the executives caved in, not because they saw the light but because if they wanted to get Lucy, they had to accept Desi. She wouldn't do the show any other way. Although it was a groundbreaking program in its easy mixture of white and brown skin, part of *I Love Lucy*'s humor played off Arnaz's broken English. His character was highly sympathetic and well loved, but he was a conspicuous foreigner in their midst.

Of course most Hispanics in the United States would never know the lucky breaks and fabulous wealth that came Desi's way. They weren't stars, but they were prototypical Americans. They were hard workers looking for a leg up in the fields, kitchens, and hotel rooms of their adopted country; strivers searching for a better life for their children; and seekers, looking to be more than background players.

The daring, dangerous job of a jockey perfectly suited talented Hispanic immigrants who were desperate to leave behind their old lives. Not unlike Ronnie Franklin, they gladly took on the most dangerous and difficult job in sports in exchange for a chance at a comfortable life, material wealth, and citizenship.

Hispanic Americans may have come late to the American horse racing party, but they were the perfect people to assert themselves in the moment. Riders of English, Irish, French, and Italian ancestry, with surnames like "Shoemaker," "Arcaro," and "Woolf," once dominated high atop the horses. They set the standard for the first half of the twentieth century, when the jockeys were overwhelmingly small, hungry, and white.

But with time, the ethnic groups from which those riders had emerged became more established, educated, affluent, and assimilated. The dangers and labors of whipping a horse to top speeds didn't appeal to second- and third-generation Americans as they had to their fathers and grandfathers.

On the other hand, Hispanics came to North American racing like conquistadores, galloping in for the plunder. Seemingly impervious to fear, they brought with them a new gusto for hard work and a swagger and a bravado that revved up the intensity of competition. As early as 1962 *Sports Illustrated* noted that there was a "Latin Invasion," a phrase that then had a whole different meaning. By February of that year, Latin riders in the United States were on pace to win purses worth more than $8 million.

"Sunny" Jim Fitzsimmons was a horse trainer who was born only about a decade after the Civil War. His career in racing had spanned seventy-eight years, and he had won more than 250 stakes races. He had more or less seen the entire history of U.S. horse racing. Bearing down on age ninety, Fitzsimmons made a prediction about the influx of Spanish-speaking riders. "The Latins are going to take it all over in five or 10 years," he said. "They're natural horsemen. They're bright and they're strong. Mark my words, there'll be more Latin riders around here than Americans before too long."

Sunny Jim proved to be a prophet. By the end of the decade an extraordinary group of Latin riders was among the finest in the country. They would dominate U.S. horse racing throughout the 1970s as they won nine Triple Crown races.

Given their work ethic and fire to succeed, the Hispanics' ascent to the top may have seemed inevitable. In fact, it was anything but easy. One of the best of these new riders was Jacinto Vasquez, who made his name riding, or defeating, some of the most legendary horses in history.

Vasquez began life as one of six boys and ten children born to a Panamanian farmer who raised cows and pigs in the countryside. He was only about thirteen when he left his father's modest home and sought to make his own way in the world. He departed the protection of his parents while he was still as vulnerable as he could be. He had no financial assets to speak of. And he was still remarkably small at only about 5 feet and less than one hundred pounds. But he was a nice-looking young boy with a thick head of raven-colored hair, high cheekbones, and skin that was as rich and dark as tanned leather. He had an angular, hawk-like nose and a face so finely produced that it looked like a monument carved by skilled hands with primitive tools. All of this gave Jacinto the look and bearing of a native American chief.

Out on his own, the only steady work Jacinto found with so little experience or education was in the back of a Panamanian kitchen washing dishes. But after two years, even that modest opportunity was almost taken from him. "I had a fight with a Black kid," he remembered, "and they tried to put me in jail."

From that low moment, a life of success emerged. A mature Panamanian woman whom he didn't even know happened to see his struggle with the police and stepped in to save him. She bailed him out of trouble and gained control of him. As it turned out, she was the mother of Heliodoro Gustines, a Panamanian rider who was then a success in Mexico and soon headed to stardom in the United States.

Señora Gustines looked at Jacinto and noticed how strong and feisty he was—and how small. She told him he was wasting his time washing dishes and explained that there was a far better line of work for him. "You should be a jockey," she said.

Jacinto had never heard of Gustines, and he had no idea what a jockey was. But two weeks later Señora Gustines shepherded him to the track. He watched from the stands and was mesmerized by the performance of Braulio Baeza, another future star, who won five races in a row that day. Young Jacinto turned to Señora Gustines and asked her what was, for him, the key question:

"How much does a jockey make?"

"Anywhere between $500 and $1,000 each week," she told him.

Before she could even get the words out of her mouth, Jacinto had already decided to resign from the dishwashing profession. It would be a long while before he ever rode his first thoroughbred. His initial job at the track was at the other end of the horse. He had to muck out the stalls. He eventually moved on to the duties of a groom, which he found extremely unpleasant. "I was rubbing seven freaking horses a day," he complained.

But two years later he was more mature and the ideal size for a jockey at 5 feet 2 inches and 105 pounds. So at age fifteen, he stopped rubbing horses and started riding them.

In 1960 Jacinto came to the United States to race at Aqueduct. Soon he was all over the country, making his way through the heartland and riding at tracks in Arizona, Nebraska, Colorado, and Kentucky.

As a Panamanian, Jacinto was treated to a lesson in gringo racism. He wasn't Black or of African descent, but in Kentucky in the early 1960s, being brown was good enough to get him confined to the "colored" restroom.

Jacinto had a happy, forgiving nature and he was too single-minded about success to worry about slights he considered petty. "I came here with one mission," he said, "and that was to do good. If they like me, okay; if they don't, *I don't give a shit* about it."

But while many of the American riders were kind to him, helped him, and socialized with him, the trainers were sometimes openly hostile. Jacinto eventually became highly associated with Frank Whiteley Jr., a brilliant trainer but a difficult and bigoted man.

Whiteley and Vasquez first met each other at Delaware Park in 1963. At that time the young jockey was riding intermittently for Buddy Delp and others. Scrounging for additional business opportunities, he asked one of the backstretch workers, "Who is the best horseman here?" The man pointed in the distance. "There is a gray haired son of a bitch over there in that barn behind the kitchen," he said. "No one gets along with him, but he is the best horseman here."

That "son of a bitch" was Whiteley. The next morning Jacinto went straight to his barn and got a firsthand lesson in why so few people liked him.

"Good morning, Mr. Whiteley," Jacinto politely said. "Can I do anything for you today? My name is Vasquez."

Whiteley listened to Jacinto's pitch in silence, allowing the rider to say his piece without interruption. But when it was over, the trainer laid it on the line. "You're Puerto Rican," Whiteley said, "and I don't like no goddamn Puerto Ricans. And I don't have no Puerto Ricans in my barn. Now get outta here!"

Whiteley was shoeing Vasquez away like a stray dog. But Jacinto was persistent.

"I'm not a Puerto Rican," Vasquez sputtered back. "I'm from Pan-ah-mah."

"Well you're a spic just the same," Whiteley said. "You speak the same language. I don't want no Puerto Ricans around me."

Jacinto lost the argument, such as it was, but he was undeterred. Later on, he related the whole story to his amigo, telling him all about the vicious racial slurs. "Move on," his buddy wisely told him.

But Jacinto had his mind made up. He wanted to ride Whiteley's prime horses, and he wouldn't give up until he did. "I don't give a shit what he calls me," Vasquez said. "I'm gonna get on one of those caballos."

Morning after morning Vasquez returned to Whiteley's barn with a smile painted on his face and the same pleasant question on his lips: "What can I do for you today, Mr. Whiteley?" And every day he got chased off with the same ugly rebuke: "Get outta here, Puerto Rican!"

One hot summer day, with the temperature leaping into the high 90s, Jacinto came to the track in his suit and tie, then the customary attire for a jockey reporting to work. He passed Whiteley in his car on his way in, as he always did, and he pleasantly waved to the trainer. This time, to his surprise, the trainer waved back and flagged him down.

Vasquez pulled up beside Whiteley and cranked his window down. "I need you," the trainer said to Jacinto. "I have an emergency call in the barn. Finish hosing my horse down for me."

It was a demeaning request. But Jacinto carefully folded his suit jacket and gently placed it on the car seat. And then, right there in the sweltering heat, he took the hose from Whiteley's hands and squirted the filthy horse. Sweat poured from his face and stained his dress shirt. His tailored pants and leather shoes were splattered with mud.

Meanwhile, when Whiteley finished his call, he hung up the phone, and to Jacinto's amazement the old man leaned back in his chair and took a load off instead of coming back to reclaim his horse and hose.

Jacinto couldn't believe his eyes. Finally, he'd had it. "Hey, I'm going to melt over here," he shouted at the old man. "Why don't you come get your goddamned horse?"

For weeks the old man had meanly rejected Vasquez's kind inquiries. But now that the jockey had finally had the gumption to stand up to him, Whiteley became an old softy. "You know, Puerto Rican," he said, "you're all right. I'm going to put you on a horse."

A few weeks later, Whiteley finally gave Vasquez a mount. But even then the trainer was reprehensible, demanding a kickback in exchange for the opportunity. "Don't pay your agent for this ride," Whiteley told Jacinto. "I got you this job; I want the commission."

Jacinto's persistence and discipline only underscored how powerless he was. But the same was true of all the jockeys—Black, brown, or white; Irish, Italian, or Colombian. In an era when football and baseball players were unionizing and assuring their futures, jockeys were still mostly working on one-race contracts.

There was a deep philosophical divide between the trainers and jockeys; each group felt more entitled to the purse money than the other. The trainers typically worked with a horse far longer than a jockey, but it was the jockeys who darted into tight spaces and dealt with the fears and dangers of falling and being kicked or crushed by thousands of pounds of animal force. The trainers had their hearts in the game, but it was the jockeys who had their asses on the line. "When you jump on a horse," Jacinto said, "you got one foot in the wheelchair and one foot in the cemetery."

After his early verbal wrestling matches with Whiteley, Jacinto proceeded to a legendary career. Vasquez was an unorthodox guy, and much of his great reputation was built on his affinity for a type of horse many others didn't want to ride: Jacinto liked the fillies.

Most jockeys passed on female horses because they considered them slower and less powerful than the males. Jacinto, on the other hand, shrewdly perceived an opportunity in his competitors' mistaken beliefs. He learned this by going to the track early in the morning each day, when the only other riders out there were exercise men. It gave him one-on-one time with the best trainers and a chance to test out any horse that caught his eye. So it was under vibrant orange skies that he examined the fillies and learned all about their idiosyncrasies.

And he believed he knew what it took to make them run. "They are just like women," he said. "You can't just walk over and grab their tits; they slap your face." What they needed, Jacinto claimed, was a little romance. But what he called affection was really just a different way of whipping them.

The first horse that grabbed his notice was Kittiwake, a filly in trainer Woody Stevens's stable. Jacinto noticed that all of her previous jockeys had hit her precisely as they did their male horses—smacking her haunches with the whip. Jacinto could see that it brought only negative results. When Kittiwake felt the stick on her backside, she dug her toes into the dirt and almost stopped. Stevens noticed the pause but not the underlying reason why. So he ignored her potential and considered her to be a lost cause.

When Jacinto came to him and asked to ride the horse, the trainer was befuddled. "What do you think you're going to prove?" Stevens said. "Cordero rode her. Baeza rode her. Turcotte rode her. What are you going to do that they didn't?"

"I'm a very romantic guy," Jacinto told him, "I get along with the fillies."

Stevens gave Vasquez the mount, and the clever young rider experimented. He hit Kittiwake in a different spot, an area he called "the gertz." It was track lingo for a place between her rib cage and stomach, near the spot where his foot rested.

Kittiwake responded. With Jacinto aboard, she surprised everyone and won two races in a row. Later, when schedule conflicts forced Jacinto out of her saddle, his old friend Gustines replaced him and continued to reel off the wins with advice form Jacinto.

All of this gave Vasquez the rock-solid reputation of a lady's man. Even Frank Whiteley, that old hater of "Puerto Ricans," gave Vasquez the mount on the best horse he would ever train, the beautiful but doomed filly named Ruffian.

With Jacinto up, Ruffian won all of her races and broke speed records. She only ever fell behind in a single race, her last one, when she broke down in a match race at Belmont Park. Vasquez desperately tried to keep her upright to save her life and his. The sight of his careworn face and his vain attempts to protect his horse became one of the most enduring and poignant images in the history of racing.

Later Jacinto would also work with another legendary filly, trainer LeRoy Jolley's Genuine Risk. Jolley initially gave the mount to Jacinto, and she ran well under his guidance. But Jolley demonstrated how vindictive a trainer could be. He wanted Vasquez to ride another of his horses; when Vasquez refused that mount, he removed Jacinto from Genuine Risk too and instead gave the promising reins to Laffit Pincay.

This time the loss of opportunity had nothing to do with racism. Pincay, like Jacinto, was Panamanian. And he was also an elite and deserving rider. None of that made any difference to Jacinto, who was furious at his removal from the horse.

A measure of revenge came Jacinto's way when Genuine Risk regressed without him. It all came to a head when she hit the far turn at Hialeah and bolted toward the outside fence. After that, the owner and trainer were convinced that no one could control her or ride her effectively except Jacinto. Jolley and Genuine Risk's owner, Bertram Firestone, found the jockey at Hialeah and tried to get his attention so they could speak to him. But to no avail.

"Hey, Vasquez," Jolley shouted. "I want to talk to you."

Jacinto stopped but only to give them a piece of his mind. "Fuck you!" the jockey shouted at them. "I don't want to talk to you. You took me off your horse for no reason."

With that, Vasquez hurried on. But the powerful owner, Firestone, chased him down and caught up to him. "Vasquez, you know we got a problem with this filly," Firestone said. "We'd like you to go back and ride her."

"Yeah, you guys want me to straighten your freakin' horse out," Vasquez said. "And then you're going to put someone else on her. No way! Screw you guys."

Vasquez left.

But in the afternoon Firestone and Jolley, who were highly unaccustomed to bowing and scraping to little brown foreign riders, reapproached

Jacinto in the jockeys' room, and they took another crack at convincing him to ride their horse. "Look, if you help us and straighten her out," Jolley promised, "you'll ride the horse"—meaning Vasquez would be her regular rider.

Jacinto had heard it all before and knew better than to trust them. Once the owner and trainer got what they wanted, they would give the horse to anyone they chose. There was no loyalty and their promises meant nothing.

Jacinto decided to take a calculated risk anyway. "Look," Vasquez said, "I'll straighten your horse out, but I don't want to hear no shit afterwards. Because I might be mad. And then I'll try to kill one of you guys."

True to his word, Vasquez exercised and examined Genuine Risk. The first thing he noticed was that she was burdened by an excessive amount of equipment on her face. It was a proliferation of hardware that had accumulated over time to correct a litany of perceived problems. "Take all of that shit off of her," Jacinto ordered.

Next, he slow galloped her so that he could examine her exact behavior. In doing so, he found that her mouth was painfully cut up, probably from the devices he had just ordered removed. "She needs to see the dentist," he said.

After his suggestions were adopted, Genuine Risk felt better and ran like her old self.

With his filly back on her feet, Jolley packed her up and took her to Gulfstream. He entered her and another filly in two different races there. Jacinto went too, naturally assuming that he would be her rider. But when he got to the track, he was in for a little surprise. The listed rider, for both of Jolley's fillies, was Angel Cordero Jr. Jacinto was beside himself with rage. The next morning, he got out of bed at 5 a.m. and went down to LeRoy Jolley's barn with a scowl and a baseball bat. Jolley wasn't there yet, so Vasquez told the foreman to deliver a message. "When you see LeRoy," Jacinto told him, "you tell him I'm waiting for him. Over there."

Jacinto went to the tack room and sat, seething, for about an hour. At around 6:30 a.m., Jolley finally appeared. When he came into the tack room, Jacinto quickly locked the door and stood between the trainer and the only exit, the Louisville Slugger resting on his shoulder like he was waiting for a fat pitch.

Then Vasquez, breathing heavily, addressed the double crosser. "Listen to me, you mah-thah-fuck-ah," he said. "You put Cordero on that horse? After all the work I did?"

Jolley threw his hands in the air. "Oh, no-no!" he shouted. "You're going to ride the horse."

"I better," Jacinto told him, "because otherwise I'm going to break that bald head you got with this baseball bat."

Next, it was Angel Cordero's turn to be enraged. Jacinto's return to Genuine Risk's irons meant that Cordero was removed.

Jacinto would go on to win the Kentucky Derby on Genuine Risk, making her the first victorious filly in the Derby in sixty-five years. But Cordero would not celebrate that victory nor forget the slight. He reemerged in the Preakness Stakes, on Codex, and challenged Genuine Risk.

Cordero and Codex were in the lead at the far turn when Jacinto and Genuine Risk came rushing on the outside, threatening to overtake them. Cordero pushed his horse into Jacinto's and "took her out to the parking lot"—racing jargon for very far to the outside. What's more, Angel used his riding crop to viciously whip Genuine Risk in her face. He whipped her so hard that he lacerated her eye.

Angel did his damage and then pulled away to win the race. Jacinto, Jolley, and Firestone were heartbroken. Angel was vindicated; he had avenged his removal.

Buddy Delp would soon make his mark in the ongoing struggle of trainers and jockeys. As Spectacular Bid clocked one unbelievable time after another, the horse drew the interest of virtually every name-brand jockey in the country.

Delp succumbed to this siren song and went looking for a better fit for his superhorse than his eighteen-year-old apprentice. But by merely doing the prudent thing and looking for the best rider for his horse, he would unleash a wide range of the very worst aspects of human nature—rage, jealousy, insecurity, greed, and ethnic rivalry; they were all headed his way.

Everyone in Buddy Delp's world would soon learn just how ugly horse racing could be. And many dreams would be crushed.

8 *Follow the Money*

Buddy Delp had a hard decision to make.

Spectacular Bid's scintillating performances had changed every possible expectation and equation. Ronnie Franklin had ridden the horse to near perfection, winning races, beating great riders, and breaking records. But Buddy Delp had decided to look for another jockey anyway. In fact, the better his horse ran under Franklin, the more he was convinced that a different rider was necessary.

Members of the racing world weren't surprised. Despite Franklin's successes, both on the Bid and on Delp's many other horses, there were plenty of negative whispers about the boy from Dundalk who was getting so much attention. He was too young for a horse like Bid, they said, too inexperienced. Others dissected his riding skills and found fault in just about every move he made. And then of course there were those who gave all the credit for Franklin's accomplishments to the talented stable for which he rode.

Buddy often spoke publicly and wistfully of engaging Willie Shoemaker, the sensational and legendary rider then entering the autumnal years of a highly significant career. By the late 1970s, Shoemaker had already won ten Triple Crown races and thousands of others. "If Bill Shoemaker were six feet tall and weighed 200 pounds he could beat anybody in any sport," the most well-respected sports writer in the United States, Red Smith, once wrote. The fact that Shoe was only 4 feet 10 inches tall and ninety-one pounds didn't bother Smith. "Pound for pound, he's got to be the greatest living athlete," Red said.

In short, Shoemaker was the polar opposite of Franklin. Ronnie was still a teenager; Shoemaker was bearing down on fifty. Ronnie was still an apprentice who'd come out of nowhere; Shoemaker was as famous, experienced, and successful as any rider in the country. He already had more than six thousand trips to the winner's circle in his career.

Once, when Delp was asked if the California-based Shoemaker would want to come east just to ride his horse, Buddy answered with the flippant arrogance for which he was fast becoming known. "Is a blue bird blue?" he asked.

Despite that confidence there was already one prominent rider who had turned down an opportunity to ride the Bid. Stevie Cauthen was among the first riders Buddy reached out to as a possible successor to Franklin. Like Ronnie, Cauthen was only a teenager, but his circumstances were already vastly different. For one thing, Cauthen had just won the Triple Crown, masterfully riding Affirmed to three whisker-close victories over Alydar (ridden by Jorge Velasquez) in one of the most intense duels in the history of racing.

Cauthen's precociousness and all-American good looks had made him more than just a jockey. He had quickly become an ambassador for his sport and an American icon. By the late 1970s the Hispanic riders already dominated American racing, but Cauthen, born and raised on a farm in Kentucky, briefly restored a sense of Caucasian dominance and middle-class values.

The tracks and training facilities were filled with high school dropouts and poor people. Cauthen's winning smile yielded more than a white gleam; good grammar came peeking out from behind those teeth. He presented a sense of social class that was well within the understanding of America's job holders and bill payers. Suddenly, with Cauthen on the throne, horse racing was pasteurized and homogenized, shrink wrapped, and packaged. It was, in short, a lot less spicy than it had been for twenty years, but that suited American tastes.

Thanks to Cauthen's many virtues, he enjoyed opportunities that few people in racing had ever known. He leapt from the starter's gate to the covers of major American magazines and starred in commercials for blue chip brands. "Do you know me?" he asked hundreds of millions of Americans. "I won the Triple Crown, but people still think of me as a kid. With the [American Express] card," the diminutive boy said as he mounted a horse, "people look up to me, and not just when I'm up here."

But a peculiar prejudice cost the brilliant young rider a second-straight chance at a Triple Crown. When Delp put in the request to speak to Cauthen, his agent, the usually prescient Lenny Goodman, told Stevie not to bother.

"What do you know about Spectacular Bid?" Stevie asked him.

"Not much," Lenny responded. "I think he's some New Jersey horse."

Cauthen and Goodman said thanks but no thanks, and they passed.

If Delp couldn't have Cauthen, he turned to the next best option, the man Stevie had barely defeated in the Kentucky Derby, the Preakness, and the Belmont. That rider was Jorge Velasquez, who also went by the Anglicized moniker "Georgie."

Stevie, Georgie, and their horses had just engaged in a duel so intense that there were few precedents for it in racing—or anywhere else. Affirmed versus Alydar was only vaguely reminiscent of Seabiscuit and War Admiral. It was no one-act play; it unfurled in ten brutal installments. In the intensity and drawn-out ferocity of their confrontation, they had more in common with exhausted and bleeding pugilists than anything on four legs. They were two fighters so skilled and fearsome that nobody else could or would challenge them, so they kept going at each other.

The horses and their riders and especially their rivalry unlocked the potential of their sport. They captivated the nation with high-speed daring and contrasting styles. Affirmed inevitably set the pace, while Alydar chose to save something until the end.

In the 1977 Champagne Stakes at Belmont, a race for two-year-olds and a key early indicator for the Kentucky Derby, Alydar and Velasquez came charging from the outside and swooped past Cauthen and Affirmed to win. It was less a sign of things to come and more of a wake-up call for Cauthen.

In the next season's Triple Crown races, Stevie used Velasquez's and

Alydar's tendencies against them. Victory in the Champagne Stakes had taught Velasquez that the best way to beat Affirmed was to hang back and then kick it into high gear. With enough gas left in Alydar's tank, he believed, he could outgun Affirmed to the finish line. But it was Cauthen who had unlocked the secret to victory. If he could get to the inside and save enough ground, he believed, he could stave off his magnificent competitor long enough to win. He put that strategy to work in the Triple Crown, where he outmaneuvered the more experienced rider. In all three races, Cauthen found the rail and saved just enough millimeters around the oval to defeat Alydar's frantic and fearsome late charges.

Those second-place finishes notwithstanding, Velasquez was about as formidable and sensible a choice for Spectacular Bid's mount as any race rider in the country. Like Jacinto Vasquez, Georgie was a Panamanian who had made a big name for himself in the United States in the 1960s. In 1967 he won more races than any other jockey in the country. In 1969 he was the nation's top money winner.

So Georgie Velasquez was Buddy's man, the experienced and battle-tested rider chosen to take the Bid's reins like a baton from Ronnie Franklin. Georgie was supposedly getting the mount of a lifetime, one better than Alydar or, for that matter, Affirmed. Spectacular Bid was a horse, it seemed, that would bring him even greater fame and financial fortune than any he had ever known before.

But who would really want to be in Velasquez's boots?

While the Bid was unquestionably great, the situation was not. In replacing Ronnie, Velasquez was taking over for a rider who had already performed admirably on the same horse and for the same trainer. Franklin was not only under contract to Delp, but he also lived with him, supposedly as a son. In Franklin's last race on the Bid, the World's Playground Stakes in Atlantic City, he had galloped to an incredible fifteen-length victory.

For the new rider, following in the footsteps of a success and one who was apparently dear to the boss was virtually guaranteed to be a poor situation. And yet, given how extraordinary the Bid was, how could Velasquez or anyone else turn down the mount?

In his first race on Spectacular Bid, Georgie took the reins for the 1978 Champagne Stakes, the race he'd won on Alydar only the year before. Delp's advice to him was oddly more about appearances than substance. "Don't let [Spectacular Bid] loaf," Buddy told Velasquez. "Show them in New York who's the champ from the quarter pole home."

The Bid indeed finished fast. He was just two-fifths of a second off the stakes record recently set by Seattle Slew. Nevertheless, the Bid barely beat the field, finishing less than three lengths ahead of the second-place horse. It was a striking contrast to Ronnie's recent fifteen-length victory.

After the race, Velasquez might have also provoked Delp a little when he very lightly criticized Spectacular Bid's ride. "He didn't break too sharp," Georgie said about the horse's emergence from the second turn.

It was a mild statement and typical of a jockey's observation, but Delp was cultivating an image of perfection for his horse and didn't like his jockey speaking out of school. Velasquez's wife didn't help either. She got on Buddy's nerves too when she exuberantly pushed her way into the winner's circle photo. Nevertheless Velasquez was back in the saddle a little less than two weeks later when the whole crew went to New Jersey's Meadowlands for the Young America Stakes.

Delp's team arrived just as the New York Yankees were returning to the tri-state area from Los Angeles with the 1978 World Series trophy. The Bronx Bombers won their title memorably, but only after firing their popular but erratic manager, Billy Martin, and falling fourteen games behind the Boston Red Sox in July.

Spectacular Bid entered the starter's gate in New Jersey soon after the Yanks had been feted with a ticker-tape parade in Manhattan. Like the Bronx Bombers, the Bid endured some struggles before crossing the finish line. When the gate opened, a horse called Port Ebony took a hard-right turn that threw off several riders including Velasquez, who was forced to stand up in the irons. He recovered masterfully and continued on, but as he ventured through the race, he encountered more trouble as he ran into traffic. For a few desperate moments he was locked inside, and ahead of him was Strike Your Colors, a colt that had beaten the Bid at Delaware Park only two months earlier.

Velasquez, a calm and expert rider, patiently waited out the traffic jam until a hole appeared. Exploiting the sliver, the Bid bolted into daylight and emerged from the tight quarters cinema-style, in the nick of time. In the end, the Bid won, but barely. He had prevailed by a neck.

Buddy wasn't pleased with the small margin of victory, but that was less disconcerting to him than the jockey's contention that the animal was hard to control. Buddy had always seen the horse as a "natural" that needed little correction or coercion.

Yet Velasquez was emphatic. He told Buddy that the Bid required two radical pieces of equipment to perform properly. He insisted on an extended blinker, for focus, and a burr bit, to keep the horse from lugging in. Delp couldn't disagree more with both suggestions. But the notion of a burr bit particularly irked him.

A burr bit is an uncomfortable piece of equipment with pronounced bristling brushes that go on the side of the horse's face. It was considered a severe solution that was usually utilized only for incorrigible horses. It is painful by design, but it gives the rider maximum control of the animal.

Buddy saw this as a typical suggestion by a Hispanic rider. He believed that as a rule they sought more forceful control over their animals and had no qualms about handling the animals more roughly.

Buddy believed that Spectacular Bid was a more talented horse than any other he'd ever seen, and he'd seen a million of them. In his mind there was no need for extreme or cruel measures. In fact, on a horse like the Bid, the less equipment, the better. Delp believed the jockey's number one job on the Bid was to sit back and enjoy the ride. Up to that point Spectacular Bid had never been outfitted with anything more elaborate than a "D bit" and a simple leather bridle, the most basic equipment in the game. It was a minimalist approach and, as far as Delp was concerned, the right one.

Delp thought about the difference of opinion between himself and Velasquez on the car ride back to Baltimore. He knew, however, before he even reached the Delaware Memorial Bridge that he was going to make a change. "Georgie's fighting the horse out there," Buddy told his sons as they zoomed past the endless exits of the New Jersey Turnpike. "He's not the right fit."

Back in Baltimore, Delp aggressively did what he had to do to move on. He called Velasquez's agent and delivered the bad news in a terse, dispassionate conversation. That's all it took to do the deed and sever the tie. There were no scenes, no arguments, and no baseball bats.

Velasquez's bad news was good news for Ronnie Franklin. Delp returned the boy from Dundalk to the mount, allowing him to reprise his role as the luckiest man on earth, at least in the eyes of the Hispanic jockeys. Whether he truly was unprepared and undeserving, as they said, it was nevertheless undeniable that no one knew Spectacular Bid better than Ronnie Franklin did. The horse and the boy had been together from the beginning.

It wouldn't be until a few weeks later that the wisdom of returning him to such a rare and coveted mount would be tested. That's when the two-year-old horse and the eighteen-year-old jockey were reunited for the Laurel Futurity.

Great horses like Honest Pleasure, Affirmed, and Secretariat were all recent winners of the Laurel Futurity. It was a highly prestigious race for two-year-olds, and it would be a stiff test for both horse and rider since they would be pitted against a small but promising field of four of the nation's best up-and-coming thoroughbreds. The real showdown, however, would be with just one horse. General Assembly, Secretariat's well-regarded son, was also in the race, and Stevie Cauthen would be in his irons.

As everyone anticipated, the two horses and their young jockeys were neck and neck for much of the race. They were still that way as they went around the second turn.

Because the race was an important one, with the eyes of the horse community following the action, Buddy was eager for everyone to see what his special horse was capable of doing. In his pre-race instructions, he told Ronnie, "When you straighten him out into the stretch, ride him out, keep on driving."

The jockey followed Delp's directives to the letter. Ronnie pressed the Bid and whipped him on the haunch ten times down the stretch. And the great beast responded. Having been asked for more, Bid provided it, accelerating past his rival as though General Assembly was a claimer and not the son of Secretariat.

The Bid-Ronnie rocket ship finished the race in a minute forty-three and three-fifths seconds. From the second turn to the wire, Bid opened up eight and a half lengths between himself and General Assembly, and more than twenty on Clever Trick, the third-place finisher.

Spectacular Bid had not only beaten General Assembly, but he had eclipsed that colt's illustrious father too. Ronnie and the Bid clocked the fastest time yet recorded in the long and storied history of Laurel, more than a second faster than Secretariat had run the Futurity just a few short years before.

Even the hardened trackmen who'd made long careers in and around racing could barely believe what they had just seen. Buddy and his crew, however, had no problem fathoming it. The Bid's implausible speed catapulted all of them into a state of euphoria.

Delp was so happy that the cranky old man actually became giddy and planted a kiss on his talented young jockey in front of everyone. And Ronnie wasn't the only one to get a little unexpected affection. Posing right next to Buddy for the last picture of the day was none other than Raymond Archer, Delp's stepfather, the man who had so kindly taught him everything there was to know about racing and then had so cruelly cast him aside.

In the exhilaration of the moment they had all lost themselves.

The horse was doing the hard lifting and generating the happiness. The Meyerhoffs, Buddy, and Ronnie were all raking in big money and developing huge reputations because the stars were in alignment for them. They had crossed paths with the golden horse like Pharaoh's daughter had lifted Moses from the Nile. They hadn't created the horse, but they had found him. And with his special qualities he was changing everything.

But lost in the huge victory and the incredible display of equine speed was the relative ease of the race. Although the field consisted of excellent two-year-olds, true contenders, there were only four of them. That meant that Ronnie and the Bid had a mostly clear path to show off the horse's genetic superiority. Beating the great and famous Stevie Cauthen was certainly a point of pride, especially for Franklin, who had come under so much scrutiny. But as fine a rider as Cauthen was, he might have been one with whom Ronnie could cope.

Cauthen wasn't bellicose or intimidating. As his public image suggested, he was straightforward, a clean competitor. Like Ronnie, Stevie was a teenager who'd been allowed to pilot the very best talent and to compete in the most prestigious races. He'd already won the Triple Crown, and he was the current hottest commodity in the business. Stevie might've been the only rider in America who had no axe to grind with Ronnie, and of course, he felt no jealousy for him.

But now that everyone could see the greatness of Spectacular Bid, now that the superlatives were stacking up and Bid was the clear frontrunner among the two-year-olds, all that he had really earned was a big fat target on his back—for himself and Ronnie.

Buddy finished out 1978 by taking the Bid to one last lucrative race. At the Heritage Stakes in Pennsylvania Spectacular Bid, with Ronnie aboard, won by a gaping six-and-a-half-length margin. When the year finally ended, the highest recognition came pouring in. The Bid won the Eclipse Award as the "Two-Year Old Male Horse of the Year." And Ronnie was named the "Outstanding Apprentice Jockey of the Year."

But Franklin could barely enjoy the professional validation. His personal life suddenly became far more complicated when he got a call he never expected. It was from Shirley Campbell, the young woman with whom he'd had a single, quick sexual encounter earlier in the year.

Shirley was nervous and uncertain. She made small take with Ronnie for a moment, and then she blurted out the real reason for her call. "You're going to be a father," she bluntly said.

Ronnie didn't reply.

He expressed no happiness and showed no anger. He didn't deny anything or urge her to put the child up for adoption. He didn't demand that she have an abortion. He simply said nothing.

Shirley could sense his fear. She was scared too. Awkward and unsure of herself, she attempted to fill the petrified moment with the same soothing question a young wife might ask her husband in the same situation.

"What would you rather have, a boy or a girl?" she asked Ronnie.

"A boy," he said.

And that was it; they said nothing more to each other, and they hung up the phone.

Shirley never heard from Ronnie again throughout the months of her pregnancy. And he wasn't present in December either, when she gave birth to the boy he said he wanted.

Without Ronnie there, Shirley was free to name the child whatever she liked. She called him Chris, and gave him her last name, Campbell. It was a way to honor the father whom she loved so much, her father.

Chris was the only son Ronnie would ever have, and he was a dead ringer for his dad, but he was a Campbell and would never be a Franklin.

The appearance of a son would only apply financial pressure to Franklin, and by all appearances he now had plenty of money to cope with that. But the truth was that even as he was under contract to Buddy Delp, riding excellent horses on a daily basis, dominating area race tracks, and winning and making national headlines, he had very few assets. Since he had first tried cocaine with Buddy and Gerald in the "playroom," he had developed a real taste for it. He regularly got high with them and others at Buddy's house.

Although living with Buddy was portrayed as wholesome and protective in the media, it was actually draining. Ronnie paid the bill for the coke consumption of the whole house. And the white powder was so pervasive at Buddy's that one housekeeper accidentally used her vacuum tube to suck up a mound of it on a table, believing it was talcum spillage.

In that house, they smoked pot and swallowed a variety of pills and drank booze by the bottle. And Ronnie, the young guy with the big paydays, shelled out for most of it. There were also other costly vices. Ronnie lost piles of money at the poker table, and Buddy was known to be a great poker player.

Although the track was supposed to be the place where Ronnie made his money, he lost a significant amount of it there too. Hank Tiburzi, Tony Franklin's best friend, the man who had brought Ronnie to Pimlico that first time, continued to watch over the boy and do odd jobs for him. From a distance, he once observed Buddy solicit $2,000 from Ronnie for a horse bet. Tiburzi decided to shadow Delp as the trainer made his rounds through the track and see what he did with the money.

Buddy never went to the windows with it and never placed a bet. In fact, the money remained in his cavernous pants pocket, where it never saw the light of day again. But when Buddy got back to Ronnie, Tiburzi heard him deliver some sad news. "Your horse lost," Buddy told Ronnie. And just like that, two grand of the kid's money had evaporated.

"This was an old trick," Cathy Rosenberger said, "usually perpetrated by an unscrupulous agent on his client-rider. They'd take the money from the jockey, supposedly to lay down 'the bet' for them, but instead they'd keep it. If the horse won, the agent would tell the jockey that he got shut out of the window, didn't get the bet down in time, and would simply give the money back. But if the horse lost, the agent kept the entire stake for himself."

Ronnie was young and vulnerable, but even he knew that he was being duped. But what could he do about it? For that matter, what could his parents, do? They weren't going to confront Buddy, so they merely chose to see it as the cost of doing business with him. The Franklins were all too painfully aware what they owed Buddy Delp. Without him, Ronnie would still be at the fast food fryer or God knows where.

For better or worse, Buddy was Ronnie's font of opportunity, his future, and his identity. Everything Ronnie had—the roof over his head, his friends, his career as a jockey, and his celebrity—were all owed to Buddy. And Buddy could end it all in a moment's notice, at his whim. That was the power dynamic.

Ronnie had the ability to walk away from any of these unfair situations, but it would have cost him everything to do it. And for what? A little coke money or some stupid bet on a horse? It was all just part of some unfair dues he had to pay to get to the top. He had to see the big picture; there were years of good times and easy paydays ahead. Anyway, as long as Buddy was getting a regular taste out of Ronnie's till, there was every incentive for the trainer to keep feeding the young rider good mounts and especially to keep him on Spectacular Bid.

9 *Retribution*

Right out of the starter's gate Spectacular Bid clanged into the side of the unforgiving steel opening; he did it with so much abusive force that Ronnie Franklin was almost jarred clean off his wide, strong back. The young rider might have fallen under the pounding hooves, but with his great physical strength and fortitude he managed to stay in the saddle, and after only a few strides the horse and rider had recovered and were in top form.

That hard crash was only the beginning of an extremely trying race and day.

As Ronnie and the Bid ventured further into the loam of Gulfstream Park and the prestigious Florida Derby, a key stakes race and an indicator for the Kentucky Derby, the path would only become more treacherous.

It was a small field, but among the group of riders was Georgie Velasquez. When last Ronnie and the Bid had seen him, Georgie had been their friend and teammate, wearing Hawksworth Farm's familiar black-and-blue silks and riding the Bid to victory in two pivotal races.

When Buddy Delp removed Velasquez from the mount, the rider seemed to walk away professionally and without rancor. But as Ronnie was the first to find out, the veteran rider wasn't at all happy about losing his place on the Bid. In fact, he was still livid. Much of his rage stemmed from the humiliation of losing the special horse to the young and inexperienced Franklin, a rider he did not respect.

The depth of Velasquez's wrath and his capacity for revenge were both about to be revealed. He and his friend Angel Cordero Jr. were intent on torturing Franklin in front of the entire racing world, thwarting the mighty Bid, and paying back Buddy Delp.

Ronnie was oblivious to all of that. After the Laurel Futurity, where he had bested Secretariat's time and defeated Stevie Cauthen, the hottest name in riding, he was calm and confident. In the Futurity, it had all been so simple.

Here at the Florida Derby Franklin tried to employ the same tactics, but things played out far differently. Just as he had done at Laurel, he let Spectacular Bid languish far behind the leaders without a worry in the world. But when it was time to make his move, he ran into a different style of racing than he had ever encountered before.

He whipped the Bid and gave the horse his marching orders. "Let's go Big Daddy!" he shouted in the Bid's ear. With that, the steel gray accelerated and gobbled up the ground between himself and the others. The first rider he encountered on his trek to the front was Angel Cordero Jr.

Angel, who liked to have his name pronounced Spanish-style, *Ahn-hel*, was a jockey unlike any other Ronnie had seen before. By 1979, Angel was already firmly established as one of the finest riders in the country, and perhaps one of the greatest across the centuries. Both Black and Puerto Rican, Cordero grew up poor on the island, in a little wooden house that sat behind the stable area of the track. Despite his family's lack of wealth, he had a happy upbringing. His father, Angel Cordero Sr., was a highly respected man who had emerged from a huge family of horse people.

Angel Sr. was just one of forty-nine Corderos listed as jockeys in Puerto Rico. He distinguished himself from the crowd of his own family and, for that matter, all of the other Puerto Rican horse professionals to emerge as one of the most distinguished jockeys and trainers in the history of the island.

In Cordero Sr.'s era of racing the men were so tough and fearless, so desperate for opportunity, that they often raced without helmets. Angel Cordero Sr. was among the greatest of these natural horsemen, an adept rider who scored more than a hundred victories on one horse alone. After his riding career was over, he became even more well known as a winning trainer.

Angel Jr. regarded his *papi* as a kind and loving man who taught him almost everything he would ever know about riding. Angel's mother, Mercedes Hernandez, also came from horse people. Her father, too, was a jockey and a trainer, as were all of her brothers.

Living at the track from birth and with so many family members in the profession, Angel Jr. found that horses and riding came naturally to him. He was familiar with the huge animals before he could say "cat." Years later his mother still had albums full of photos of Angel on the *caballos*, in the saddle, grinning, when he was still barely old enough to walk.

It is interesting that even with his pedigree and God-given horse-riding ability, Cordero harbored another dream. He loved baseball as much as racing and fantasized about playing in the World Series every bit as much as he did riding in the Kentucky Derby. From his home on the island he followed the pennant races in the American and National Leagues and worshipped the stars who fought all summer for the October glory.

Angel's baseball ambitions were fueled by the kids he ran with. He counted Roberto Clemente and Orlando Cepeda among his childhood friends. Like Angel, they were Black and Puerto Rican and intensely driven with a hot fire for success. But while Clemente and Cepeda went to the United States and became All-Stars and Hall of Famers, Angel learned the hard lessons of sport. Though clearly a superb athlete, he didn't really have much to offer the scouts. He was good enough to play some semipro ball on the island, but physically he was never going to cut it. At age twelve he was so small that many people believed that he was a midget. At eighteen, he was but 5 feet tall and weighed seventy-eight pounds. No one had to tell him that there was no future for him in baseball. "I was just too small to do anything but ride," Cordero said.

But the path wasn't as clear as it might have seemed for him to be a great rider. For one thing, his mother was dead set against it. In fact, despite her own background and immersion in racing, Mercedes Hernandez Cordero wanted her little son to be anything else but a rider. In her eyes he was tiny and vulnerable. She lived in fear that her Angel would get hurt or killed on the track. Her anxieties were only heightened when her husband finally, inevitably, came to her and asked the question that she had long dreaded: "May I take Angel to work with me?"

Before she gave her consent for him to even go, she made her husband promise to keep her boy off the horses. He agreed, and more than that, he obeyed. He personally saw to it that Angel Jr. never got a leg up. And he made it clear to all of his workers that his son was not to ride the horses when he was away.

But Angel Jr. was already a determined kid and a rule breaker. When the old man left the premises, he hopped aboard any old horse that appealed to him and rode without regard to parental rules. So Angel Sr. soon learned the same lesson that countless others in the horse world would find out the hard way: Angel Cordero Jr. did what he wanted.

Unable to stop the boy from riding, Angel Sr. used his son's dogged determination for his own simple needs. "Buy me a beer," he told his son, "and I will put you on a horse." So young Angel saved his money and delivered cold bottles to wash the hot dust of hard work out of his old dad's dry mouth. And of course he got his race-riding lessons.

Later, the clever father demanded one more thing. He used riding as an inducement to get his kid to school. He wanted Angel Jr. to have enough education that he wouldn't be forced to the irons to make a living. "If you finish school, I might think about letting you ride," he told his son. "But we'll have to convince your *mami*."

Angel finished school, or at least more school than most of the men who worked at the barn or the track ever had. He got his high school diploma and went on to a semester of community college to boot.

Mercedes was delighted that Angel was getting an education, although she never knew about his backroom deals with her husband. They never told her that Angel Jr. was also training to race ride.

Mercedes only found out that her son was a jockey on the day before his first race. By then, she was forced to accept the fact that he was a rider and there wasn't much she could do to prevent it. But while she accepted it as a fact, she never quite reconciled herself to it. That was true even after he became a star on the mainland.

Because riding was second nature to Cordero, he drove his horses with an urgency, ferocity, and daring that few others could rationally attempt. His riding style and combative nature both kept him in constant conflict with track officials, and he came to the mainland only because he faced a long suspension in Puerto Rico. Had he stayed there, he would have been out of work for months. So he made a deal with the stewards. They agreed to lift their punishment if Cordero agreed to leave the island.

He complied and moved on to the United States.

Angel had no idea what to expect on the mainland. Clemente and Cepeda told him about the terrible prejudice aimed at Blacks and Latinos in the states. They recounted how they had to take different buses than their white teammates and stay in different hotels.

At first, Angel thought their stories were exaggerations. But when he landed in the United States for the first time in 1962, the civil rights movement had not yet reached its zenith, and he actually found life on the mainland worse than his friends had described it.

"They treat me like shit here," he confided to his parents, and there was plenty of reason to think so. At the track, white riders who were punished for some infraction typically received a five-day suspension. But Angel noticed that if he (or another Latino) was involved in a similar violation—and he was always involved in something—his suspension would generally last ten to fifteen days.

He was also ordered to speak English in the jockeys' room. The Latinos were generally forbidden from speaking Spanish. Worst of all, he had to take the pain of being called "nigger" and "spic." He heard those words applied to him both at the track and outside the gates. On occasion, in an attempt at self-deprecating humor, he even referred to himself as "the little nigger." Certainly that's how he was seen and treated. Away from the track he was second-class. He was turned away from "white" restaurants and bathrooms. These things didn't happen only in the South; he experienced similar treatment in New York.

Later on, riding in California and enjoying financial success for the first time, Angel hoped to live the American dream and purchase his own home. On two different occasions he picked out a house only to be told he couldn't buy in a "whites-only neighborhood." "Spanish guys was very mistreated in this country in the sixties; womens, too," Angel remembered with some bitterness. "America in the sixties was meant for white mens only."

Going hand-in-hand with the racial and ethnic abuse was class warfare. The monied interests were always working to suppress Angel's upward mobility. Riders were required to have agents for their own protection, but Angel wasn't allowed to speak to his in private. It was required that someone official always be present to listen into their conversations.

These slights and insults only enraged Cordero and fueled the aggression and ambition that came so naturally to him. He wasn't in the least bit ashamed of who he was. On the contrary, he had a rock-solid sense of self, and he sure as hell hadn't come all the way to the mainland to be a pin cushion for demeaning epithets. And no matter how unwelcome he was made to feel, he had no intention of going back home to live in some race track shanty like his father did, with the smell of horseshit and poverty in his nose night and day.

He had come to New York for good, and he had come to win.

Angel wanted the money, and he wanted adulation. He was in the game for groceries but also to show the world his talent. If you didn't give him your respect, he would take it from you against your will. He could beat you and break your heart with his whip because he was willing to take his horses to places you were too afraid to take yours. But, if by chance, you were feeling a little courageous and willing to ride in the dangerous places too, he would make you pay for that.

Fear, and potentially pain, were merely implements in Angel Cordero Jr.'s toolbox. No matter who you were, he could almost certainly outride you. But if that didn't work, he was more than willing to out-crazy you. Even Angel's most ardent admirers knew that.

Angel was the type of guy who would go to the wall for a friend, help him in private, and even aid and abet him out on the track. But should your self-interest collide with his, all bets were off. "He had a motto for himself," Angel's close friend and fellow jockey Ruben Hernandez said. "'Number one, Angel. Number two, Angel. Number three, Angel. Number four, Angel.'"

Hernandez admired Cordero and considered him greater than any other jockey in the business. But encountering him in a race was no picnic. "He was the type of rider if you come in the inside, well you picked the wrong place to be. He won't let you in there. But if you come outside he push you out."

Cordero reminded Hernandez, a Panamanian, of another strong athlete he knew back home. "Angel was like Roberto Duran in a saddle," Hernandez said, referring to the wild man of the boxing ring who had once unnerved and defeated Sugar Ray Leonard. Duran was as much about pre-fight psychological torture as he was about his whipping, whizzing hands of stone.

Ruben idolized Cordero but knew that he was wild and brutal too. "Most of the time Angel do it the right way," he said, "but a lot of time he overdo it a little bit. He not only ride his horse, he ride your horse, too." By that, Ruben meant that Cordero could make an opponent's horse follow his instructions instead of his own jockey's. Angel also had no compunction about using his crop to whip another rider's horse.

But Ruben also saw Angel's cerebral side. He knew that his friend's greatest strength lay in his understanding of every crevice and nuance of his game. "Angel always examined the other horses," Hernandez said. "When he rides he always looking to his surroundings. He looking to the left, he looking to the right. He cover every angle, when he was riding a horse."

Intelligence and intensity carried Angel to victory many times even when he wasn't on the best mount. "Angel take the maximum ride of the horse," Ruben said. "That's one of the best achievements of him. It doesn't matter if he ride a favorite or a 10–1 shot, you would see him riding with the same enthusiasm." Ruben continued, "Angel was very patient. He wasn't the type of guy who move after the 3/8th pole. He can wait and can wait and then check you around, look where you are especially when you ride the favorite. If he's not riding the favorite and somebody else ride the favorite, he look for you because he want to beat you."

Even Angel's friends could suffer at his hands. At times, it seemed he punished other riders for simply doing what they were paid to do and trying to win.

Jacinto Vasquez had a colorful name for it. He called it "barbecuing."

If you got pushed or shoved into a rail, a fence, the parking lot, or a hedge; if something endangered you and made you feel like you would be thrown, kicked, maimed, or killed, that was getting "barbecued."

Angel might as well have worn a "Kiss the Cook" apron instead of silks. He did more barbecuing than anyone in racing. Even so, most of the other Latin riders liked and revered him, and they tolerated his cunning tricks. "We didn't call [Cordero's style] dirty," Hernandez said. "We called it horse riding."

For many of the old Anglo-style Americans in racing Angel epitomized everything they believed about Hispanic jockeys. One story about an old trainer trying to make a jockey out of a young Irish boy summed it all up. When asked about the Irish kid's prospects, he was pessimistic. "Ah, he's such a nice, good little Irish lad," he said, shaking his head sadly. "Little son of a bitch will never make a goddamned nickel. In this business you gotta be nasty. You have to be some common little spic to make a living."

It was a despicable story, but it explained how the white riders and trainers saw it. In their eyes the Latins were more daring or, perhaps, more desperate. They were liable to do anything out there. Cordero understood that and played off their fears and insecurities about what he was willing to do. Ronnie Franklin was simply too young and inexperienced to know just how complex, dangerous, and difficult Cordero was.

The two jockeys rendezvoused at the first turn. Angel was a length or two ahead of Ronnie and straying to the outside. Right away that presented Franklin with a choice. Cordero showed him a yawning gap between his horse and the rail. Franklin could go around Cordero, but that was taking the long way. When Ronnie peered into that hole, he saw exactly what he had hoped to see: the pure Florida sunlight shining on the other end.

So far as Ronnie could tell, it was a short, inviting tunnel to a sure victory. But as soon as he charged into the gap, he realized he'd fallen into something. What he had perceived as a path was in fact the jaws of a vicious predator. He and the Bid were the prey.

So he tiptoed into the opening like a baby into a disaster. Meanwhile, Cordero was a stoic hunter. He waited for Franklin to venture far enough into the hole to the point that there was no easy escape route, and then he clamped down with the teeth.

Cordero, on Sir Ivor Again, swiftly pointed his horse's nose to the left and shut the aperture. Ronnie knew that he had been duped; he was trapped with nowhere to go. He didn't just see it; he could feel it. With every step Sir Ivor Again galloped, Cordero shoved Ronnie and the Bid closer to the terrifying rail, where everything was tight, claustrophobic, and dangerous.

Ronnie still had viable options. He might've taken his chances and bolted through the flickering sliver of light, but that was a huge risk that could have spooked or even damaged the Bid had Cordero continued to squeeze him. Or he might have elected to bide his time, maintain his ground, and wait until the varying speed of the horses caused a natural reopening of the gap. The latter required a certain cunning and patience, a belief that the horse could still win despite the long impediment.

But Franklin was still too inexperienced to know which was the better path.

Fearing both the rail and Buddy's rage if he lost the race or damaged the horse, Ronnie made an extraordinary and dangerous decision that no experienced rider would have attempted. He pulled the Bid's reins, slowing the mighty horse in mid-gallop. He so desperately sought to maneuver outside that he panicked and cut across the heels of Sir Ivor Again and Cordero.

Ronnie treated the Bid as if he were equipped with a break, a clutch, and an accelerator. He was variously stomping on all the pedals in a frantic attempt to explode his way out of Cordero's iron grip.

To his credit, he escaped Cordero, but in doing so, he came incredibly close to clipping hooves with Sir Ivor Again. Had that happened, Franklin, Cordero, and several tons of babied horseflesh would have all tumbled to the unforgiving dirt. The horses would have most likely shattered their femurs, and the riders might have been kicked in their skulls or crushed under the weight of tons of tumbling horse. And with two horses still behind Franklin and Cordero, the calamity would have been significant.

And yet Franklin got away with it all. Not only did he avoid the heels, but the Bid actually responded to his crazy demands. After his forced slowdown, the great horse accelerated, regained his momentum, and took aim at the leaders, who were still a ways off in the distance.

Almost any horse in the Bid's shoes, having had the reins pulled, would have lost the race—and lost it badly. But the Bid had a peculiar engine. Apparently, he was more Ferrari than thoroughbred. He seemingly went from 0 to 60 in no time. And Ronnie, despite the mistakes of a lifetime, somehow had his horse gaining ground with every stride. Cordero and Sir Ivor Again, who had been so menacing just seconds ago, were now mere specs in the distance and relics of the past.

Set free and out into the open, the Bid made up fourteen lengths against some of the best horses of his generation. Improbably, he found himself neck and neck with the three leaders.

Ronnie approached those front runners near the second turn. But instead of staying to the outside, where he'd just found so much success, he inexplicably ducked back into the hole on the inside. And that's where he and Georgie Velasquez, riding Fantasy 'n Reality, became reacquainted.

Velasquez was galloping side by side with the other two leading colts to form an impenetrable wall. He met Franklin's move inside in much the same way Cordero had. He showed the boy the opening and then squeezed him tight when he took it. And Franklin responded in the same exact way. Unbelievably, he tugged on the Bid's reins yet again, but this time he cut across the heels of not one but three horses!

Miraculously, Ronnie avoided all of them, and once more he found the wide-open outside. At this point the Bid had traveled an incredibly long distance on his four spindly legs, not only going forward but also zigzagging back and forth across the track. And yet somehow he still had the wind for victory. With the encouragement of Franklin's frantic whip and verbal pleadings the horse rocketed past the field.

Ronnie and the Bid somehow won the Florida Derby by five lengths, going away. But they did it only after one of the most manic and erratic rides in the annals of professional racing. For the horse, it was a magical journey. After the first turn, Spectacular Bid made up nineteen lengths and did it after his reins were pulled and he was steered erratically.

It was a stunning race in its danger, its speed, and, of course, its sheer malevolence.

While the crowd roared its approval at Ronnie's theatrical display of riding—something more reminiscent of a rodeo than a race—Buddy Delp stood and watched it all with his jaw open and his blood pressure popping. He was seething and horrified by Ronnie's recklessness. And with newsmen all around him he kicked his composure and opened a window into his true nature. "I'm going to put a size 10½ shoe up his ass so far it'll take a dozen doctors to get it out," Delp bellowed.

Then, rushing down to the track, Buddy confronted Ronnie, who was still trotting to the winner's circle. His "son" had not only just won one of the most prestigious races in the country, against the most well-bred competition, but he had also beaten some of the best jockeys in the world.

Yet Buddy Delp pelted him with mean abuse. His succinct message to his boy was as direct as it was crude. And it was all highly public. "You fucking, idiot!" Buddy raged at his victorious rider. "You fucking, idiot, I ought to put my foot in your ass!" The trainer's unbridled rage and loss of control escaped from his mouth right in front of the Meyerhoffs, Franklin's fellow riders, his parents, and members of the press corps, who were delighted by the horrifying spectacle and printed every humiliating word (at least the ones that were printable).

Though Harry Meyerhoff actually owned the valuable horse, he was more gentlemanly and composed in his reaction. Calm and collected in his sport coat and tie, with his beautiful young wife and strapping son by his side, Harry responded to the inquiries of the writers in the manner of a CEO reporting sunny results to nervous shareholders. He cited the bottom line: "[Franklin] won the race, didn't he?" Harry asked with a confident smile.

Meanwhile, Ronnie complained to both Delp and the press that he had been the victim of collusion. He appeared paranoid, claiming that every single other rider in the race was in the same conspiracy to get him. "They teamed up on me," he said. "What can you do? Six riders against one." Ronnie said their motive was his horse or, more precisely, the mount. They all wanted to ride Spectacular Bid so badly that they made him look bad in the hopes that he would be fired.

Buddy might've fallen back on his many years of experience in racing to calm his rider and defuse the explosive situation. Instead, he dumped gallons of gasoline on it and then casually lit the match. Right in front of a reporter, Delp placated Mrs. Meyerhoff by explaining to her how unintelligent his own hand-picked rider was. "Ronnie is smart enough to know that he's not that smart," Buddy said.

Another reporter, who hadn't heard Buddy's profane rant firsthand, asked him what he had said to Franklin. "In essence it was something like this," Buddy said. "I told him he was a dummy and rode a stupid race on a horse who could've won by twenty lengths."

After berating Ronnie some more, Buddy urged his protégé into the jockeys' room. He wanted him to confront Cordero and Velasquez with his fists. Physical altercations were not uncommon in the manly sanctuary of the jockeys' room. That's where the men who strove against each other on the track for victories and in the barn for decent mounts, and who intimidated and endangered each other in competition, settled their scores. They didn't always even need a provocation to fight. Sometimes they merely hauled off and cracked each other just to establish psychological dominance.

Ronnie, though a successful fist fighter back in the nooks and crannies of his old high school hallways and on the streets and alleyways of Dundalk, didn't punch anybody. Instead he did something really dangerous. He slurred Cordero and Velasquez. Shouting at the top of his lungs in rage, he called them both "spics."

Velasquez knew Ronnie personally. He looked past those ugly words, perhaps understanding the frustrations that led to their utterance, and without admitting anything, he said that Ronnie was probably right in his wild accusations "Everyone's always after the best horse in the race," Georgie said. "Everyone takes his shot at him. [Spectacular Bid] is the best horse around—everyone wants him."

After the tumult was over and Ronnie and Buddy had humiliated and embarrassed themselves, they went their separate ways. Buddy moved on to an after-race party and then came back to the barn to check on the health of his horse.

The old man was intoxicated, of course, after almost drowning in a half-dozen vodkas, and he made the unfortunate decision to drink and talk with a reporter by his side. He would've been safer behind the wheel and speeding down the highway.

Soaked in booze, he suddenly turned from ass-kicker to gooey sentimentalist. Buddy regaled the reporter about his feelings for Ronnie. "He's my man," Delp said. "He'll always be my man. Give him a hug and tell him I love him."

It was the revolting and mawkish blabbering of a drinker whose every word was fermented in a vat. So the worst luck Buddy had on this evil day was maintaining his consciousness. He hadn't even had the good fortune to pass out before he'd opened his big mouth.

And now something really telling was about to slip out.

"I'm going back to the house now and see Ron," Buddy said. "I may be going to party with him."

"Going to party" was an odd expression for a man nearly fifty to use in connection with a teenage boy. "Party," used as a verb, was Baltimore high school slang for getting high. When Gerald and Ronnie said that they were "going to party," they meant that they were going to inhale cocaine or, as they said it, "snort some blow."

Buddy had used their nomenclature to tell the journalist that he hoped to go back to his rented Florida house, find the teenagers, and use illicit drugs with them.

That didn't happen. When Buddy got home, Ronnie wasn't even there. In fact, nobody knew for sure where he was. Franklin, near tears, had been so humiliated when he left the track that he simply disappeared. By the time Buddy returned home, Franklin had been gone for hours and had yet to resurface.

Without his "man," Buddy quickly passed out in bed. Meanwhile, with no one paying attention to him, seventeen-year-old Gerald Delp sat in the living room and did lines of coke all by himself. His enjoyment was disturbed only when he suddenly heard a loud crack out on the porch.

Gerald opened the front door to see what had caused the racket. It was Ronnie. Intoxicated, he'd tried to lie down on the porch's hanging glider and had fallen off. Once on the ground, he decided to use the hard floor as a makeshift bed and go to sleep.

But Gerald walked out and roused his best friend. Ronnie sat up, his head spinning, and told Gerald that after fleeing the track, he had scored some coke of his own and gotten stoned. That was how he dealt with the incredible stress of his horrific day.

"But, what're you doing out here?" Gerald asked him.

"I was afraid to come home," Ronnie said. "Buddy was so mad."

"Don't worry about him," Gerald said. "Anyway, he's asleep. Come on inside."

Ronnie entered the house, and he and Gerald sat down on the sofa and enjoyed the remainder of the cocaine together. They also drank their hard liquor and popped their pills. Those activities occupied the boys the rest of the night until Ronnie's pain was sufficiently numbed, and they went to bed.

But a good night's sleep didn't solve much. In the morning, matters were as complicated as ever. Despite Buddy's drunken pronouncements the day before about Ronnie being "his man," the trainer informed the media that the Bid's mount was under review. Delp told the press that he had given the Meyerhoffs a list of several riders for consideration, and asked them, as the owners, to make the definitive decision. Buddy's register of appropriate riders included Willie Shoemaker, Darrel McHargue, Jacinto Vasquez, and Chris McCarron. He said that Ronnie was also still in the mix and, in fact, Delp himself had recommended Ronnie as his choice to remain.

And then, as if he could simply not stop his mouth, Delp lit off the mother of all firecrackers. He said that there were two riders who were definitely not on his list: Georgie Velasquez and Angel Cordero. "I wouldn't use [them] on a Billy goat," Buddy said, in another one of his clever zingers. He told the reporters that he agreed that Cordero and Velasquez "were out to intimidate Franklin and our horse. Georgie is hot about me taking him off Spectacular Bid." As for Angel Cordero, "I wouldn't know him if I saw him climbing out of a banana tree."

It was the lowest and ugliest blow yet, far worse than the use of the word "spic." "He basically called Angel a chimpanzee," Ruben Hernandez said. The comment did nothing to hurt Cordero, who had already absorbed and endured much worse during his time on the mainland.

And yet Buddy's slur was so incredibly vicious and public that it couldn't help but elevate the feud among the riders to a far more personal level. Buddy spoke up in a misguided attempt to protect his horse and to deflect criticism from his rider. Instead he birthed a terrible animosity right there and at that moment. It had the net effect of putting a target on both the horse and the jockey. Thanks to Buddy, they were assured of getting extra attention from the most intense and ruthless rider in the country.

And Cordero was a man who relished target practice.

Buddy did the talking, but it was Ronnie who had to stare down the barrel of the furious men in the jockeys' room. It was Ronnie who would have to go out on the track and ride in close quarters with Cordero and the other Hispanics. Now pretty much all of them would have a grudge, and of course they would all be on the backs of animals that weighed in excess of half a ton—animals that could be aimed at another man and fired like a canon.

But even without Buddy's explosive comments Ronnie still had a lot to endure. The next day one of Washington's major newspapers published a cartoon of him on the Bid, in mid race. The jockey whipped his horse while Buddy sat right behind him and whipped Ronnie with a crop that was the size of a golf club.

Even more troubling, in a segment for ABC's *Wide World of Sports* program, Ronnie faced the music for his strange ride. His professional credibility and competence were questioned for the world to see by two eminently reasonable and expert men. Host Jim McKay and his racing sidekick, legendary jockey Eddie Arcaro, broke down the film of Franklin's disastrous day.

Arcaro, likable and articulate and one of the biggest winners in racing history, gave his ostensibly unbiased third-person assessment of the race. He basically exonerated Cordero and Velasquez. Arcaro never explicitly mentioned collusion and didn't address it, though it was clear as day that it had occurred. Instead, he blamed Ronnie alone for all the trouble.

Going through the race film frame by frame, Arcaro dispassionately analyzed the controversies. First, taking note of Ronnie's rendezvous with Cordero, he said nothing of Angel squeezing the boy and the Bid against the rail. Instead, he implied it was an empty worry. "It looks like you could move a small Toyota in there," Arcaro said, speaking of the gap.

At the point in the race when Ronnie complained about Velasquez, Arcaro again stopped the film and appeared to peer into the same small space Ronnie saw. "There was room in there, Jim," Arcaro said to McKay. "There was absolutely room in there."

Like the excellent reporters that they were, McKay and Arcaro sought comment from the principals: Cordero, Franklin, and Delp. And all three of them said revealing things.

First, Franklin, more in the glare than anyone else, was surprisingly calm and poised on camera. Looking younger than his nineteen years, he spoke from high atop Spectacular Bid with a rider's protective helmet on his head.

With his smooth baby's face and fractured grammar, Franklin radiated a childlike vulnerability. Despite his position and talent and all of the success and attention he had amassed so far, it was easy to see that he still had the fragile psychology of a boy. "Around the first turn, when Angel Cordero shut me off, he was intimidating me," Ronnie said. "I was taking care of my horse. I didn't want [Cordero] to bang [Spectacular Bid] up against the fence and everything, which he would've did."

As Ronnie spoke, his shoulder jerked and twitched in involuntary spasms—a sign, perhaps, of the pressure that he was under or maybe of the high quantity of illicit drugs that were coursing through his system.

Buddy also spoke to the crew from ABC and offered his own theory as to what might be making the young jockey so nervous. "I want the monkey off of Ronnie's back," Delp said, utilizing an old euphemism for drug addiction. But then he clarified and said, "The monkey being Bud Delp." Speaking of himself in the third person, Buddy said, "I think Bud Delp has intimidated Ronnie Franklin to a degree; he wants to please Bud Delp."

Finally, Angel Cordero had his say, but he provided it on paper instead of in person. Feigning an innocence that belied his uncanny mastery of the track, Angel wrote, "I was never close to [Spectacular Bid], and I found no problem with the race. I was two or three horses away. Franklin wanted to go around me. I couldn't see what was going on behind me. You could look at the film and see there was no problem. There was plenty of room between Franklin and me."

Finally, Arcaro spoke up again and reported the conversation he'd had with Florida's chief state steward, Walter Blum. He informed the audience that Blum was "a former rider and a good one." Arcaro said that Blum also felt that Cordero and Velasquez were "never near" Ronnie and the Bid.

It all seemed so comprehensive, and it was a professional take on the events from highly credible men, and yet it utterly ignored the fact that Cordero was a known badass. Every jockey in the business knew he had done exactly what Ronnie accused him of doing. In a sense it was poor journalism since it never even bothered to address the key question: Were Cordero and Velasquez in fact targeting Ronnie Franklin?

Jacinto Vasquez didn't need a reporter to tell him what was what. He was friends with Cordero and Velasquez, and he had battled both of them many times. He admitted that Angel had deliberately "crowded Franklin." Jacinto knew that Hispanic riders regularly ganged up on the English-speaking jockeys, coordinating their efforts to defeat them. "We did it many times," Jacinto said.

More than that, Jacinto also knew that Cordero and Velasquez would collude against *any* other rider, regardless of ethnicity, if that rider had succeeded in ousting one of them from the mount of a coveted horse. "They even did it to me," Jacinto said.

According to Vasquez, Angel was the ringleader of the shenanigans. "Velasquez was the nicest guy to ride," Jacinto said, "and Cordero used to abuse him all the time. Then Angel would come back [to the jockeys' room] and say, 'I'm sorry, papa. My brother.'"

"My brother?" Jacinto roared. "You asshole!"

"Cordero was a nasty little prick when he was riding," he said.

Jacinto easily knew from hard experience what McKay and Arcaro didn't know and hadn't bothered to learn. Angel and Velasquez had deliberately tortured Ronnie out there as payback for Buddy Delp's decisions and choices.

Jacinto also knew how inappropriate aiming angry, coordinated, and complex retribution at such a young rider was. "Leave that freakin' kid alone," he had advised Cordero and Velasquez.

Jacinto said it, but no one was listening.

10 *Coke Was It*

The buzzards were circling.

After Ronnie Franklin's calamitous ride at the Florida Derby journalists were widely condemning Franklin and Buddy Delp for their racist language and out-of-control behavior. It was all extreme and bizarre and yet, in its total, delicious theater.

A handful of the nation's greatest jockeys followed the drama closely. They were waiting by their phones, eager to get a call from Buddy Delp. They hoped to find out that the suddenly vulnerable Franklin was deposed and that one of them would ascend to Spectacular Bid's mount on the largest stage in racing, the Triple Crown races.

While they all hoped to be chosen, most said nothing and did nothing. They kept a respectful distance from the decision makers and the process. But there was one man under consideration who showed no fear of making his presence felt. That was Jacinto Vasquez. He came to Delp's barn as he always did, brimming with confidence and vigor. But he didn't come to romance the trainer or to cuckold the mount from Franklin or to get a leg up on the other hopefuls. He arrived at the barn for the oddest reason of all. He was simply concerned about the young and fragile Franklin, and he came to console him and offer a little veteran advice.

Jacinto, of course, was known for his ferocious sense of competition and his success in gaining and maintaining the mounts he wanted.

Riding Spectacular Bid would have meant a huge financial windfall for him, not to mention another boost to his already formidable reputation and legacy. Yet he sat down next to Franklin, put an arm around him, and talked him through the difficult situation he had just encountered in the Florida Derby. "When you get boxed in," Jacinto told Ronnie, "there's nothing you can do anyway, so stay in there. There's a next time."

It was an unusually generous moment, especially considering that Jacinto was also a "spic," the ugly ethnic slur that Ronnie and Buddy had used only recently against Angel Cordero and Georgie Velasquez. Jacinto was a proud man, but he had a high tolerance for certain insults and a pragmatist's capacity for forgiveness. Jacinto was also as greedy for victory and recognition and a nice payday as any of the other successful jockeys, but he was able to put it all aside and help the kid. Vasquez simply had a talent for being brotherly and magnanimous.

But Jacinto took no such credit for being a nice guy. He chalked up his warm behavior toward Ronnie, when so many others were against him, to a kinship of the saddle. "That kid was just like us," Jacinto said. "He was just trying to make a living."

Jacinto wasn't the only one who let Ronnie off the hook. Harry Meyerhoff, believing that his colt and the boy had a special bond, retained the young rider. Yet the public wouldn't know of that decision until almost a full week after the Florida Derby.

Even though there wasn't any real news to announce, Delp called a press conference and milked the opportunity to spend more time in front of the TV cameras. Standing where he was most comfortable—at the front of the room with all eyes on him—Buddy discussed Franklin and rolled through a gauntlet of emotions.

First, he was maudlin, choking up and almost breaking down into tears. Then he made a fast transition into hard-ass, falsely claiming that he had been violent with his protégé. "I've knocked him across the room," Buddy said, "but I couldn't knock him off the horse." And then, with tears in his eyes, Buddy proclaimed for the world: "Everyone in the Delp organization loves Ronnie Franklin."

It was a gushy and gross performance, all to announce something that needed no announcement—that the current rider would continue to ride the horse. But Buddy had what he wanted, and that was the attention of the press.

Many racing insiders watched with disbelief. They were fascinated by the decision. How could Delp and the Meyerhoffs possibly retain Ronnie Franklin, young and inexperienced as he was, after that spectacularly poor performance in the Florida Derby?

Almost all of them felt that with "a more competent rider" the horse was a sure thing to win the Triple Crown. Those who adhered to this school of thought also minimized the importance of chemistry between colt and rider. It meant nothing to them that Ronnie and the Bid had been together since Middleburg; that they had been taught by the same brilliant trainers; or that they had amassed an impressive stakes-race winning streak with record-smashing times that bespoke dominance. They chose not to notice that when Franklin was removed from the Bid's saddle for two races, the horse simply did not perform as well for Georgie Velasquez, though Velasquez was widely acclaimed as one of the best riders in the nation.

The fact was that Ronnie had demonstrated superior riding skills. He won on the Bid. And he was also a winner on a slew of other horses.

The bottom line for Buddy and the Meyerhoffs was that Franklin achieved their goals and made money for them. He was a young man without the long resume or battlefield savvy they would have preferred, but he demonstrated that he was more than capable of snatching purses for all of them. Every time he took the irons, their wealth and prestige increased, and their dreams came closer.

But while everyone pondered whether or not Ronnie was good enough for Spectacular Bid, very few stopped to ask whether the Bid was good for the boy. It was a fair question too, considering that the kid had grown up in what basically amounted to a small village, raised by unpretentious parents who did their best to shelter him from the uglier sides of life.

Did Ronnie have the maturity and mental stability to handle the national spotlight and a pushy press corps that celebrated and then heckled anyone with the talent to stand apart? Given that his life was just beginning, did he have the emotional steel for an inherently dangerous and terrifying job that could kill or paralyze him at any moment?

Ronnie also had an additional pressure that that few others did. And that was Buddy Delp. Living with and working for a man so volatile and intimidating, owing him so much, was Franklin's most difficult challenge.

But no matter how excruciating the pressure was, Delp had a talent for making it even far worse. There were the insults he aimed at the competition, the constant bragging, and the predictions of victory. And of course there were the racist taunts that made national news.

No doubt Buddy saw himself as a latter-day Joe Namath or Muhammad Ali, predicting victory and backing it up. Only he forgot that it wasn't he out on the track pulling it all off. That fell to the horse and the rider.

Buddy did most of the talking, but it was Ronnie who had to dodge the dangerous and sometimes coordinated moves of rivals who were enraged by Delp. Franklin would be the one to stare them down in the jockeys' room. And if necessary, Franklin would be the one to exchange hard fists with them.

Within racing circles Buddy's worst traits stuck to Franklin with a stubborn persistence. Buddy was a braggart, loud and abrasive, so the other riders and the trainers saw Franklin that way, only in silks and a saddle.

It made perfect sense that Ronnie would pay the price for Buddy's bad behavior. The riders were in the habit of getting along with and pleasing the trainers. That's how they made their meat and potatoes. No one wanted to feud with a powerful man like Delp, who controlled a huge stable of talented, well-trained horses that won purse money. Jockeys who wanted to win and get rich spent their days kissing ass to guys like Buddy, not alienating them. So Ronnie became the proxy, the man to aim for when they didn't want to take on the man himself.

But even without these complicating factors it was clear to anyone paying attention that Ronnie was an unsophisticated kid and wholly out of place in the adult world. Cathy Rosenberger knew it. She spent a great deal of time alone with Ronnie, transporting him to the stables and working with him. On afternoons when Ronnie was racing, Cathy "ponied" him, calmly leading his horse on the long trek from the paddock to the gate.

In all of these activities there was a great deal of opportunity for companionship or at least a little banter between the two colleagues.

Even more so since Cathy was in her late twenties, loquacious, attractive, physically fit, and passionate about horses. She had already been married to a blacksmith and trained a racing stable of her own. In short, Ronnie and Cathy had everything in common but very little to say to each other. "In all the time I spent with Ronnie I can't remember ever having had a single interesting conversation with him," she recalled years later.

The silence that stood like a wall between them was more than just a lack of personal chemistry; it was a sign of how out of place the teenager was in the adult world. Ronnie was only just then emerging from boyhood. Had he stayed home with his parents, he might've eased into a grown-up's life with community college classes or a low-level job where the money, stress, and expectations were all more manageable and commensurate with his ability to handle them. But instead of being under the watchful eyes of his mother and father, Ronnie was housed and harbored by other adults who had a stake in his talent. What was it that bound Ronnie to these grown up companions?

The thrill of celebrity. The allure of money. And ultimately the seduction of cocaine.

So instead of cleaning his room or taking out the garbage, Ronnie was sparring with the national media, coping with Triple Crown pressures, and hiding from Buddy Delp's explosive temper. Thanks to Buddy, Franklin also had a contingent of grown men gunning for him, especially Angel Cordero and some of the other Latin riders who were outraged by the racial slurs that Franklin and Delp dropped so easily and publicly. Everyone knew—press, public, and horse professionals alike—that there was every possibility that fists and full-speed horses both might soon be aimed at Ronnie.

As he contemplated the growing dangers of his situation, Ronnie also had a baby son to think about and that he'd yet to see. The boy's mother was reaching out to him, but he barely knew her, and anyway he blamed her for the predicament that they were all in. He might've taken some solace in the vast sums of money he was honestly earning, but it was all slipping from his grasp like a fistful of water. But all of these problems paled in comparison to just one other, and that was the coke.

For Ronnie, cocaine was new and decadent, but it was a drug that had been around to amuse the bored and lonely for a long time. A century before Franklin discovered its pleasures, Arthur Conan Doyle described it in his debut Sherlock Holmes detective story, "A Study in Scarlet." Doyle used cocaine, per se, in a way that would surprise modern audiences. In his world, his London, cocaine wasn't the inventory of a loathsome criminal bent on distributing it or the habit of a depraved junkie. It was the hobby of his hero, Holmes himself, the brightest and most moral man in Doyle's universe. Holmes was characterized by his bravery and broody brilliance, but when he wanted to unwind, he rolled up his shirt sleeve and injected cocaine into his muscular arm.

By the 1970s cocaine was considered illicit, but it was growing in popularity anyway. The mania for it was a sign that American demographics, perceptions, and attitudes had all rapidly changed. Previously illegal drug use had been viewed as a fringe behavior, scandalous and embarrassing. Like everything else in America, it also took on a taint of racism as the white-bread middle class convinced itself that hard-drug addiction was a ghetto behavior confined to inner-city Black populations.

But in the 1960s marijuana and LSD weren't the special province of outliers; they were popular with middle-class suburban Boomers who were less willing to be controlled than their neck-tied and Brylcreemed fathers. The new generation created a counterculture in which sex, music, and recreational drugs were all expressions of a peculiar rage aimed at a society that was supposedly free and prosperous yet self-suffocating in the thick air of its own conformity.

The same young people who wanted to change society were thwarted from total freedom by their parents' values, which demanded love of God and fealty to country. Militarism was part of the deal, the price one paid to be an American. There was a sense of purpose and duty in service, even though it was compulsory, and a moral awakening in war.

But when the war ended in disgrace and the unpopular draft had stopped, the nation's youth turned to decadence. Young people, without the obligation of service or the fear of premature death on a battlefield, could suddenly do as they pleased. And freedom was no longer something to protect; it was something to be enjoyed. And theirs was a life of pleasure.

One of the most popular movies of the era, *Saturday Night Fever*, brilliantly depicted this change. The main character, Tony Monero, was played by an envelope-thin and elastic John Travolta. Monero had a lot in common with Ronnie. He lived in Brooklyn, New York, then a blue-collar town much like Dundalk. By day, he was a clerk in a hardware store who seemed destined to a lifetime of hard work and low pay.

A couple of decades earlier the same life Tony Monero rejected was precisely the kind of life Tony Franklin had embraced. After completing his military duty, he had come home and fulfilled commitments as a husband, a father, and a bill-paying consumer. He didn't run from hard work; he added to its burdens with night jobs and weekend enterprises.

Ronnie Franklin had a lot more in common with Travolta's character than Tony Franklin did. Ronnie also wanted to run away from drudgery and give his life purpose and recognition.

In the era of *Saturday Night Fever*, popular music was no longer raw or anthem-like or political, as it had been in the 1960s. The new sound was sanitized and uncomplicated. It required nothing from the listener intellectually or morally. This new music was all about the beat; if there was any message at all, it wasn't about politics; it was about pleasure. The songs, by and large, were about dancing or having sex after dancing.

For Travolta's character the dance floor was his saddle, and for Ronnie the saddle was his stage, the place where he could show the world he had talent and purpose.

The fictional movie character and the all-too-real boy both yearned to be someone. But on the authentic dance floors and race tracks of the era cocaine was a sign of arrival.

The capital of the disco world was located on Fifty-Fourth Street in Manhattan in an old CBS television studio. The building was a throwback to the early days of TV. For many years it had hosted the Captain Kangaroo show. When the building was abandoned by CBS, two entrepreneurs snapped it up and created the most exclusive club in the country, a place they called Studio 54.

At Studio 54 the mediocre were banished behind an inviolable velvet rope while the beautiful people and the rich and powerful businessmen all glided through the front doors.

The interior of Studio 54 was so full of coke users that the powder hung in the air like a poisonous fog. Even when the place was empty, the walls were skim-coated with a thin but perceptible layer.

But the drug user's experience wasn't only for the people who glittered. A variety of drugs was being used by ordinary Americans all over the country. One of them was Judith Grisel, who, much like Ronnie, spent her own formative years as an addict. With her long, lustrous brown hair and bright eyes, Grisel started life with the fresh and wholesome look of a 4-H beauty queen. But she also had a secret life in which she harbored a craving for the illicit. Much later she managed to overcome the disease of addiction and became an expert in its neuroscience. She wrote a best-selling book on the subject called *Never Enough*.

Grisel enjoyed her first taste of intoxication when she was only thirteen, guzzling half a gallon of wine in her girlfriend's basement. Soon after that she was drinking before, during, and after school.

Alcohol was only Judith's gateway drug. After a short while, she was regularly using marijuana, cocaine, and meth. She was high at her high school graduation and, in her own words, "wasted" at one of her grandparents' funerals. Eventually she was kicked out of college and estranged from her parents, who withdrew their financial and emotional support from her. They felt hopeless to help their daughter and feared that any money they gave her would be used to fuel her drug habits.

Without her mother and dad around and without their help, Judith was often jobless and homeless. She found herself scoring in dangerous places such as public housing projects, where she'd go to an apartment and get high in a bedroom with a man while his wife and children were on the other side of the wall watching television. Her addiction was so intense that she ripped off stores and stole credit cards to get the money she needed to get high.

By age twenty-three Judith was already many years removed from a completely sober day. Feeling suicidal, she finally committed to going to a rehabilitation center. She expected it to be a spa-like experience. It wasn't that. She spent a month in that facility and then three months in an old convent converted into a halfway house. Treatment made her miserable, but she learned how to control her addictions. She recovered so well that she ultimately went back to college and earned a PhD in neuroscience. Her passion was not only to understand the relationship between addiction and the brain but also to explain it to others in plain language. In her book *Never Enough*, she chronicled her own redemptive journey and clarified for ordinary readers the neuroscience behind the problem.

And Judith understood why cocaine was so well liked in the horse racing world. It was the perfect drug for a jockey because it provided a jolt of energy without any corresponding hunger. But more than that, Judith said, "Cocaine is like sex, with everything but the orgasm."

When Ronnie and Gerald snorted their coke, they experienced feelings of intense pleasure. But for them the drug was particularly harmful. At their young ages, their brains were still in a state of development. "Between puberty and age twenty-five, peaking at about fifteen years old," Judith said, "there is a proliferation of changes in the brain as new pathways and circuits are being made. The drug organizes how the brain develops and can permanently change things such as mood or cognition." So Ronnie's and Gerald's essential natures were changed with every snort, affecting their ability to think and learn and especially experience pleasure for the rest of their lives.

A more mature cocaine user might experience only temporary changes. Someone beyond twenty-six has a brain that is already developed and solidified. But for young guys like Ronnie and Gerald, chronic and heavy cocaine users as teenagers, the drug had far-reaching effects. The huge pleasure of coke made them less sensitive to ordinary pleasure. They kept using because they hoped to recapture the happiness they experienced at first use. They didn't understand why, but they came to know that goal was impossible to achieve.

As Mackenzie Phillips, a famously addicted actress of their era, eloquently put it, "[Cocaine is] an endless cycle of give and take. [It is an] instant thrill and surge of ecstasy that . . . promised, delivered, and revoked all in the course of half an hour." After that, she said, "The race to recapture that unimaginably good feeling would begin, again and again, until the supply ran out and the thrill turned to a dark, hollow absence, a bleakness so opposite and dreadful that more cocaine wasn't just desirable, it was necessary."

That is the essence of addiction: going back to cocaine, hoping to recapture pleasure, knowing full well that one could not. For addicts like Ronnie and Gerald there was simply no pleasure to be found.

And without pleasure where was happiness?

Ronnie was achieving things few other riders ever could. He was entrusted with the finest horse in the country, maybe the greatest horse who had ever lived. He was a national celebrity, stacking up the stakes race victories. He was setting new records on a daily basis. He was earning bushels of money. And he was winning prestigious awards. Everything he did was news.

For just about any man these public achievements would have been proof positive of his worth to the world. But for Ronnie, a kid reminded again and again that he'd been a dropout from a working-class neighborhood, who was labeled dumb, who was bullied and beat up because he was small, it should have been luscious vindication.

And yet he was quite literally unable to fully enjoy his substantial achievements. It was the coke that had robbed him of that. Where the joy should have been, there was a great emptiness instead.

If there was any excuse at all for Ronnie's addiction, it might have been that drug use was so pervasive in his world. Experienced horse professionals described the backside as "a candy store to an addict." The jockeys' room was a virtual bazaar, with vendors doing everything they could to lighten the jockeys' pockets. They came with anything and everything, including customized saddles, gold watches, jewelry, furs, and drugs. Pills, coke, and everything else were widely available right there in the inner sanctum of the track for the jockeys to buy.

The riders used the drugs in great quantities and for more reasons than just one. They wanted recreation, yes, a diversion, but they also used laxatives and amphetamines to suppress the appetite and maintain or reduce weight, they took pills for energy and alertness, and they smoked marijuana or swallowed other drugs to reduce pain from a variety of injuries. Drugs were an essential accessory to celebration in moments of triumph, and they were self-medication for chronic pain and depression.

Virtually all had their stories. Cathy Rosenberger remembered leading one horse to the gate with a rider so stoned that he fell off the mount and landed in the mud before the race could even begin. That hapless jockey was dragged to a first-aid station while a new rider was quickly called in to replace him.

In 1979 Jacinto Vasquez spent the winter in New York, where rampant drug use by others regularly interfered with his ability to make a living. "There were some guys taking that shit," Jacinto said. "It was a bunch of bad boys, hopheads. They couldn't function without the shit. They got stoned every day before they [went] out. The sons of bitches. I report[ed] 'em to the stewards one time. And I told 'em, 'All of these guys are on some kind of frikken dope.'"

What bothered Jacinto the most was how the riders' drug habits affected the day of racing. "The [stoned riders] refused to ride," he said. "They used to take off because they said it was too cold. The stewards was canceling races every day. I said, 'Hey, I stay here in the winter not because I am waiting for good weather. I don't give a shit about the weather! I came here to ride. If I wanted good weather, I'd go to Miami. I don't like to ride with these guys. They don't know what the hell to do. They all messed up.'"

Sick of seeing his paydays canceled, Jacinto rounded up the "bad boys" one day and marched them all into the stewards' office. "These guys on some sort of shit because they don't act normal," Jacinto said.

One of the stewards asked, "What do you mean, they're drunk?"

Jacinto didn't know exactly what they were on, but he knew it wasn't booze. "Why don't you take them all over there and give them a test?" he responded.

It didn't do much good. Jacinto's belief was that the drugs were so universal that even the powerful white guys, the supposed watchdogs who ran everything, were on them too. "A lot of the commissioners used to go out to the meetings and tell us, 'Say no to drugs,'" Jacinto recalled, "and the next day they was taking those drugs themselves."

Ronnie was embedded in a world of rampant drug use. Not only could he see it at the track, where the more experienced riders were users; not only was his mentor, Buddy, a user and an abettor, but he could even look to the wealthy and successful Meyerhoffs and see that the so-called respectable people, the better people, the wealthy people, enjoyed drugs too.

Ronnie was well aware that Harry Meyerhoff always had a drink in his hand, and it was a source of amusement for the Delps and Ronnie that the "old man" liked to smoke his pot. Teresa Meyerhoff was, for a time, a casual cocaine user.

But for Ronnie and Gerald cocaine and pills, marijuana and booze, all clearly had a different meaning than they did for most of the drug-using adults who were around them. When Buddy Delp introduced Ronnie and Gerald to cocaine, he put the two teens on the fast track to a serious and lifelong problem. "Eighty percent of all addictions begin before the age of eighteen," Judith Grisel said.

Gerald not only became a habitual user, but he also manned the supply chain. He could easily acquire any kind of drug the boys wanted. Because of that, Ronnie took to calling him "Doc," an old-timers' nickname for a pharmacist.

In the end, whatever issues Ronnie had as a rider or as a young man, Harry Meyerhoff chose to return him to Spectacular Bid's mount. Like most of Harry's business decisions, it appeared to be a golden one.

Ronnie was back in the saddle for the Flamingo Stakes in late March at Hialeah, and the crowd jeered him. Clearly understanding now that he had the best horse by a long shot, he made no pretense about fighting with the other jockeys for position on the inside. In fact, he was quite content to take the scenic route.

Ronnie was four wide at the clubhouse, meaning that he was going a very long distance to get to the wire. But it didn't matter. By the time he reached the far turn, he was in front of the other leaders. He widened the gap with every stride and crossed the finish line twelve lengths in front. It was an impressive victory, but in the eyes of the press and many in racing, the glory all belonged to the horse. Franklin's ride from the outside told them nothing about his ability.

The Bluegrass Stakes at Keeneland in Kentucky was Bid's last great tune-up before the Derby itself. It went much the same as the Flamingo. Ronnie stayed to the outside. The difference was that Bid was in last place of the four-horse field for a while, though Ronnie was whipping and goading him all along. Finally, nearing the turn at the top of the homestretch, he moved into first place by two lengths.

But for the longest time the horse appeared complacent, as though he wasn't even challenged. With Franklin whacking his haunches the whole way, the lethargic horse finally picked up the pace and sprinted to a seven-length victory.

In the final two races before the Kentucky Derby, with Ronnie aboard, the Bid won by a combined nineteen lengths. The ease with which Spectacular Bid beat the other horses, the huge distances he put between himself and the others, made it almost appear as if he was a completely different animal than they were. He fought through his own yawning indifference to slaughter them all.

The people around Spectacular Bid may have started to show just how fragile they were, but the horse's only addiction was for victory.

11 *Derby Days*

Flying Paster's father was named Gummo, in honor of the only Marx Brother who was not in the least bit funny. And indeed, the Paster was a serious horse. He had bolted from the American West with a long list of impressive stakes victories and a growing reputation. Even in snobby, superior Louisville they regarded the California-bred animal as the only horse left in America with a legitimate shot to beat Spectacular Bid in the Kentucky Derby.

Flying Paster and his team cut quite a contrast to Spectacular Bid's crew. His owner, Bernard "Ben" Ridder was as different as he could be from Harry Meyerhoff, the Jewish entrepreneur from Baltimore. Ridder was a northeast elite with blood as blue as the endless sky. He grew up in a privileged New York family where business opportunities and great horses were both merely a matter of fine breeding.

In his youth, Ridder had been an excellent rider. He was at home in the saddle as either a polo player or a fox hunter. His experience as an owner of thoroughbreds, such as it was, started with his father, Joseph, who owned a supposedly small and modest stable, though its workings were overseen by Louis Feustel, Man o' War's own trainer.

Ben Ridder's entrée into racing ownership came later, when he was in his early forties, after he and his wife had packed up and left their East Coast home and moved to Southern California. It was there that Ben took over the publisher's duties of the Pasadena *Independent-Star News*, a Ridder-family property.

The best horse that Ben ever produced was three years old in 1979, a bay colt, ostentatiously muscled and with an elegantly long neck. He gave it the aerodynamic but industrial name, Flying Paster. Newspaper people understood the reference. A "flying paster" was a device attached to the rumbling presses; it affixed thin sheets of newsprint to each other at blinding speed.

Like the horses' owners, the trainers cut quite a contrast. Paster's conditioner was Gordon Campbell, sixty, a Canadian veteran of World War II. Campbell had grown up on race tracks and was considered a solid and experienced man. But he was as taciturn as Delp was noisy. Reporters could barely get a decent quote out of him. In the days leading up to the Derby, he told reporters that Paster was the finest horse he'd ever trained. That was about the extent of his braggadocio. Delp, of course, had a flying paster of a mouth.

If there was a real difference between the two teams, however, it was in the jockeys. And that was the one area where track people and horse writers alike saw a potential Achilles' heel in the Bid.

Whatever reputation equity Ronnie had built as an Eclipse Award–winning apprentice or whatever records he had smashed on Spectacular Bid's back, it had all been wasted or at least greatly dissipated with his erratic ride at the Florida Derby. Now, often as not, the press viewed Franklin as a liability on an otherwise unbeatable horse.

On the other hand, Paster's rider, Don Pierce, was seen as an expert, as battle-hardened as Ronnie was green. He'd been riding out west for almost twenty-five years and was in the prime of an accolade-filled career with many impressive stakes victories already on his resume. In fact, Pierce had been around so long that he had actually ridden Gummo in the 1960s, when Ronnie was still a child in Dundalk.

Although Pierce was an established star, he could understand better than most Ronnie Franklin's pressures. He'd been there himself. In 1964 Pierce was the young, hot rider with the horse that everyone else coveted. Aboard Hill Rise, he'd peeled off a string of big victories leading up to the Derby, including the California Breeder Stakes, the San Felipe Handicap, and the Santa Anita Derby.

Unfortunately, Pierce might've performed a little too well. Under his guidance Hill Rise had become a national sensation and the favorite to win the Derby. While that brought a great deal of gratifying attention Pierce's way, his work also didn't escape the notice of one man in particular who had the power to crush his dreams. Willie Shoemaker, then the country's most well-respected rider, saw what Hill Rise could do, and he reached out to the horse's owner, George Pope. Shoemaker was already riding Northern Dancer, another Derby favorite, but he told Pope that he wanted the mount on Hill Rise.

Pope was flattered by Shoemaker's attention, and he was star struck. He didn't waste any time in firing Pierce and hiring Shoemaker to replace him. The young jockey was devastated and burst into tears. He had earned his opportunity, but now, at the last second, with no real reason or warning, he was humiliated and cut loose.

Pope was unmoved by Pierce's histrionics. He summed up his decision in purely mercenary terms. "I feel very strongly that you can't win big races like the Derby if you don't have everything going for you—and that includes the best jockey," Pope said. "If . . . Shoe got into trouble in the Derby and we lost[,] I'd still say that we had the most experienced rider in America trying his best for us. If Pierce got into trouble and we lost[,] I would forever blame myself, because I had the best rider in America ask to ride my horse and I turned him down."

Pierce lost the horse and was denied the opportunity, but he didn't have to wait long to find a little vindication. In a moment of karmic justice Hill Rise, with Shoemaker aboard, lost the Kentucky Derby. In fact, he came in second. Northern Dancer, Shoemaker's old horse, rumbled past him with jockey Bill Hartack aboard.

Ronnie did what Pierce couldn't; he held off Shoemaker and kept his famous mount. But in the Derby, he would have to contend with Pierce himself, who at forty-two was a potent and cunning rider. The writers and some of the best-known trainers took great delight in pointing out that it wouldn't be easy for the panicky Franklin they had seen in Florida to beat the mature Pierce, at the top of his game, with a horse roughly equal to Spectacular Bid.

The Derby was in a strange place in its history, both ascending to its highest level and yet at the same time also falling into a kind of disrepute.

In recent years the race had taken on greater meaning with Secretariat, Seattle Slew, Alydar, and Affirmed all turning in extraordinary performances. Those horses had raised the level of competition and drew greater interest in the race by the media and the fans.

But not all of the increased awareness was positive. It was also an era in which the Derby had taken serious blows to its reputation. In the culture wars of the late 1960s and 1970s, as the majority of Americans were awakening to their country's serious racial inequities, the Derby for many felt less like a glorious tradition than an embarrassing anachronism. The horses raced beneath gothic spires, the fans sipped mint juleps, and the vibe was purely old plantation. One of the Derby's most sacred events, the playing of "My Old Kentucky Home," was a national-anthem-like salute to a maudlin tune that harkened thoughts of a bereaved Confederate soldier pining for the safety of his parents' hearth. (In fact, it was a ditty written for a minstrel show by some guy from Pittsburgh.)

In 1968 all the greatness and revulsion of the Derby—the decadence and the drama, the racism, hypocrisy, and legitimate thrills—all congealed. That year a Maryland-bred horse, Dancer's Image, with jockey Bobby Ussery up, bolted out of last place and hugged the rail to beat thirteen other horses and win the roses.

It seemed to be a triumph for both racing and the Derby, but a couple of days later it all came crashing down. It was revealed that Dancer's Image had failed the post-race drug check and tested positive for phenylbutazone, more popularly known as "bute," a pain killer.

Bute was perfectly legal in many parts of the country, and it was even permissible in Kentucky. But the Derby was a different story. The rule was that the chemical had to be out of the horse's system by race day.

Dancer's veterinarian, Dr. Alex Harthill, was more than a giant in his field; he was a genius more or less acknowledged by all. He admitted giving the thoroughbred a dose of bute earlier in the week, on Monday. He said it was necessary because the horse's two forelegs were sore and the drug, an anti-inflammatory, would relieve the pain. But Dr. Harthill, widely hailed as a brilliant chemist, was adamant that any bute given to the horse on Monday would have easily cleared the animal's system by Saturday.

Dancer's owner, Peter Fuller, went from the dream of a lifetime to a gross ignominy. His horse was the first to ever be disqualified from the Kentucky Derby, and the race directors demanded that he immediately return the winner's trophy, something that he deeply coveted, and also the full purse, almost $125,000.

But the worst was yet to come.

There was a persistent question hanging in the air, and the answer was potentially quite ugly: If Fuller and Harthill had not given Dancer's Image the bute that had disqualified him, who had?

Fuller didn't profess to know the exact answer, but he clearly understood the motivation. Earlier in the year, Dancer's Image was in Bowie, Maryland, where he won the Governor's Gold Cup, a lucrative victory with a $77,000 purse. It should have been a joyful moment, but in 1968 the race was run under a dark cloud as it came just three days after Dr. Martin Luther King Jr.'s assassination in Memphis, Tennessee.

That murder sparked rioting all over the country but also a noble impulse in Fuller. He donated his entire Gold Cup purse to Coretta Scott King, Dr. King's widow, to help support the family that was left behind. It was a generous gesture, an act of American reconciliation coming as it did from a privileged white New Englander to the country's most bereaved southern Black family.

The Kings had impoverished themselves for their righteous cause, and now they had given to it, as it were, their father in the prime of his life, their provider. In essence they'd given everything they had to the cause of social justice.

Yet Fuller's magnanimity was met with rage in Kentucky.

Dr. King had gone to Louisville too, in 1967. He had gone there to protest housing discrimination, a topic the Meyerhoffs knew all too well. Dr. King chose the week before the Derby, to attract maximum publicity. Many of the locals were outraged. They looked past the injustice that necessitated his protest and instead saw only a disruptive grandstander upstaging their state's most important week and biggest business opportunity.

Fuller didn't get accolades for supporting Mrs. King in her hour of need; he got death threats. And more than mere words came his way. An arsonist torched one of his barns. Even Dancer's Image was not immune to the crude abuse. Wherever the horse appeared, he was showered with racial epithets and vile profanity.

Fuller felt, until the end of his life, that racists had either drugged his horse or tampered with its urine. He believed it was all done to sabotage the victory and humiliate him—a payback for the kindness he had shown to Mrs. King.

The real taint, however, wasn't on Dancer's Image or Peter Fuller or even on Alex Harthill; it was on the Derby, and it lingered. That old southern charm that was once so appealing was starting to look nakedly racist. The event itself took on the taint of hypocrisy.

Just two years later journalist Hunter S. Thompson, at the beginning of his weird and brilliant career, came calling. Thompson was a Louisville native, but it wasn't hard to see that he had an agenda to further expose the sham values that Fuller's situation brought to light.

Thompson was still young, but he had already been a failure in almost everything he had tried. He had been honorably discharged early from the air force though he had been branded a troublemaker there. In private life, he had already been fired from a variety of jobs.

Thompson was a nice-looking young man in a conventional sense: tall, thin, and darkly colored, though with a hairline that was already receding. But he was odd too. He wore aviator-style sunglasses everywhere he went, like the Lone Ranger wore his mask. And he chain-smoked cigarettes from a long-stemmed holder.

Writing didn't come naturally to Thompson, but he found it was the only thing people were willing to pay him to do. He taught himself the craft by typing the works of masters like Hemingway, Fitzgerald, and Faulkner. He believed that he could unravel the secrets of their great prose by feeling their rhythms on the keyboard. There must have been something to that theory because Thompson developed one of the most distinctive and interesting styles in American literature.

But genius wasn't the only side to Thompson; he was also a barbarian, a sodden miscreant whose every stunning word dripped with whiskey; his manic sentences and paragraphs mainlined with mind-altering chemicals.

To his credit, Thompson didn't hide his issues. "I don't recommend my lifestyle," he once said, "but I don't deny it either." The biting reality of who he was and what he did led his editor, James Silberman, to tell him, "Your method of research is to tie yourself to a railroad track when you know a train is coming to it and see what happens."

For one assignment on the road Thompson described the contents of his luggage as an illicit pharmacy: "Two bags of grass, 75 pellets of mescaline, five sheets of high-powered blotter acid, a salt shaker half full of cocaine, and a whole galaxy of multicolored uppers, downers, screamers, laughers…and also a quart of tequila, a quart of rum, a case of Budweiser, a pint of raw ether and two dozen amyls." It was enough to bring down a 747.

This radioactive man infiltrated situations and then brandished his pen like an ink-filled shiv, stabbing at the seamy and the vulgar, the violent and the ugly in American life.

In an essay for *Scanlan's Monthly* in 1970, Thompson went to the track. But he arrived as only he could, smoking a cigarette firmly twisted into his holder and with a bummed drink in his hand. The first thing he did upon deplaning was to head for the airport bar, strike up a conversation, and lie to a random stranger. Thompson told the first rube he met, a man from Texas who had come to the Derby to get away from his wife, that he was a photographer from *Playboy*. He told the gullible fool that he'd come to cover an expected race riot at the Derby.

The essay he produced, almost by accident, was "The Kentucky Derby Is Decadent and Depraved." Immediately upon publication, it was hailed as a seminal piece of American journalism. Although Thompson's self-descriptions were almost barbaric, he had the whole educated country talking about his wit and originality. He basically described how he'd fried his own brains in a pan, and yet the literary world was bowing to his superior intellect.

In Louisville he met up with the brilliant British illustrator Ralph Steadman, who'd come to sketch prototypical American faces at one of the nation's most iconic events. Neither one of them had any interest in the race. "We didn't give a hoot in hell what was happening on the track," Thompson reported. "We had come there to watch the real beasts perform."

Those animals, of course, were Americans.

Motioning to the infield the day before the race, Thompson told Steadman that it would soon turn into a medieval lunatic asylum. "That whole thing," Thompson said, pointing to the grassy expanse, "will be jammed with people; fifty thousand or so, and most of them staggering drunk. It's a fantastic scene—thousands of people fainting, crying, copulating, trampling each other and fighting with broken whiskey bottles."

That was the infield. Inside the clubhouse Thompson claimed there would be "thousands of raving, stumbling drunks, getting angrier and angrier as they lose more and more money. . . . The aisles . . . slick with vomit; people falling down and grabbing at your legs to keep from being stomped. Drunks pissing on themselves in the betting lines."

In the end, Thompson and Steadman found nothing more disturbing at the Derby than what they saw in the mirror. "We came down here to see this teddible scene," Steadman told Thompson in his proper British accent as they drunk-drove their way to the airport, half naked and reeking, "people all pissed out of their minds and vomiting on themselves and all that . . . and now, you know what? It's us."

Who knows what Hunter S. Thompson really saw at the 1970 Derby. His testimony was a little tainted. He had given Steadman his first-ever hit of a hallucinogenic there, and they were admittedly drunk and stoned the entire time. Yet his descriptions were so arresting as to be hypnotic. In a few magical paragraphs Thompson had taken an event that was a century old, with rock-solid traditions, and redefined it on his own nasty and repulsive terms for generations to come.

Most took it for granted that Thompson's version of the Derby was fictionalized and embellished, but it was hard to write it off as outright lies. Everyone knew that on some level he'd put his finger on something that was somehow more truthful than the actual truth.

Moral decay was in fact at the heart of the Derby, a Dionysian festival of excessive drinking, internecine drug use, compulsive gambling, violence, scams, whores, and masses of stinking humanity. The Derby is a grotesquery, Thompson seemed to say; but like it or not, the Derby is America.

Buddy, Ronald, and Gerald came to Louisville almost a decade later, but it could have been the next, hazy day. They made it their business to stay out of the tumult. Creating the appearance that they were focused on the race, they rented a house in the wooded countryside and made themselves scarce. Even Buddy was on the down low. He avoided the spotlight and asked the Meyerhoffs to take his seats and stand in for him at a Derby-week press dinner for trainers.

Harry and Teresa projected a certain glamor out on the town. Although their age gap yawned between them, they were a natural and winning couple. Harry's power was only amplified by Teresa's great physical beauty and charm. He radiated success and superior ability, and her presence beside him was a beautiful and breathing embodiment of his achievements.

After dinner, Pete Axthelm, the wise and wry writer from *Newsweek* who covered horse racing on ESPN and who had written a classic sports book, *The Kid*, about Steve Cauthen, kicked off the questioning by getting a little belligerent with Harry: "Is it a matter of heart, or is it perhaps a matter of overconfidence . . . or supreme confidence that you don't think anything—even poor judgement by a jockey—could get [your] horse beaten?"

That question was loaded, and though it was posed by only one man, it was typical of the ugly stance many writers had taken about Ronnie Franklin. One Baltimore newsman who had covered twenty Kentucky Derbies going all the way back to the 1950s said, "I have never . . . seen as much written about a jockey as was carried here about this 19-year-old kid from Dundalk. Not Arcaro, not Shoemaker, anybody. And not much of it was complimentary."

Axthelm's question was the type that would have set Buddy off on a headline-making diatribe. But Harry, as always, was cool and composed, imperturbable. He answered the question simply and with a smile. "We're sticking with [Ronnie] because we think he's the best jockey for the horse," Meyerhoff said. "I think he's already proved that. What else can I say?"

Avoiding the limelight went against Delp's grain, but it was a sound media strategy for the Derby in light of his Florida meltdown. His loud, abrasive, and ostentatiously racist rants there and his constant crowing about Spectacular Bid's invincibility had all ratcheted up the pressure on Ronnie, and the kid was already in the cooker.

Avoiding the press like Buddy did or taking the wind out of the writers' sails, as Harry just had, didn't mean that the press couldn't still present significant challenges to Bid's team.

Hunter S. Thompson was long gone from the scene, but Andrew Beyer of the *Washington Post* was there, and he was ready to make a little trouble of his own.

Like Thompson, Beyer fancied himself something of an agitator. He didn't brag about drug use, but his vice, if in fact it could be called one around the racetrack, was gambling. Beyer first started going to the racetrack as a Harvard undergraduate. He was well respected enough to be named sports editor of the *Crimson*, Harvard's student newspaper, where he succeeded his future boss, Donald Graham.

Beyer's career as a student was stunted by his interest in gambling; it superseded his academic work. Instead of going to class, he spent as much time as he could at the track, wasting entire days and evenings there. On the nights he couldn't get to the track, he was up playing poker.

All of this came to a head at the end of his senior year. In an episode that must have made his father's heart sink, Beyer blew off a final examination on Chaucer in order to go to the Belmont Stakes and place a bet. As it turned out, he picked the winner, Amberoid, but the cost may have outweighed the benefit. "Although I blew a $12,000 education," Beyer later wrote, "I did collect a $13 payoff . . . , cutting my losses for the day to $11,987." It was humorous in the retelling but a wink and a nod to something that wasn't quite healthy.

Though it might have been difficult to imagine such a man influencing the next generation of students, Beyer gave serious consideration to a career in teaching. Before he could get started, however, he applied for a job writing sports at the *Boston Globe*, and he was hired there. His work was clearly good, so much so that after only a few months in New England he was offered a better position at the *Washington Post* by long-time sports editor Shirley Povich.

In Washington, Beyer covered a wide array of teams and leagues, but none of the work pleased him. He soon realized that his only real passion was for the track. And even his enthusiasm for racing was limited to the gambling. He didn't really care that much about the sport itself. He liked the people he met at the windows, "characters with a tale of woe or larceny," as he put it. But the fact was that it was the gambling, not the gamblers, that intrigued him.

Gambling may have brought many a man low, but for Beyer it was his ticket to the top. His prowess at the windows made him a star. When he was still a young reporter, in 1970, he spotted what he thought was a sure thing at the old Liberty Bell Park near Philadelphia. That's where Sun in Action, a 20–1 shot, was scheduled to run. Beyer, employing a mathematical formula he'd devised himself, was positive that the nag would win. So he told his readers, and everyone back at the sports office, not to worry about Christmas money; he had them covered.

Beyer bet $200 of his own cash and $200 pooled by his friends at the office. And wouldn't you know it, Sun in Action lost the race by a whisker. But it wasn't over yet. Due to a disqualification, Beyer's horse was named the winner anyway, and Beyer and his assemblage of colleagues each won $4,000.

That unlikely victory, and Beyer's generosity in sharing the tip, all catapulted him to a kind of national prominence. The *Daily News* put the whole story on its front page as though it was an international sensation.

In 1975 Beyer's fame grew even more as he expanded beyond daily journalism and authored his own book, *Picking Winners*. Touted as "a horseplayers guide," it detailed his mathematical approach to sleuthing the victorious. The *New York Times* gave Beyer's book a humorous and enthusiastic review, though it acknowledged that even if the author's method worked, and it seemed that it did, it was no fun. To the reviewer, the work of figuring out the winners utilizing Beyer's method was as arduous and boring as regular work. Nevertheless, Beyer's book was a hit, and his career took off.

But this success only brought Andrew's ego to the fore. He referred to those who followed his gambling advice as "Beyer disciples," and he professed a belief that he had changed the culture.

The Meyerhoffs were well aware of Beyer but weren't impressed. They felt that he had a certain disdain for Spectacular Bid, and especially for Ronnie Franklin, based solely on the fact that he had bet against their horse early on and lost. For all of Beyer's supposed knowledge, the Meyerhoffs laughed about his whiffing on the Bid and how it had stuck in his craw.

Beyer was still a young man then. He had long, stringy hair and glasses. He also cultivated a bristly, unkempt mustache that looked like it belonged in a push-broom hospice.

In 1979 at the Derby, his ego was once again on display as he wrote a condescending column for the *Washington Post* that trashed the city of Louisville. "From the perspective of any urbane visitor," he sniffed, "the city is a wasteland." He called Louisville "tiresome, tawdry, and maddening." And he did something that no other Washingtonian in history had ever done and referred to Baltimore as "sophisticated." That was meant more as an insult to Louisville than a compliment to his gritty East Coast neighbors on the Chesapeake.

Beyer's attack on Louisville had overtones of Hunter S. Thompson, yet his piece lacked even a trace of the wit and style or originality of Thompson's work. There was no real edge to his derivative essay, no iconoclasm. It was merely a mean-spirited cry for attention, material proof that a bully had arrived.

Beyer struck a nerve in Louisville, as he had clearly intended to do. The outrage his column fomented briefly and inappropriately over-shadowed the lead-up to the race and somehow also brought negative attention to Spectacular Bid. Kentuckians mistakenly saw Baltimore, the Bid's home, as a Siamese twin to Washington, Beyer's home. So the column only added to the anger many fans already felt for Spectacular Bid's trainer and rider.

More swirling controversy was the last thing Bid's team members needed. In fact, they had gone out of their way to avoid it since they had gotten to Louisville. Buddy, Gerald, and Ronnie were tucked away safely, in the bubble wrap of a handsome farmhouse far out of town with a gag in Buddy's mouth.

And that's where they all were on Derby's eve, squirreled away in the idyllic Kentucky countryside. Outside a symphony of cricket strings, croaking frogs, and ratcheting cicadas filled the cool, spring air. Inside,

Spectacular Bid's men, on the eve of the biggest day of their lives, were inhaling lines of cocaine. They wiled away the evening hours that way. At around 9:30 p.m., Buddy Delp, nearly fifty years old, was pooped. He announced that he was going to bed. As the father of one of the teenagers with whom he was "partying" and the employer of the other, he didn't depart until leaving some parental instructions. "Make sure you are done by midnight," he said, and then he ascended the stairs and was off to sleep.

Even that simple directive was too much for the out-of-control boys to follow. They enjoyed the coke so much, they continued doing their lines well into the night, not stopping until they had exhausted Gerald's entire supply. When they finally went to bed and fell asleep, long past midnight, their heads were still buzzing, like coked up Cinderellas who had left the party a little too late.

It had been a rainy week in Louisville, but Derby Day was dry and promising. The track surface still bore the scars of the wet days. The trainers and jockeys examined it to determine how it would race. All agreed it was "cuppy," track slang meaning that the surface would clump up under the horses, filling their hooves and forcing them to labor. The track condition was more of a worry for Flying Paster than Spectacular Bid since the Bid had already raced effectively on a variety of surfaces, while the California-bred horse had not.

The track speed would be a subject of discussion for the rest of the day.

The circus of uncivilized behavior that Hunter Thompson had spoken about a decade earlier was somewhat on display in the local Derby coverage. One Louisville reporter literally took a video camera into the men's room and interviewed fans as they relieved themselves, mid-tinkle.

A lot of the rest of it was celebrity-focused. CBS anchorman Walter Cronkite, the most trusted man in America, was there, and he took the opportunity to plug a new television show that starred his actress daughter. And then there was Phyllis George. The former-beauty-queen-turned-NFL-pregame-show-reporter had recently left her job at CBS and moved to Kentucky to marry John Y. Brown Jr., the impressive millionaire who had purchased Kentucky Fried Chicken from Colonel Harland Sanders himself. Brown transformed KFC from a nice business with a tasty product into one of the biggest restaurant chains in the world. He had just been elected governor of the Blue Grass State, and the glamorous George was his first lady.

One person very few others were talking about was Angel Cordero Jr. That was surprising since Angel was usually the center of attention wherever he went. Not only that, but Cordero had also won two of the last five Kentucky Derbies. The first time, on Cannonade, was in 1974. The second time was the bicentennial year, 1976, when he was aboard Bold Forbes.

Cordero was still nursing a grudge for Franklin's violent outburst and racist remarks, but no one seemed to think that mattered since he was on Screen King, a 9–1 shot. Experts believed he had only an outside chance to win the race. As always, he took himself very seriously, and he came to Kentucky telling anyone who would listen that he knew the secret to beating the unbeatable Bid. "I know a lot of things that [Spectacular Bid] doesn't do well," Angel said.

What were those things? Cordero's explanation was half Sun Tzu and half obnoxious child. "You don't tell in public the weakness of your adversary, right?" he said. "It's only for me to know, and for them to find out."

Cordero also found out a few things that Ronnie Franklin knew. On Derby Day, in the seventh race, Angel rode the favorite, Julie's Dancer. He squared off against Ronnie, who was on Seethreepeo. Like the Bid, Seethreepeo was a Hawksworth Farm product belonging to the Meyerhoffs.

They raced most of the way with each other, but no hard words were exchanged. But in the end, Cordero's favored horse finished in last place while Ronnie and Seethreepeo went to the winner's circle.

Ronnie's victory against Cordero only underscored that the Derby had been oversimplified by the media. Their narrative was that Spectacular Bid was the best horse, but he had the least experienced and worst rider in the race. Flying Paster was a little under the radar but had a canny veteran aboard.

Franklin showed his rhetorical acumen and refuted all that. "I have as much experience on the Bid as [Don Pierce] has on Flying Paster," Ronnie said.

The truth was far more complex. As always, the Derby was filled with the wiliest jockeys and the most experienced and respected trainers from all over the United States. The horses were bred from the finest stock. As everyone learned in the Florida Derby, reputations aside, anything can happen out on the track. Great jockeys were known, on occasion, to force an outcome no one expected.

The Derby field included enviable teams under any circumstances. The who's who of riders, trainers, and well-bred horses included Cordero and trainer Luis Barrera with Screen King; Laffit Pincay and LeRoy Jolley with General Assembly, a Secretariat product; Sandy Hawley was riding Golden Act for Loren Rettele; and the ostentatiously named Cash Asmussen was aboard King Celebrity for trainer Robert J. Taylor. Any of these top professionals and their horses were capable of pulling off a surprise if Franklin or the Bid were having something less than their best day.

In fact, many credible voices rose up to say that they believed Flying Paster would win the race. One of them belonged to Lucien Laurin, whose training of Secretariat had made him among the most highly respected men in racing. "To be honest, I think I'd have to take the California horse," Laurin said. "Flying Paster is getting better and better."

And then Laurin went on to say something that many others also felt: "I think they are close enough where the jockeys could make a difference," he said. "In jockeys, I'd have to give the edge to Don Pierce, especially if it's a close finish."

Ronnie and the Bid had their defenders too. Woody Stephens, Derby-winner Cannonade's trainer from 1974, said, "Franklin is all right, though. I think the horse runs for him."

Billy Turner, who had won the Derby with surprising Seattle Slew, agreed with Woody on the subject of Ron Franklin. "I think Buddy Delp deserves credit," Turner said, "for standing behind Ronnie Franklin as his jockey. Spectacular Bid runs for that rider."

It was not surprising that all the trainers who were actually in the race claimed that their horses were talented enough to match strides with Spectacular Bid and Flying Paster.

But Buddy wasn't having it. In speaking to Howard Cosell, whom he addressed by his first name as though they were old friends, Delp said that he had merely feigned the idea that it was a two-horse race. "I didn't want the glory, the glamor, or the fun to be taken away from [the Derby]," he said.

But . . .

"My horse is superhorse," Delp continued. "If Flying Paster is as good as Secretariat he'll make a race out of it. But he's got to be that good, and what's the odds on that?" It was a foolish thing to say, of course, but that was one skill where Buddy excelled.

Many experts expected that the race would feature shenanigans by the jockeys, and why not? Cordero had proven in Florida that Ronnie was vulnerable and that such maneuvers could unnerve him and inhibit the Bid. The conventional wisdom was that Pierce would also take advantage of Franklin by boxing him in. Everyone believed that Pierce would do whatever it took to keep Bid away from the outside, where he would find a clean and easy lane to the wire. The inside was the equalizer since in those crevices a jockey could be exposed, and even a great horse could be constrained by those ahead of him. Even the Bid could not simply jump over the backs of the other horses to find his best gear.

When it was finally post time, Spectacular Bid showed the demeanor of a dressing-room pugilist. He was a little nervous and volatile and even kicked dirt on the immaculately dressed Meyerhoffs, who had come to the paddock to wish him well.

Mo Hall, Bid's groom, the valet, and Delp had a hard time saddling the horse, who acted up even more when he appeared before the crowd. Eventually, Hall used a blanket to shield the huge eyes from the throngs, and the horse quickly calmed down so that he could be dressed for the battle.

The final accessory placed upon the horse was Ronnie Franklin himself. He looked heroic in the rustling blue-black silks of Hawksworth Farm, high off the ground, with his head in the fluffy white Kentucky clouds. At nineteen years of age, he had hair that was thick and swept across his forehead, and his face was uncreased and perfect. Once he settled into the saddle, his familiar presence calmed the Bid, and the horse went to the gates without further incident, slipping into the small steel enclosure "like a man," as broadcaster Eddie Arcaro said.

Ronnie promised that he would send Spectacular Bid away from that gate as quickly and as fast as he could. His goal, he clearly stated, was to be in first, second, or third at the first turn.

When the gates finally opened and they were off, a different story unfolded. Spectacular Bid didn't rush to the front of the pack; in fact he was knocked around a little out of the gate. He recovered, but he was stunned a little and proceeded slowly and sluggishly before he settled in, out of the fray, in seventh place. And there he stayed for an uncomfortably long while.

For all of the talk of strategy before the race, Don Pierce paid Franklin no mind at all. In fact, he seemed to forget about him while he and Flying Paster did exactly what Ronnie had promised to do. He came out of the gate strong and kept pace with the leaders. He was in third place.

At the first turn Pierce and Paster were nose and nose with the two horses in front of them, General Assembly and Shamgo. At that point Spectacular Bid was far behind and losing ground. That moment may have been a terrifying one for the Meyerhoffs and Buddy Delp. Flying Paster hadn't even kicked it into high gear yet. Given his reputation for greatness, it was reasonable to wonder if even Spectacular Bid could catch him.

And then things got a little worse.

Just past the half-mile pole, Pierce made his move. He encouraged Paster to quicken his pace, and the hero of the West showed what he was made of as his great speed was put on display. The horse gained ground on those in front of him, the booth announcer shouted and threw spittle into his microphone, and the crowd thundered its approval.

Paster was in the moment; he looked his finest and his best, but it was he who planted the seeds of his own destruction right then and there. The ruckus his movement created only awakened a very important horse and rider still long behind him.

Ronnie clucked in the Bid's ear. "Let's go, big daddy," he said, and Spectacular Bid heard the call to arms, and his stride widened and the rhythmic thunder of his hooves quickened.

The Bid accelerated with such glorious ferocity that he seemed to change species right there in the middle of the race. He was no longer a horse but a predator stalking the helpless animals ahead of him. Each one, in his turn, was about to experience the terrifying sensation of being the weakest in the herd.

No one took it worse than Flying Paster. He sensed the Bid's pursuit from many lengths ahead, and what had been his charge was soon his labor. When the Bid finally caught him, at the approach to the far turn, the two great animals were eye to eye, and the fiction that Pierce could box Ronnie in, Cordero-style, was as dead as any of the other prey.

Ronnie had held his horse back for so long that he'd snuck up on Pierce and Flying Paster. And now the Bid was in exactly the position Franklin, and especially Delp, would have hoped. He was on Paster's outside shoulder, unfettered, and free to do as he pleased. The soft, late-afternoon sunlight splashed down on Spectacular Bid's steel-wool-colored coat, and to the eyes of the crowd the bounding horse was a conductor, electrified and sparking.

Meanwhile, Flying Paster, finally confronting an animal even more dominant than himself, was cowed. As the two horses made their way around the far turn, the Bid's approach menaced him. They stared at one another until the Paster could not take it. He meekly spit the bit and gave up on his rider. He had been a hero in the West, but in Kentucky he wasn't quick enough on the draw.

With the Californians behind them, Ronnie and the Bid turned their attentions to the leader, General Assembly. Secretariat's direct descendant was less afraid and did his best to compete, but he was simply no match for Franklin and his horse. Had the Bid been a mountain lion he would already have been in the infield veldt, feasting on General Assembly's flesh and enjoying the taste of his marrow.

Ronnie and the Bid encountered General Assembly at the head of the stretch, when he was in full stride. They were neck and neck when the Bid exposed him and robbed him of both his rapidity and his lineage.

General Assembly was beautiful and a royal son, but next to Spectacular Bid he seemed more like the progeny of a hobbyhorse. Perhaps General Assembly was running for fun instead of glory? He had no legs at all. His defining feature in the biggest race of his life was stillness; he seemed locked in place, as in a photo, as the Bid whooshed right by him in real time.

Though Ronnie had broken the race open, he left nothing to chance. He cudgeled the Bid with his left hand, and the gap only widened. The only thing left in front of horse and rider was the wire. "And Spectacular Bid is going to win the 105th running of the Kentucky Derby," the track announcer screamed into his microphone. "Spectacular Bid does it, Ron Franklin aboard!"

When it was all over, Spectacular Bid had won by two and a half lengths going away. General Assembly, of course, was second, and the others were far behind. Pierce and Flying Paster finished fifth, far outside of the money. And Angel Cordero Jr. and Screen King were so far out of it, in sixth place, they may as well have bought tickets to the show.

With the victory came the megawatt celebrity. When Buddy went for his on-camera interview with Howard Cosell, he was the image of respectability in a solid blue blazer, striped necktie, and white V-neck sweater. Somehow, in the moment of his greatest victory, Buddy appeared . . . humble, a word he barely knew. Cosell asked him if Spectacular Bid was better than Secretariat. Instead of his usual stream of hyperbole, Buddy demurred. He said he would have to go back and look at the track conditions before deciding that.

Cosell then turned his attention to Ronnie and compared him to last year's nineteen-year-old hero, Stevie Cauthen. It was high praise. Ronnie projected a boyish exuberance. Howard teed up the ball for the young jockey to say something vindictive, but the kid was too elated to take the bait.

"All the talk about the crafty and very fine jockey Don Pierce outmaneuvering you didn't come to pass, did it?" Cosell asked.

"Well, no, not really," Ronnie replied with a big, happy grin; and he wisely left it at that.

No one, however, lit up the screen more than Teresa Meyerhoff. On the victory stand she was flanked by her husband and stepson, her business partners. But the sunlight found her and shone down on her like glitter so that the world could see her success. She was young and beautiful. Her long blond hair cascaded down onto a modish orange dress with a bold geometrical pattern. After a few perfunctory remarks by Harry, Jim McKay asked Teresa for her thoughts. She murmured her pleasure. In a breathless voice she modestly said that she was merely glad that Spectacular Bid had finally proven that he was the best horse in the country. Teresa was beaming but composed; she didn't say much, but she put a highly appealing face on a team that at times had been awfully hard to like.

In the jockeys' room, the real celebration began, though not for poor Angel Cordero. The Puerto Rican eminence, widely hailed as a genius in his craft, had just had a poor day by anyone's measure. He had lost twice to Ronnie, a rider he did not respect. It was no wonder then that he was uncharacteristically sullen. He sat and silently fed himself after the rigors of competition, a comfort to all men when the workday is done.

One enterprising reporter had the gumption to approach Angel and remind him of his claims from just a few days earlier that he had the formula for beating the Bid.

"What happened?" the reporter asked.

"I never got to see the race," Cordero responded. "I was too far back."

How could Ronnie understand Cordero's middle-age defeatism? The young victor was garrulous, and why not? A little more than twenty-four months earlier he was working in a fast food shop. Now, for one day at least, he was the biggest story in the country. Along the way he had absorbed put-downs and insults that were both whispered behind his back and blared on national television.

Trainers, other jockeys, the press, and the fans all wondered aloud if Ronnie was merely "lucky," a kid who had run across the right trainer at the right time even though he didn't have the maturity or the talent to ride for the Triple Crown. He had been called an idiot by his own trainer, and he had almost been removed from a horse that he had ridden since the time they were both babies.

But Ronnie knew he was no different than the Hispanics that everyone hailed as "natural" horsemen. He'd come from hard beginnings himself, and like most of them he never wasted a moment with books or teachers. His classrooms were the stalls and the shed rows. His apprenticeship was shoveling mountains of horseshit and hot walking thousands of horses. He'd isolated himself far from home and slowly learned to ride, the hard way, from the ground up.

In Middleburg he had been mentored by one of the most brilliant and knowledgeable people in the horse business anywhere in the world: Barbara Graham. He had listened, and he had learned, and he had worked, and he had earned his way. Now the Kentucky Derby trophy was in *his* hands, and it was a sweet vindication.

But Ronnie Franklin couldn't quite enjoy his big moment. He clutched the trophy and gave the world a big smile, but he didn't embrace the big picture; his mind was on the minutiae. He couldn't stop thinking about the seventh race, where his victory meant less than another man's defeat. "I have to admit," Ronnie Franklin said, "it was fun beating Cordero earlier in the day."

And with that the nineteen-year-old boy got up and loudly asked if anyone knew where the vodka was.

12 *Coming Home*

No one was happier to return home to Baltimore than Harry Meyerhoff. He had enjoyed himself immensely on the road, watching his team's success, showing off his tall and handsome young son and his beautiful wife, and sitting for interviews in which the biggest names in print and broadcast journalism came to him and hung onto his every word.

Despite these heady days, Harry could never be entirely himself when he was on the road. He didn't quite fit in with the other owners. Although he was rich like they were, he always felt a little out of place in their company. At the Flamingo Stakes, where Bid had won by twelve lengths, all of the other owners were invited to a soiree called the Flamingo Ball.

All but Harry.

At the Kentucky Derby, Harry and Teresa attended a dinner party in a restaurant one evening, but when they returned to the exact same place a day or two later as private diners, they were turned away in their nice clothes and refused service. Harry knew what it was all about. He ascribed these anomalies to anti-Semitism. They didn't want him around because he was a Jew.

Baltimore was more than a hometown or a safe harbor to Harry. In Baltimore, he called the shots. He and his family were aging, but they were still prime movers.

Nineteen seventy-nine kicked off four years of major Meyerhoff family accomplishments in Baltimore. There was the Bid, of course. A year later, Harry's father and his organization, the Rouse Company, unveiled Harborplace. It was only a shopping center, but it was Baltimore's first major downtown retail and restaurant venue in many years. In 1982 Harry's uncle, Joseph, revealed his pet project, the Meyerhoff Symphony Hall. It opened to great acclaim. More than mere wealth was involved in achieving these goals; it required powerful connections and the capability to get things done.

In Baltimore the Meyerhoffs were like town fathers. If anyone gave a damn that Harry once went to Hebrew school, they kept it to themselves; Baltimore, in a very real sense, was his town.

Being back in Maryland also meant that Harry could return to his beloved farm on the Eastern Shore, far away from the eyes of others. He could drink all day there, as much as he wanted, and smoke a little pot too. At Harry's farm no one but his family was there to look in on him and judge him.

The other members of the team were happy to be home too. Buddy returned like a colossus to the racing scene, where he had labored so long and hard with claimers and where he had fought the other trainers for supremacy. Now they could all see for themselves what he was capable of accomplishing under the right circumstances. He was showing them all who the top dog really was. Many of the other trainers had achieved great things in their careers too, but Buddy had the Kentucky Derby winner in his stable now, and he had trained the horse *and* the goddamned jockey too!

The greatest redemption story in Baltimore belonged to Ronnie. He went back to his parents' home to find Dundalk lit up like Christmas with colorful congratulatory signs hanging off the row house porches, each one containing good wishes just for him, blessings for his success and bright future. Even more impressive was the front parlor of his parents' home. In the last twelve months it had become a shrine to Ronnie, his own personal hall of fame, filled with saddles, trophies, horse blankets, and other hard-won memorabilia from his sensational, almost miraculous career.

When Ronnie's parents went out to dinner, to the same simple haunts they had enjoyed for years, they were no longer the same simple people.

They were gawked at, congratulated, and toasted by their own neighbors. They were asked to sign autographs and fielded requests for Ronnie to make personal appearances at the mall and car dealerships.

Dundalk's newspaper, *The Eagle*, did a front-page feature on the new favored son. There was a big illustration of his boyish face, surrounded by a horseshoe of victory flora. Businesses bought up print ads and spent their marketing capital just to congratulate him and find some way to associate themselves with his magic name.

As far as Spectacular Bid was concerned, everything was cute and sweet and positive as it could be. The local politicians, of course, latched onto him. They came out to have their pictures taken with the wonder horse and grab a little of the refracted glory for themselves.

Baltimore's mayor, William Donald Schaefer, a rising star with a flair for the dramatic, went so far as to write a proclamation naming the Bid an honorary citizen of Baltimore. He read the official copy to the assembled press and got himself—bald head, suit, tie, and all—in the papers next to the superstar equine.

But as Bid's team was about to find out, celebrity and publicity cut two ways. For instance, when members of the press came to Hawksworth Farm to see Harry and Teresa in their natural habitat, they quickly and inevitably noticed Harry's hands, the ones that always carried a drink. No one came right out and said he had a problem, but every one of them devoted at least a sentence or two to his ever-present beverages. In essence, they described a functional alcoholic.

Worse than that, very few could resist delving into the Meyerhoffs' relationship. Of course many of the details were highly personal and embarrassing. The writers often alluded to the fact that Harry and Teresa were in a liaison before his first marriage had ended. The wide gulf in their ages was considered fair game and inevitably brought up by every reporter. They wrote with wide-eyed astonishment about the jumbo-size diamond in Teresa's engagement ring. And the highly offensive expression "gold digger" resurfaced again and again.

Some noted that the young, glamorous Teresa looked better suited to Harry's elegant son, Tom, than to Harry himself. At one point, poor Tom felt compelled to say, "At the end of the day, there is no confusion as to who goes to bed with Teresa." It was a pseudo-Oedipal admission pushed out of his mouth by an invasive press scratching and clawing at the family to find some new angle on an over-covered story.

At least the coverage of Buddy and his outsized personality was understandable. There was a comically prototypical photograph of him in all of his bald-headed swagger. A long cigarette holder was clenched between his teeth, pugnaciously jutting from his mouth into the world. He wore a polyester polo shirt with a long and wide collar. The tails of his shirt were neatly tucked into the wide waistband of his dress pants, which were pulled way up above his navel, old-man style. His globous belly was encircled by his belt like a wide leather equator. No one could deny that the photo had captured the animal himself in full swagger.

Even that picture paled in comparison to the one painted by an enterprising reporter who sought out Buddy's rival Maryland trainers to hear what they had to say about him. These men described the Delp they knew. One journalist noted their grudging admiration. "[Buddy] is not universally liked," he wrote, but "he is universally respected by his peers."

Those peers were mostly willing to give the devil his due. All of them acknowledged the extraordinary work Buddy did with both the Bid and Ronnie. But it didn't take them long to also light into his massive ego and bellicose personality.

Nate Heyman, an assistant to King Leatherbury, one of Delp's most prominent Maryland rivals, brought up the fact that Buddy had only recently thrown a punch at an exercise rider whom Buddy believed had endangered Spectacular Bid during a workout. Delp was suspended for that one, but Heyman chalked it up to Buddy's being Buddy. "[Delp] flew off the handle," Heyman said. "He does that, blows his stack."

That aggressiveness also manifested itself in truculence, something the others believed came naturally to Buddy. "He's shooting off his mouth," Heyman said, "and enjoying it."

If Delp was loud, he didn't appreciate the same quality in his employees. They knew better than to say anything at all that might set him off. And they feared his wrath. "A whole lot of times he has gotten on me,"

Mo Hall, Bid's groom and a loyal Delp employee, said, "but I don't pay him no mind. If you say something, that's when you get in trouble."

The reporter also dredged up Raymond Archer, Buddy's racing mentor and stepfather, just to hear his thoughts on the man of the hour. Raymond was eighty, and he and Buddy had been estranged for years. Whatever bad blood there was between them, Archer allowed that he was "rooting" for Buddy. But he also took a shot at his "son." "I guess this horse makes him feel awfully big," Archer said.

But the worst thing anyone said about Buddy came out of his own mouth, though no one seemed to notice the implications. "I play just as hard as I work," Buddy revealed, "and that's pretty hard."

He was alluding, right there in the family newspaper, to his hidden dark side, the drinking and cocaine use alongside his own sons and Ronnie. It didn't much matter. The incurious reporter didn't bother asking Buddy to elaborate on the meaning of "playing hard."

There was no concern shown about how Delp's recreational habits might be affecting the boys who were in his care. Anyway, the press was also inflicting its own damage on Ronnie. The Tuesday before the Preakness the *Baltimore Sun* wrote a piece about him, complete with a jubilant photograph of Tony and Marion Franklin beaming in front of their Dundalk row house with a flock of neighbors cheering them on. The article was supposed to be flavorful and congratulatory. But the writer turned into a junior Woodward or Bernstein. He investigated to uncover a once "bratty kid," and his article went into some detail about Ronnie's youthful indiscretions. He quoted one of Ronnie's old schoolteachers, who unprofessionally and ungenerously reminisced that Ronnie had been a boy who "was wasting his time going to school." Another one recalled how he refused to sit down in class. And still another brought up the fact that tiny Ronnie had been a target for bullies. The article was chock full of negative anecdotes that would have embarrassed anyone.

As the Preakness drew closer, it was even newsworthy, at least in Baltimore, that Ronnie had waited too long to acquire reserved tickets for his parents, putting their ability to attend the race in doubt. The story subtly suggested that Ronnie was an ungrateful or neglectful son.

This mean view extended beyond Ronnie to his whole community.

It was as though white-collar Baltimore was looking down its nose on blue-collar Baltimore. Given the fact that Franklin's ascendancy on Spectacular Bid was a big moment for the entire unglamorous town, the semi-insulting coverage was an act of self-loathing.

Of all the responsible people making editorial decisions, no one seemed to consider the various parties' ability to weather embarrassing publicity. The rich, beautiful, and worldly Meyerhoffs personified power and success. They could simply retreat into their huge farm and ignore the noise. Anyway, their persona was pure confidence. A week before the race they had already planned a huge victory celebration at Baltimore's swanky Prime Rib Restaurant, paying to have the entire place shut down on a Saturday night so that they and their friends could enjoy the afterglow of a victory that had not yet been won.

Buddy Delp was also unperturbed by negative press. He was a veteran of the service and of the horse wars at the track. He was an experienced, even bare-knuckled, practitioner of his trade. Whatever people wrote or broadcast about him, he could take it, and he could dish it back out.

But what about Ronnie?

Unlettered and unsophisticated, Ronnie was just a boy, really. Could he possibly handle the media scrutiny with the same savoir fare? He had pens, pads, and microphones, hot lights and huge audiences, shoved in his face night and day. How could he be expected to deal with all of these pressures? And all of that didn't even consider the many secrets he was also harboring.

The members of the media were not distinguishing between fully-formed adults like Delp and the Meyerhoffs and a young man like Franklin still in the midst of emergence. The mere presence of the press was a tightening vice on all of them, yet no one thought to accommodate the least experienced and most vulnerable person in the mix.

In comparison to the media hordes, the race was starting to look easy.

The Kentucky Derby had had ten horses crowded into the field. But at the Preakness the owners of the fastest horses in the United States saw the hopelessness of racing Spectacular Bid. The Preakness field thinned out like Buddy's hair. There were only five horses entered, including the Bid. It was the smallest field since the great Citation had beaten only three other rivals in 1948.

All of this was great news for Ronnie and Spectacular Bid. Franklin's strategy was much as it had been in the Derby. All he needed to do was find an opening on the outside and then stroll to victory. His horse was that good.

As the day of the race drew near, controversy kicked up. The Preakness had traditionally been a public relations boon for Baltimore—and one of the few that the city had. For one spring day every year, the eyes of the sporting world turned to this decaying city, and they did so in an admiring way.

The Preakness was steeped in tradition and full of mystery. Only in Baltimore was the most compelling question of the season answered: Did the winner of the Kentucky Derby have a chance to win the Triple Crown?

But in this year, when the favorite lived at Pimlico, and his trainer, rider, and owner were all Baltimoreans, the publicity machine went a little awry. First, Edwin Pope, a highly respected veteran columnist from Miami, revealed a little secret about Pimlico that most people around the country didn't know. "Aesthetically," Pope wrote, "Pimlico rates a zero—a scenic cipher with the rim rubbed off. It is little more than a large structure fronted by what appears to be a cow pasture edged by a dirt strip."

It was a mean statement but true. In the years since the track's heyday, when its antebellum clubhouse was the most magnificent and dramatic backdrop in racing, both Baltimore and the rich men who controlled Pimlico had let the entire facility fall into a calamitous state of disrepair. By 1979 the venue was a magical name and little more. The mere mention of Pimlico harkened back to mythological horses and great and flawed men, but that was all that was left; it was a discarded shell filled with nothing but stories.

The dilapidation of both Pimlico and Baltimore became the subject of a column by the *Louisville Courier-Journal*'s Billy Reed. Reed looked like a gentile, cigarless Groucho Marx with his large glasses, bushy black eyebrows, and long black mustache.

To pay back Andrew Beyer for his tasteless column about Louisville, Reed did a literary hit job on Baltimore. Never mind that Beyer had gone to school in New England and worked in Washington; for some reason Reed felt that bashing Baltimore was some kind of retribution.

Toward that goal Reed wandered the town in search of material and found plenty. He slandered Baltimore for everything from overpriced crab cakes and liquor to its sleazy red-light district, known as "the Block." His puritanical revulsion for the Block didn't stop him from spending a few hours and a fistful of reimbursable dollars there, gazing at the strippers. He became well acquainted enough with the place to ask for the whereabouts of Blaze Starr, a famous but fading exotic dancer who was by then closing in on fifty.

Later on, Reed saw two men kissing in his hotel parking lot. He was disgusted by that sight of ordinary love between two adults and included it in his list of grievances against Baltimore. To him, it was further proof of the city's decay and depravity.

The ugly sentiments that the puerile journalists hurled at each other had no bearing on a race run by animals, but they did make for a discordant moment for the racing industry. The sport was at its apex in excellence and interest. Three Triple Crown winners had already arrived in the decade, and some thought Spectacular Bid might be the fourth, better than any of those who had come before him.

Instead of enjoying the moment for their beautiful and fascinating sport, Beyer and Reed cannibalized it. Meanwhile, their petty and theatrical columns missed the real story, the one unfolding right in front of them.

There were no questions or articles about Ronnie Franklin's state of mind or how he was handling the pressure of the moment. No one inquired about the efficacy of his living with and working for the same man and what the negative implications of that might be. No one knew or asked if Buddy Delp was providing a healthy environment for his young rider, though he himself seemed to hint that he wasn't.

No one asked pertinent questions about Ronnie, even though there were clues everywhere that he was working in a toxic culture. In all those puff pieces that everyone wrote and ran, the journalists could see plenty that might concern them. Harry drank all day. Buddy was a bully, a brawler, and an admitted "partier." Ronnie was erratic and asking for vodka in the jockeys' room.

The journalists were on the spot and hungry for stories but found the mystery of how many carats were in Teresa's diamond a more intriguing question than anything about Ronnie's state of mind, finances, or care. It was as if every single sports journalist in the country was asleep on the job. Perhaps some were too focused on the race, while others, like Beyer and Reed, had their professional senses dulled by ego and pettiness, so much so they didn't notice the big story.

Ronnie Franklin, the boy everyone was talking about that magical springtime in America, was on the verge of coming unglued.

Jerome Blum was an unfamiliar name to horse racing fans, but in 1979 the strategies that he had devised in the weeks and months leading up to Preakness Day would change the trajectory of everything.

Blum was a Baltimore-based lawyer who handled a variety of issues, including domestic cases. Robert Campbell had just such a case for him. It was Campbell's daughter, Shirley, who'd had a single midday tryst with Ronnie at a motel near Pimlico and gotten pregnant. She had given birth to their son, Chris Campbell, in December 1978.

In the six months since his son was born, Ronnie had neither acknowledged nor supported the baby boy. He hadn't even seen him. Shirley, who was still just seventeen and working at the track, would have liked both. She felt that the child needed his father in his life, and she had so little money to raise him that she had to live at home with her parents.

Her father's chief concern was Ronnie's money. He said he wanted it for his daughter, but even Shirley suspected he wanted at least some of it for himself. And Ronnie looked like he had plenty. He was all over their TV sets day after day. The newspapers were full of stories of his victories on Spectacular Bid and many other horses. Campbell and his lawyer could infer that Franklin's purses must have added up to a tidy sum.

Jerome Blum believed that celebrity and publicity were the keys to Ronnie's money. "Ronnie Franklin is a public person," Blum said, running his fingers through his thinning hair, "so let's take this public." The plan, Blum explained to Campbell, with his diploma framed and hanging on the wall and his shelves of law books behind him, was to serve Franklin with paternity papers in the jockeys' room on the day of the Preakness. He told Campbell that he also intended to release the news to the press.

The embarrassment and distraction were meant to humiliate Franklin and to put maximum pressure on Delp and the Meyerhoffs to encourage a quick and generous settlement. No one, Blum reasoned, would want a major distraction in the heart of the Triple Crown. Too much was invested in the success of the horse and rider to see it all go down in a scandal, especially one that could quickly be resolved with a few fat checks from people who could easily afford to write them.

All of this notwithstanding, Shirley herself still wasn't entirely sure who the father of her baby was. She had had only one quick and meaningless encounter with Ronnie. But she regularly slept with her boyfriend, jockey Edwin Canino.

One of the things Shirley's team was asking for in the papers that were being prepared was a blood test to determine paternity. The child could still technically belong to either rider, though little Chris did not have swarthy Hispanic coloring, and he already bore a strong resemblance to Ronnie. Certainly Robert Campbell and Blum knew who they were rooting for. If Franklin was the one in the winner's circle, they would finish in the money. Or so they thought.

Ronnie was served in the jockeys' room, the papers pressed into his chest and punctuated with a jaunty "Have a nice day" by the server. It was a humiliating and scary moment on what was supposed to be the biggest day of Franklin's life. Nevertheless, there was nothing to be said or done about it, so he went out and faced the day.

To help him acclimate for the big race, Ronnie was scheduled to ride a couple of tune-up races. Having the jockey ride in one or more of the preliminaries was a common practice. It allowed the rider to get a feel for the track conditions and an adrenaline rush for focus.

In the fourth race, Ronnie's horse, Bear Arms, was the favorite, but he had a rough ride. Starting from the number one post position, Bear Arms broke out of the gate and was immediately out of control. He veered right and went into the horse next to him, permanently removing that horse from contention. Franklin regained control but rode erratically for the rest of the race, going in diagonals instead of straight lines before finishing second.

Franklin rode again in the seventh race. He and Angel Cordero were side by side on two horses with similar names. Angel was on Bold Ruckus, while Ronnie was aboard Bold Road, a Delp-trained horse.

Cordero was up to his old tricks. At the quarter pole he brushed Franklin's horse with enough force to enflame Ronnie, and the two men fought it out all the way to the finish line. Cordero's Bold Ruckus edged out Franklin's Bold Road, but Ronnie made a foul claim related to the action at the quarter pole. The stewards were ambivalent. They deferred to Angel, disallowed the claim, and the results stood as originally posted.

Regardless of what the stewards saw, Franklin was livid. But there was little time to dwell on it. The next race was the Preakness, and the horses were already in the paddock.

Between the seventh and eighth races a huge, portentous black cloud had appeared and swallowed the wide sky above Pimlico. It menaced the proceedings, threatening to soak the infield throngs and utterly change the track conditions.

It was under this cloak of darkness that Buddy gave his final instructions to Ronnie Franklin. The trainer was dressed well in an elegant camel-colored sports jacket, a brown and white tie with wide stripes, and nicely tailored brown dress slacks.

The tall trainer jammed his fists into his pants pockets so that no one could see them and sternly leaned into his young protégé's face. He glared at the boy and spit out the ingredients for success to him one more time: Don't do anything stupid. Steer clear of trouble. And don't get caught on the inside. The horse is good enough to take care of the rest.

Franklin listened intently, but the day's pressures began to show on his face. He was wide-eyed and could not hide the fear and stress, the fright, of everything that had happened so far and that still might happen.

As Angel Cordero got a leg into his irons, he knew Delp's strategy, had known it for some time, and felt that he could cope with it, if not defeat it entirely. He was ready to take on Franklin, Delp, and the Bid and use their strengths against them.

The five horses paraded to the post without incident, each one looking gallant and game under a brilliant jockey. First were Flying Paster and Don Pierce in his pink silks; next was the Bid, looking calm and content with the familiar Franklin on his back; after that came the highly respected Canadian jockey Sandy Hawley and Golden Act; number four was the indomitable Angel on Screen King; finally, the five horse was General Assembly with Laffit Pincay Jr. up. It was an extraordinary collection of riding talent. Every single jockey in the race, save Ronnie, was a future Hall of Famer.

Because there were so few horses, everyone expected an easy run. The animals did their part to comply; each one in his turn was loaded with ease. But the thunder clouds were a better indicator of what was about to come than the docile horses were. Nature's anger only foreshadowed the hot and swirling winds of human rage that were about to present in jagged bolts of spiteful energy.

And then the gates opened.

The well-trained horses burst out of their confinement with passion and purpose. General Assembly and Flying Paster predictably took the lead; they were neck and neck and setting an extraordinarily fast pace. At the quarter pole they were at twenty-three and two-fifths seconds, tied with Pimlico's track record.

The Bid was immediately "in good stride," Ronnie said later, but he was also content to be second from last and many lengths behind the leaders. Any keen observer could easily see that Ronnie hoped to employ the same relaxed tactics that had worked so well for him in Kentucky. He was biding his time and hoping to sneak up on the leaders.

But that wouldn't happen in Baltimore. This time Angel Cordero was between Spectacular Bid and the leaders, and he knew exactly where Ronnie was.

At the first turn Cordero finally revealed the strategy he'd long claimed would defeat the Bid. When Ronnie's horse leapt to the outside to make a move on the leaders, Angel, directly in front of him, sensed Franklin's desire and made a move of his own, maneuvering Screen King to the outside too, kicking dirt in the Bid's face and blocking his path.

At this point, Ronnie was forced to decide. He could continue on the outside of Cordero, but that would mean taking the longest possible path to the wire. It would be a risky move considering the excellence of the other horses in the race. His other option was to find the inside hole on the other side of Screen King, but that would mean potentially getting ensnared in another Cordero web with slow horses in front of him and the rail to his left.

With the embarrassment of his panicked Florida Derby ride still fresh in his mind, Ronnie remained calm and maintained his composure. He made the calculated decision to go farther outside, confident in the belief that no matter how wide he went, the Bid was rapid transit and more than enough horse to come home first.

But as the two horses worked their way around the backstretch, Cordero continued to herd Spectacular Bid to the outside. It was as if Angel was riding a collie instead of a thoroughbred. Farther and farther out they drifted, practically to the parking lot.

Finally, Ronnie had had enough. He was side by side with Screen King, but the Bid had gained the upper hand. With that advantage Franklin pushed back on Cordero and aimed the Bid right at him. Screen King was the one forced into a small, suffocating pocket of air right behind a gassed out General Assembly. Ronnie was on Cordero's right, bearing in on him, and the grinding rail was to Angel's left. With nowhere left to go, Cordero turned to theatrics and stood up in his irons.

Ronnie lingered there momentarily, sadistically, so that Angel could taste a generous helping of the Baltimore clay flying off the filthy heels of General Assembly and right into his face. Franklin, on the other hand, got to savor the sweet flavor of revenge. And then, with a gust of air, he was gone.

In a fraction of a second Cordero and Screen King were distant memories. A heartbeat later, Flying Paster and General Assembly went from thundering pacesetters to has-beens. In a violent burst of electricity, the Bid whooshed by them at the head of the far turn and opened a gap that demeaned the other horses.

With extreme suddenness it was obvious that Cordero could not win the race, but his day was far from over. Boiling underneath his festive helmet, he found himself stride to stride with Golden Act, though he was far to the outside while Golden Act was on the rail. It was already abundantly obvious that both of them would finish many lengths behind the Bid, though an ignominious third place was still at stake.

It was there that Cordero's impotent frustrations got the better of him. While the rapt attention of everyone in the grandstand and infield was focused on the Bid's burst of speed, Angel sharply moved to the inside, going a long distance to intimidate Golden Act and Sandy Hawley. In a move as fast and destructive as a snakebite, Cordero darted in a violent burst and pushed Hawley against the rail. Then, just as quickly, Cordero bolted out. It was venomous aggression misapplied by a thwarted bully in need of an outlet.

When Ronnie and the Bid crossed the finish line, acres of North Baltimore seemed to separate them from the other horses and riders. They were only a fifth of a second off the track record and had run a faster Preakness than either Affirmed, the celebrated winner from the year before, or the sainted Secretariat, who had buried the field in 1973. (Later it was determined that due to an equipment malfunction that incorrectly determined Secretariat's time too slowly on the day of his Preakness, Secretariat was the real Preakness record holder.) Had Ronnie not wasted time encumbered with Cordero, Spectacular Bid surely would have smashed the record. But what did that matter? Ronnie got to hold the shiny Woodlawn Vase, the Preakness trophy, like it was a golden calf.

The Preakness winner's circle featured the Meyerhoffs, Buddy, Ronnie, and the Bid but no Gerald. Buddy's son missed the historic photo because he was already on his way to find his regular drug dealer and score some "blow" and other treats for later.

As soon as their photo was snapped and the Bid was safely in Mo Hall's capable hands, Ronnie and Buddy hustled over to meet Howard Cosell and Jim McKay on their makeshift ABC Sports set so that they could take the broadcasters through the highly eventful race.

Buddy started off by complaining about Cordero's behavior, how his horse had lingered in front of the Bid and thrown dirt in his face. "It didn't bother [Spectacular Bid]," Buddy said. "It just made him a little bit mad."

And then Ronnie took over. Like Buddy, he was impulsive and overly candid about the things that bothered him out on the track. He complained, of all things, about Cordero's ability to play nicely. "He brought his horse way out," Ronnie told the American people. "He took him clear out to the outside fencing. To me, that's not really good sportsmanship."

It was an exaggeration but not by much. Cordero had taken him out about thirty feet. Cosell, as always, stirred the pot. He sensed the drama of the moment and probed, hoping to get even more from Franklin. "So you felt Cordero was out to make trouble for you?" the great broadcaster asked Franklin.

Hearing Cosell put it more bluntly than he liked, Ronnie walked back his remarks a little. He took a breath, smiled a boyish grin, and then changed the script in his distinctive grammar-resistant dialect. "No, no I'm not goin' to say that," Ronnie responded. "I don't want to start no trouble or nothin'."

And then, in an attempt to undo the damage, the young jockey laid it on a little thick. "[Cordero] is a nice guy and everything," Ronnie said, alibiing for the jockey whose shenanigans had just robbed him of the track record. "He's just doing his job."

But back in the jockeys' room it was a different story. Ronnie reminisced with pleasure about how he had been the aggressor, shoving Cordero behind General Assembly and making Angel swallow his own bitter medicine. "Payback is payback!" Ronnie loudly crowed, and the phrase, in its vengeful, spiteful simplicity, delighted the laughing scribes.

But when the writers went to Cordero and told him what the kid had said, Angel failed to find the humor. Instead, a fuse was lit, and a burning fever stoked inside the brilliant Puerto Rican's brain. He was livid, but he couldn't do what he surely would have loved to do: bust Ronnie in the chops. So instead he aimed his profane rage at the reporters. "You fucking guys write anything you fucking want," he sputtered.

When they told the great rider that Ronnie had called him a poor sport, Cordero laid it all on the line. "He better not say that to my face," Angel warned, and everyone knew that he meant it.

Ultimately Cordero's "conversation" with the press degenerated into a shouting match. He became so animated that a Pimlico security guard had to be called over to break it up.

The crux of Angel's argument was: "It's my ground, my race track. I can go where I want to go." He also accused Franklin of "cutting up [his] horse" when Spectacular Bid shoved him behind General Assembly. He had a point, but as usual he had taken it to extremes. He could ride Ronnie way to the outside if he wanted, it was technically legal, but it meant that he was going way to the outside too.

Why would he do that if his goal was to win the race?

That was Luis Barrera's question. Luis, Angel's trainer for the Preakness, didn't necessarily see things the same way Angel did. About the cut legs of his horse, Barrera said, "Cordero tell me it happen at the half-mile pole and that it's Spectacular Bid [who did it]. I don't know."

Barrera was a little bit more certain when it came to the subject of Angel's questionable ride. He said it had cost his horse "seven or eight lengths." His horse had had to "go around all the [other] horses," Barrera said, and he had had to do it "with cut legs."

It was an embarrassing moment for Cordero. He'd lost to Franklin—again. And now he was being chastised by his own trainer for a poor ride.

Was it possible that Ronnie was in *his* head?

Cordero was convinced that Franklin was a terrible jockey. "He's an asshole rider," Angel said. And yet he was obsessed with Franklin too. It had become clear to everyone but Cordero that his fixation was self-destructive. He was more interested in ensuring Ronnie's defeat than he was in gaining his own victory.

If Angel was in a foul mood and tormented, at least he wasn't alone. Buddy, too, was spoiling for a fight; instead of enjoying his historic victory, he had Cordero on his mind like a migraine. Buddy accused Angel of trying to "sucker" Ronnie to "make [him] go inside." When one of the old-guard New York columnists, Dick Young of the *Daily News*, asked Buddy what would have happened had Ronnie taken that inside path, Delp gave him a cold glare and a few hot words.

"That's a dumb question," Buddy barked.

"Okay," Young responded, "I'm a dummy."

"Well, I don't answer dummies," Buddy shot back.

A more introspective man than Buddy Delp might've asked himself how and why he could be so angry on the most triumphant day of his competitive life.

Regardless, the battle was over. Bid's team was at home in Baltimore and on top of the world. There was nothing left to do but celebrate. "I'm just going to party," Ronnie told one of the stodgy old white men who covered him. "I think there will be some partying going on in Dundalk tonight."

"The word party was equally prominent in the conversations of Delp and the Meyerhoffs," one clueless writer pecked out for his column. "The whole gang of them had one coming and you can bet it was a prize-winner."

For the Meyerhoffs that meant hosting their friends at the fancy restaurant they had rented just for themselves. Among their many invitees there were two prominent no shows: their trainer and their jockey.

Ronnie did indeed go home to Dundalk. He stopped in to briefly enjoy the moment with his family and his ardent fans in their world of steelworkers and other organized laborers. He let them all enjoy a sliver of his refracted glory, and he understood how much it meant to them. But then he was called to another place to answer a different siren. He left his mother and father behind and went to Buddy's house, his adult home, to convene with his new inner circle. It was there that the Delps and Ronnie celebrated their way.

Buddy and the boys, the new rock stars of horse racing, went into the "playroom" and shot pool and played ping pong. They drank whiskey straight out of the bottle and mixed drinks. And they did line after line of cocaine. Eventually, they were so spent that they popped a few Quaaludes and went to bed.

13 *Out of Control*

The pressure that had been building on Ronnie Franklin before the Preakness only intensified after it was over. With each ride he was watched more closely and criticized with greater intensity. The strain and wear inflicted upon him in public only added to the miseries that afflicted him in private.

And it was all beginning to show in the form of highly erratic performances at Pimlico.

About a week after the Preakness, in the eighth race, Ronnie rode an unruly mount called Big Vision and had difficulty controlling him. After initially streaking for the finish line, Big Vision suddenly and inexplicably took off in the direction of the outside fence. Ronnie appeared powerless to redirect him, and instead of enjoying an easy victory, the young riding wizard ended up embarrassed and in fifth place.

After the race, Fred Colwill, the chief steward, happened by the unsaddling area and saw something deeply disturbing. He watched as Ronnie raised his boot and kicked Big Vision in the stomach. That was highly uncharacteristic behavior for Franklin, who saw himself as an animal lover and a man who enjoyed a special rapport with Spectacular Bid and other horses.

So what might have driven a kindly disposed kid to such a despicable and aberrant act of animal cruelty? No one asked that question or even bothered to look for a deeper meaning. No one asked if maybe too much was being heaped on the young rider or if he had other emotional issues that were affecting him.

When Colwill confronted him, Franklin didn't bother to deny the incident. He was fined the paltry sum of $100, and that was an end of it. Apparently, in the eyes of the Maryland Racing Commission, he was rehabilitated.

But only about a week later Ronnie was in trouble again. Riding in another race, right out of the gate he lost control of a two-year old called Croatoan. The horse immediately moved sharply to the left and interfered with not one but two horses, Fully Loaded and Ambitious Ruler. To his credit, Ronnie immediately pulled on the reins to redirect Croatoan, but the damage was done. Fully Loaded and Ambitious Ruler's chances to win had been scuttled. And there were still more surprises. In the stretch, Croatoan bumped yet another horse, the unfortunately named Feta Cheese, before crossing the wire in first place.

Needless to say, a claim was put in against Ronnie, and his number was ultimately taken down by the stewards. He and Croatoan were stripped of their first-place finish and placed seventh.

It was an unusual ruling. A rider's number wouldn't normally be taken down for something the horse had done in the first three strides unless it was obvious that the rider had intentionally ridden into someone else's path.

The disastrous ride aboard Croatoan put Franklin under review for suspension. That was standard procedure for a jockey in a disqualification. But on another level the situation was highly unusual since a suspension would disqualify Ronnie from riding in the Belmont Stakes, which was then only less than a week away.

Buddy Delp came roaring into the situation, of course, and made it all about himself. About steward Clinton Pitts Jr., who was in the stand that day, he said, "I'm sure he hates my guts"—as though that factored into it. Buddy often said, with more than a little paranoia, that Maryland's stewards were out to get him. In this case, he believed they were using Ronnie as a proxy.

To ward off any evil intentions, Buddy promised a big legal imbroglio if punitive measures were taken against Ronnie. "If they try to suspend

Franklin for something that he did without malice, I'll appeal it to the highest court in the land . . . to see that he doesn't serve a day," Buddy vowed.

In the end, the stewards determined that Ronnie had done enough to correct his mount, and no further penalty was warranted.

These incidents became ammunition in the hands of an intellectual assassin. Andrew Beyer had the ability, the interest, and the forum to ensure that no one overlooked Ronnie Franklin's failings. By this time Beyer was one of the most influential racing writers in the nation. Putting that prestige to work, he wrote a scathing piece in the *Washington Post* that demeaned Franklin's riding skills and discredited his legitimacy to run for the Triple Crown.

Beyer eviscerated Franklin but did so in a column full of sophistries, telling only the half of the story that supported his thesis and concealing the other half that discredited his points. For instance, Beyer wrote that Ronnie "did not display much aptitude when he launched his career at Pimlico a year ago." Somehow, in making the case for Ronnie's lack of "aptitude," Beyer forgot to mention the kid's long list of victories in 1978, his high total purse earnings, or his Eclipse Award as the nation's top apprentice. Continuing his belligerence, the columnist wrote, "He's riding even worse now [than last year]." Again, he de-emphasized an important point. Franklin had just won both the Derby and the Preakness.

Beyer attempted to justify his ludicrous statements by proving what a poor performance Ronnie's winning ride had been in the Preakness. "He went to ridiculous lengths to [keep Spectacular Bid] out of trouble," he informed his readers. Cordero was "so far away from the rail you could have driven a tank inside him. . . . If Cordero had gone into Row A of the parking lot, Franklin would have been in Row B." Beyer suggested that Franklin's fondness for the outside, his "willingness to lose several lengths," was all due to a crippling fear of trouble.

But Beyer never mentioned something that every rider in America knew all too well: Angel Cordero Jr. could be a terrorist out there, fearlessly playing chicken with any willing, or unwilling, partner he had set his sights on. Many of the best riders had fallen prey to Cordero's brilliantly conceived and executed traps, and in Jacinto Vasquez's colorful phrase, they had been "barbecued." Did Beyer believe the Preakness was the proper venue for Ronnie to prove he could handle Angel when so many magnificent and veteran riders couldn't?

The journalist might have fashioned himself an iconoclast, but there was nothing clever or illuminating or particularly honest about his piece. It felt as if it had been written by an intellectual bully.

The words on the page were ultimately more telling about the author than the youthful subject. The journalist might have seen Ronnie's recent struggles in the context of his past successes. Instead of doing backflips to prove Ronnie was a poor rider, Beyer might have used the skills of a journalist to look for the underlying causes of the kid's troubles. He had donated all of his column space to a kind of smarmy ass kicking, a man beating up a boy. Instead, he might have devoted his valuable ink and newsprint to answering the question of why this steel-plated kid was suddenly so fragile. Better yet, he could've taken the time to ask Ronnie's parents or friends, or he might have picked up the phone and demanded answers from Buddy or the Meyerhoffs or other racing professionals.

Beyer didn't do any of those things. He saw Franklin's agony and then kicked him with sadistic gusto. Unfortunately, there was no commission to review the cheap shots of writers, and no one ever got suspended or fined for kicking a kid and making him feel worthless.

Every one of Beyer's cruel and ill-considered words was accelerant to something that was already raging out of control inside the teenager's brain. At least the writer from Harvard proved one thing: education didn't inoculate a man from being obnoxious or abusive.

Ronnie wasn't the only one on his team who'd been abused a little by the press. A couple of weeks earlier they'd all been so excited to return to Baltimore, a place that loomed huge in their sentiments. And yet now departure from that same place was a delicious escape, a much-needed retreat from a town that had been far less hospitable than any place called "home" should ever be.

If New York was an exile of sorts, at least it was a swanky one. The Bid's team moved into Manhattan's finest accommodations, at the venerable Plaza Hotel. Ronnie and Gerald had their own plush rooms and a mindset that they would enjoy the big city.

At night, they relaxed their way; they snorted coke from Gerald's Baltimore supply, and they consorted with prostitutes. "Ronnie would fuck a snake," Gerald said with a laugh, though he knew his buddy wasn't the only one.

Perhaps Ronnie was giving into his animal appetites, like many a young man. Or maybe in a world that felt more and more like it was closing in on him, Ronnie desperately required someone to lie down with him and provide him the small comforts, the ones that are often sought by worried men.

The racing days following those racy nights were all business. Buddy knew that one of the blind spots in Ronnie's training was a total absence of experience at Belmont Park, the longest and most challenging race track in the country. The Bid had raced there once before, in the Champagne Stakes, but that was in the brief interlude when Georgie Velasquez was up.

Buddy had a plan to rectify that situation. He scheduled Ronnie for a few races at Belmont Park, one on the Wednesday before the Stakes and two more on Saturday, the big day itself. The Wednesday race was for two-year-olds and was interesting for one notable reason: Ronnie and Cordero were slotted right next to each other at the gate.

Angel was still seething from Ronnie's comments after the Preakness, when he had called Cordero a poor sport and shamelessly bragged that he had pushed Angel to the inside. Cordero still blamed Ronnie for the fact that his horse's legs were cut up in the race.

Now, just two days before the Belmont, Angel stomped his way to the paddock with Greg McCarron, another veteran rider, beside him. "I'm gonna drop that son of a bitch," Angel confided to McCarron.

True to his word, as soon as the gates opened, Cordero plowed his horse, Ski Pants, right into Franklin and his mount, Lorine. As two-year-olds, the horses were inexperienced and unpredictable, the type that might inadvertently interfere with each other. Nevertheless, Cordero's intent was strikingly obvious. He went straight at Franklin and made no apparent attempt to correct his horse; instead, he drove his animal hard and deep into Franklin's and kept driving until Franklin almost went down, horse and all.

In fact, Cordero's attack on Franklin had a violent ripple effect that might have brought down several horses. It was like amusement park crash cars, but the vehicles were terrified and weighed more than one thousand pounds.

"I thought I was gonna be dropped," Ronnie said, clearly shaken by the experience. "I thought I had no chance of stayin' up, that I was goin' for sure. God had to help me a little bit. I was halfway down."

"I was just glad I wasn't in between them," McCarron admitted.

After the race, Buddy Delp was understandably livid. He railed to the press about Cordero's malicious behavior. But he was also enraged at his protégé, who he believed needed to stand up for himself. "If you don't go in there and hit that son of a bitch don't bother coming home tonight," Buddy told Ronnie after the race. "'Get your ass in that room and you kick the crap out of him.'"

In his zeal for combat, Buddy seemed to forget that he was sending a boy to fight a man. Cordero was thirty-seven years old and life-hardened. He'd been a boxer in his youth and a fearless brawler ever since. Angel was one tough hombre, as intimidating and unforgiving as they came.

Ronnie was just nineteen. He had grown up on the streets of his union shop of a neighborhood, facing bullies who were the regular-sized sons of steelworkers and factory laborers, pipefitters and teamsters. He was without fail smaller than his opponent in every fight he'd ever been in, but he never walked away from a challenge.

Now there was no choice. Buddy Delp, his employer, his mentor, his father figure, demanded that he go and stand up to Cordero, and that was exactly what he did.

Whatever was bubbling up in Ronnie, however, was already boiling over in Angel. When Ronnie stalked into the room, he was immediately in Angel's eye. And nothing stood between them but sheer contempt and a murderous rage. "Te voy a matar!" Cordero shouted. ("I'm going to kill you," in Spanish.)

And just like that they went from competitors to combatants in a fight for their lives. Ronnie swung his helmet at Cordero's head and then came at the Puerto Rican with his fists swirling. He connected to Angel's head once or twice before Cordero pulled him to the ground.

There they grappled like high school wrestlers until others jumped into the fray to separate them. "If they didn't break it up," jockey George Martens, an eyewitness, said, "it was going to be a biggie."

If Ronnie and Angel were Ali and Frazier, Buddy was Don King. In other words, while the two athletes did the fighting, Delp ran his mouth and threatened legal action if Angel was not suspended. "Cordero intimidated Ronnie Franklin once, down in Florida," Delp admitted, "but he'll never do it again." And then Buddy said something really interesting and unintentionally revealed an ugly truth. "I'm the only man who can frighten Ronnie," he earnestly said.

Harry Meyerhoff did his best to throw his weight around. He told the organizers of the Belmont Stakes that if his horse and rider were in danger, he would skip their race altogether.

It was like a Mexican standoff. Everyone had his gun barrel pointed at someone else, and everyone was in someone else's crosshairs. In the end, however, it was the stewards who didn't blink. Despite the pressure that Buddy and Harry applied to them, they refused to be intimidated and did nothing to punish Angel for his outsized and aggressive behavior. In fact, they exonerated him. "Cordero's mount did come in sharply," they allowed in a written statement. "However, she hit the gate and was turned to the outside, causing Franklin to take up. Due to these contributing factors, no punitive action was deemed appropriate."

Ignoring the fact that one of the riders was in his thirties while the other was still in his teens, the stewards found them equally culpable for the post-race fight, and they fined them both $250. "THE STEWARDS DO NOT WISH TO COMMENT ANY FURTHER," a press release stated. In other words, they didn't feel like they owed anybody any explanations for their outrageous decision.

Others pointed out that there was a plausible excuse for what the stewards did. Angel was a favorite of the trainer Angel Penna. Penna trained horses for Dinny Phipps. And Phipps was the chairman of the board of trustees of the New York Racing Association, the organization that oversaw many of the state's tracks, including Belmont. To make a long story short, Cordero was closely connected to the stewards' boss.

"[Cordero] tried to bury Franklin," Buddy Delp moaned. "He wanted him on the ground. He should be suspended thirty days for this, or six months."

Buddy had a rock-solid point and he should have left it at that, but it wasn't in his nature to stop talking. "I don't understand Cordero," he continued. "Apparently, he can't stand somebody else being successful. He shows me no class whatsoever."

Steve Cauthen, the nineteen-year-old Triple Crown–winning rider from only the year before, knew how brutal the profession was. "You've got to get in fistfights sometimes, just to hold your own," Cauthen said. In a room full of strugglers and dues payers Cauthen knew that Ronnie would never be seen as anything more than lucky.

The other jockeys thought God smiled on young guys like Cauthen and Franklin who got to work with successful trainers and well-bred horses while all they got was a long, hard journey to the top and endless struggles.

There were no favorite sons in the jockeys' room, where mettle was earned *mano a mano* and never given. "Sometimes [another rider will] want to take you on just to measure you," Cauthen said. "You've got to stand your ground. Horse racing is life or death. If somebody puts your life in danger [out on the track], you let him know about it. Sometimes . . . you have to get dead serious about it." To Cauthen and all of the jockeys, "dead serious" meant attacking a brother jockey if the situation warranted it.

Cordero knew how the game worked. He could effortlessly transition from a killer in the jockeys' room to a charismatic charmer in the press room. To him, it was just one more aspect of being a successful jockey.

After the supposed steward-brokered resolution of hostilities between Cordero and Franklin, it was time to meet the press. Angel stood in front of the cameras and smiled his infectious smile and patted his young rival on the back as though he was a kindly uncle to him.

And then Cordero stepped up to the mic. The tiny Black Hispanic rider met the lily white room of tall Anglo writers, took their reins, and rode their sympathies with as much skill, dexterity, and deception as he'd ever displayed on a horse. He dazzled the boys of the media with an array of carefully chosen words. "As far as I'm concerned, it's over," Angel said with his big, toothy smile. "We shake hands and became friends."

Ronnie gave a weak smile and said nothing. And Cordero continued on. "I never caused any trouble, and I'm not planning any trouble," Angel said. "I paid $250 [in fines,] and if I'm going to fight I'll go to the Garden and get a million dollars. Far as I'm concerned, it's over."

It was a virtuoso performance—contrite without an admission of guilt and sincere enough to convince a roomful of cynical men who knew he was full of it.

Franklin, on the other hand, was transparently sullen. He was twenty minutes late for the meeting. He was good enough to pose for the propaganda photos with Angel, but after that he quickly left the premises without uttering a single word.

Cordero could fool a lot of people but not himself. He knew it wasn't "over," as he had said. In fact, it was far from over. The tipoff was his referring to Franklin, the lucky white kid who had called him "a spic," as a "friend."

Por favor.

Cordero could afford to bullshit it any way he wanted to. He had forcefully made his point to Delp, Franklin, and everyone else. He'd thumped that kid right there on the track, in front of the crowd and the cameras and the stewards, and he had come within a hair of putting Franklin, and for that matter himself, under the hooves. In case anyone didn't know already, he was letting them know: Angel Cordero Jr. was capable of anything. And he wasn't afraid of a goddamn thing—neither falling under the horses nor flying afoul of the stewards.

Worse yet, everyone could see that Buddy's running, roaring mouth and so-called prestige were worthless. Delp couldn't do a thing to protect Franklin on the track or in the jockeys' room even if he wanted to.

Now it was as if Ronnie was walking through a rat-infested alley in a bad neighborhood without a single cop in sight. And here came Angel to chase him down that alley, not with a switchblade but with a stomping horse.

It couldn't be a more dangerous game, something underscored in the next day's *Baltimore Sun,* where, wedged between stories about Franklin and Cordero, was a long piece about Ron Turcotte, the jockey who'd ridden Secretariat to glory.

Only eleven months earlier, at the very same Belmont Park, Turcotte's horse had bumped into the heels of another, and he had been launched from the saddle. He had hit the ground with tremendous force and instantly knew that something was tragically wrong. "I couldn't feel my stomach or legs," Turcotte said. Three of his vertebrae were broken, something he instinctively knew as he lay there inert amid the hoof prints; he was paralyzed and would never walk again.

And that was horse racing under "normal" conditions. Cordero was begging tragedy, playing crash cars with horses and endangering virtually everyone around him.

Yet somehow it was all good for business. The chaos and the tumult only heightened anticipation for the Belmont Stakes and the possibilities of what might happen there when the hotheaded Cordero and the impetuous Franklin met again.

The night before the race Ronnie rested alone in his suite at the Plaza. As he tucked into his luxurious bed, his worries flew away as he slipped into the sweet comfort of sleep. There, in the middle of the night, his eyes twitched rapidly beneath his closed lids, and images of himself racing flickered in his brain. In that theater of his mind he was high up on "Big Daddy," smacking him like hell, as they zoomed down the homestretch toward the wire.

There was no Buddy there to lean into him and no Cordero to run over him. It was almost like Middleburg; there was only the Bid and the track and the clouds and him. Together, the horse and jockey won the Belmont and the Triple Crown, and he hoisted the trophy high above his head.

That was his dream.

But while Ronnie hallucinated in bed, Spectacular Bid was at the stables having his own nocturnal adventures. The Bid's groom was Mo Hall, a man at midlife who was at the top of his profession and respected by everyone in the industry who knew him. He handled Buddy Delp's best horses. He was assigned the Bid after the original groom, Tots, had almost cooked the horse alive in his stall.

Mo came to Buddy courtesy of his trusted young veterinarian, Jimmy Stewart. Dr. Stewart had known Mo since they were both young men.

Back then, the groom worked for an English-born trainer named Judy Johnson, the first woman licensed to ride horses at a para-mutual track in Maryland and a steeple chase racer during World War II. When Judy retired, in 1978, Mo was without groom work for a little while. He had been relegated to the lowest job at the track, hot walking. Stewart told Buddy that Mo was available, and Delp snapped him up.

Hall's talent for his work was undeniable, but he did have one troublesome quality. He liked to drink. He hid bottles of VO all over the place. One was at the bottom of an oak barrel; another was in between where the hay was stacked. He had hiding places everywhere.

Mo's problem was usually no problem for his employer. No one could easily tell that he was drunk even though everyone knew that he was a drinker. His habit may have been self-destructive, but it didn't usually interfere with his work.

The night before the Belmont, Mo went through his usual progression of duties. He spread an extra-heavy straw bed in the Bid's stall because that was the way the star horse liked it. Next, he wrapped the great colt's swift legs with bandages and fastened them with safety pins. Because Bid could be a noncompliant customer and an unusually smart horse, Mo had to sprinkle pepper flakes on the bandages and wrap the safety pins in tape. All of this protected the four-legged athlete's delicate limbs from his own kicks and bites in the night. But with whiskey on Mo's breath, some of the small details weren't on his mind.

He forgot to tape the safety pins.

So while Ronnie dreamt of victory in the night, Bid worked to undo it. He opened one of the untaped pins with his mouth, and it fell deep into the lush straw bed. Sometime during the night his foot found that pin and he stepped on it with the full force of his massive frame, driving it deeply into the hard material of his left forehoof.

The pin traveled a good distance into the Bid's foot, at least a quarter of an inch. It was a serious and painful injury, the equivalent of a human having a pin shoved under his fingernail. In other words, it was quite literally torture.

Mo, like all good grooms, lived by the mantra, "No hoof, no horse." He obsessively and routinely checked his horses' hooves for stones or other obstructions. He found the pin and immediately removed it, but his anxiety was not assuaged. He knew the Bid was in serious trouble.

At about 5:30 a.m. Delp's limousine rolled up. Mo was already outside waiting for him. "Boss," Mo said, his face stricken and creased with worry, "you got a problem; the horse is lame."

Buddy went into the Bid's stall and picked up his left foreleg to examine the hoof. He could see the puncture. They took the Bid out of his stall and jogged him to determine if he was favoring the leg and if he was sound enough to run. "He's a little off," Gerald told Buddy.

They treated the horse themselves. First, they bathed him in warm Epson water. Then, they iced him. Even as they treated him, they were also considering their options.

There was some disagreement about the proper course. "Dad, you've got to scratch this horse," Gerald told his father.

But Buddy wasn't so sure. He'd had a long and successful career, but this was his pinnacle, his chance at immortality, and his launching pad to greater wealth. He wasn't about to let it slip away. "I'm one to nine to win the Triple Crown," Buddy said. "I'll probably never be here again. If the horse jogs sound this afternoon I'm running him."

The real decision belonged to Harry Meyerhoff, so Buddy quickly picked up the phone and called the boss. Harry was still back at his suite in the Plaza when he received Buddy's call. His face became careworn as he listened closely to Buddy's report.

Meyerhoff had made a fortune making hard decisions. And he approached this one methodically. The way he saw it, they basically had three options: they could race the horse, they could scratch him, or they could alert the stewards and let them make the decision.

"Well, what do you want to do?" Buddy asked Harry.

"Whatever you think is best, Buddy," Harry told him. "It's your call. If you don't think he should run, we won't run him."

Harry always put his horse first, but he relied on Buddy, his expert, to tell him what was best. In this case, however, Buddy had a lot on the line. They all did. Objectivity about what was "best" for the horse might be in short supply.

The Bid would soon go into syndication. His breeding rights were expected to fetch something north of the $14 million Affirmed had raised. It would be a huge payday for Meyerhoff, but he was already rich. Buddy had the most to gain or lose since he was successful but a working man. Whatever they got to syndicate the Bid, the trainer would be compensated handsomely with a nice percentage. It would be a single payday unlike anything Buddy had ever experienced before, the kind of money that would change his life.

Just how significant the money would be most likely depended on how well the Bid performed in the Belmont. The Triple Crown would be the greatest luster of all for the record-breaking horse, the final seal of approval for a thoroughbred that was not only an incredibly consistent winner but also as fast or faster than any other horse in recorded history. The Belmont was all that stood between the Meyerhoffs and Delp and all of that money.

Buddy told Harry: "We should be okay to go."

The standard procedure would have been to inform the officials as soon as possible about the horse's condition. But Buddy, in fact, did the opposite and hoarded the information. "You don't tell officials things," Tom Meyerhoff said, "because then they'll come and walk [the horse] and they'll say he's lame. They'll see what they want to see."

That was true under normal conditions. And the Meyerhoffs and Buddy were already adversarial with the New York officials. They had just had a bad experience with them in the Cordero imbroglio, even threatening to pull their horse from the race. They weren't about to entrust their hopes for the Bid to a group of men they considered to be dishonest clowns. Buddy had told Harry that the horse was sound, and as far as Harry was concerned, the horse was sound. That was it.

Buddy convinced Harry that the horse was ready to go, but he could not convince himself. He still harbored deep concerns about Spectacular Bid's health and ability to perform at peak level. Leaving nothing to chance, he summoned Dr. Alex Harthill to the Bid's stall.

Harthill was an old friend of Buddy's, and the two men shared a special rapport based on a single character trait. "They were both bullies," Harthill's daughter, Alexis, said.

"Doc" Harthill was well known in racing circles as the most brilliant and forward-thinking equine veterinarian in the world, but like many geniuses, he was quirky and problematical. Despite his many singular medical virtues, he also had a bad personal reputation and was banned from even stepping foot on the Belmont premises.

Delp nicknamed Harthill "Robin Hood," a reference to the vet's penchant for charging rich horse owners lavishly exorbitant fees yet not even accepting a nickel from anyone with a sick horse who was financially strapped. That was just one of the good doctor's many contradictions.

Harthill was born at a veterinary hospital in 1925. That facility belonged to his father, a veterinarian and Harthill's hero. Alex grew up at his father's side with an acute interest in his dad's work, but he took equine science to a level far beyond anything that his father or anyone else knew. As a result, he became one of the most respected men in the equine world. By his own estimation he had treated twenty-six Kentucky Derby winners over his long career, eloquent testimony to the esteem with which he was held.

Nevertheless, Harthill's excellence as a doctor and skill as a surgeon took a back seat to his brilliance as a chemist. It was that last skill that often put him at odds with those who policed racing. "[He] seemed to live on the edge of racing legality," the *Daily Racing Form* wrote. And indeed, in an era when human athletes were just beginning to understand and utilize performance-enhancing drugs, Harthill had already perfected their use at the track. He did so to create a competitive edge, and he had no qualms about flouting the rules.

Harthill was arrested in Louisiana for allegedly bribing a testing laboratory employee. Later, he admitted to using clenbuterol, for at least one of his patients, before the FDA had approved it. In 1964 he secretly used Lasix, which was then banned, on Northern Dancer and enabled that legendary colt to win the Kentucky Derby. All of this, in addition to the Dancer's Image episode in 1968, gave him a nefarious reputation.

No one questioned Harthill's passion to help horses. And no one could relieve their suffering, promote their healing, and help them perform like he could. But many also saw beyond the genius to a rogue, an unprincipled man who was primarily out for himself. They whispered that his great talent was a device to gain him an advantage at the betting window. Whether or not that was true, for him the ethics and rules were clearly malleable and meant to be bent or broken in order to serve his needs.

Mark Reid found out the hard way how elusive Harthill could be. Reid was just starting his career as a trainer when he traveled out to Kentucky to buy something new at the yearling sale at Keeneland. In that era, the bidders bought the horses first and then had them X-rayed to make sure that they were sound and without preexisting problems.

Reid bid on a horse for close to $50,000, which to him was a huge sum of money. He won the colt and then went with a Kentucky veterinarian to X-ray the horse. Reid saw the doctor furrow his brow as he examined the pictures of its legs. "This horse has a broken bone," the vet said.

The doctor showed Reid the photo and pointed out a break in the little loop-shaped bone that holds the ligament to the ankle. "It was broken right in half," Reid said.

Just then Harthill happened by, and Reid, who knew him a little, called out to him and asked him to also take a look at the X-ray. "Man, oh, man, look at that line!" Harthill said. "That is ug-lee."

That was all Reid needed to hear. He took the X-ray and the bill of sale to the office and asked for his money back. "Look," Reid said. "This horse has a fracture, and there are no fractures according to the Conditions of Sale."

"Alright, Mark," the official told him, "we have to have a veterinarian represent us and take a look to make sure that everything is on the up and up. We normally get Dr. Harthill."

"Great," Reid said, "have Dr. Harthill look at it."

Reid left so that the perfunctory process could play out, but he was confident. After all, it was Harthill who had just examined the X-ray. But when Reid was summoned back to the sales office, he was in for a big surprise. "You know," the sales official said, "Dr. Harthill didn't see anything wrong with this X-ray."

Reid was livid and wasn't about to get stuck with the $50,000 bill for a lame colt.

"Where's Harthill?" he asked the official.

"He just left."

Reid ran out to the parking lot, where he saw the good doctor from a distance. "Hey, Harthill," Reid shouted, "stop."

Harthill turned around, saw Reid, and made a break for it, sprinting as fast as he could through the car lanes and laughing loudly as he went. Reid took off after him. "Stop, you simple son of a bitch!" Reid screamed.

But Harthill kept running and laughing.

That was Dr. Harthill. Costing an eager, earnest, and hard-working young man almost $50,000 just to protect his own little racket at Keeneland was nothing to him.

Dr. Harthill was a severe man by anyone's measure. He was a drinker, a womanizer, and a brawler. In fact, he would challenge any man to a fight at the drop of a hat. And if someone really got on his nerves, he'd simply haul off and sock that bastard without any warning.

Harthill was brutal in his personal life too. He was verbally abusive to virtually everyone in his family, especially his wives. His first wife would call her sister and tearfully pour her heart out about the ugly things he said to her. She died when their daughter was only about five years old, and Harthill remarried, this time to a wealthy Californian.

Like his first wife, Harthill's second spouse felt forced to walk on eggshells around him so as not to provoke his "hair-trigger" temper. To them, he was a Jekyll and Hyde, at times charming but also excitable and crude. They both feared he would become physically violent.

To Harthill wedding vows were meaningless, and he did whatever he liked with women without regard to his marital status. And so it was that he met Judith Zouck, a female trainer in an era when they were mighty scarce.

Zouck's career began in 1970, at a time, she said, when "a man [wasn't] going to give a woman horses to train." So she learned to get ahead by partnering with men. One of them, Billy Christmas, was a kindly and highly experienced Maryland trainer who used his status to pick up clients for her. The work filtered through him for appearances, but it allowed her to make money, and she was always listed as the trainer of record. The situation was unfair, but given the constraints of the era, she found it tolerable and equitable.

Zouck's life changed forever when one of her horses developed breathing issues and a friend suggested that she call Dr. Harthill for help. She took that advice and found herself in the presence of a man much older than she was but for whom she felt a deep attraction. "[He was] brilliant," she said, "and those eyes!" She couldn't resist his piercing, deep-blue eyes.

Harthill's seduction was more than just physical. He was a powerful man in racing, and he gladly used his influence to help him succeed. And with Harthill's connections Zouck quickly became a hot commodity. "He got me horses from Calumet and Green Tree, and all the other huge stables," she said.

Although she enjoyed the business that he got for her, Zouck soon came to realize how highly dependent she was on him. Her professional and personal lives had become intertwined, and Harthill was at the center of both.

Just as Judith realized how vulnerable she was, the real Harthill showed up with all of his many mysteries and complications. She packed up and moved from Maryland to Kentucky to be with him. "And that's when I found out that he was still married," she said.

Harthill had hidden his status from her. When it was finally revealed, she was in too deep to make an easy decision. "I had put all my eggs in that basket," she said. "And I go to Kentucky and find out he's married, and I go, 'Oh, crap, now what do I do?'"

She gave Harthill an ultimatum: "Either you can get divorced," she told him, "or I'll just go back to Maryland."

It wasn't much of a choice: Harthill could stay with his beautiful young companion or return to his second wife and the constant fighting in their marriage. He quickly initiated a divorce. Though Zouck was technically the victor in the struggle for Harthill's affection, she soon learned that he was no prize. "He was charming," she said, "but he was evil."

Alexis Harthill understood. She loved her father deeply, but she also knew that he had two sides. "He could go off on anyone," she said. "Even his children were not immune. The only people he didn't go off on were his clients, his bread and butter."

Judith soon felt the full brunt of Harthill's ugly side. "All of a sudden, the 'new' wears off," she said. She found out that with Harthill small disagreements led to outrageous reactions. He never punched or slapped her, but he intimidated her on a daily basis. "He chased me around the house with a big-ass cattle prod," Judith said. "He threatened me. I was held at gunpoint. I had all four tires of my car slashed. My gas tank was sugared. And he tried to kill my horse."

Separating from Harthill was even more excruciating than living with him. Judith left their home, taking only what she thought were a few personal or meaningless items and established a new residence for herself in Louisville. Harthill had set her up with the top players, but she'd had her own success with them. She was confident and believed she could continue doing well even without Harthill's backing.

But where he had once been her vocal benefactor, he now stymied her. He stalked her; he called her and breathed heavily into the phone when she answered. He threatened her. And he badmouthed her all over town.

With no other choice, Judith hit the road, going farther and farther away from him at every stop. She went from Louisville to Lexington, and then to Birmingham, Alabama. She would go anywhere they raced horses and where she was unlikely to run into him.

Finally, Judith learned she could be successful without Harthill or the paternal assistance of any man. On her own, she signed a contract to train for John Franks, one of the nation's most successful horse owners. She also picked up a bevy of Lexington-based breeders as clients. Eventually, Judith amassed a stable of fifteen horses of excellent quality, and she did it all compliments of her own salesmanship and training acumen. "I was doing great," she said.

But in the spring, Judith returned to Kentucky and discovered that Harthill had not forgotten her. In fact, he was waiting for her. When she arrived at Keeneland on business he had her arrested for "stealing" two tacky beanbag chairs she took with her when she moved out.

Harthill instructed the police to humiliate her and cuff her right in the secretary's office. The officers refused to comply, apprehending and cuffing her in private and leading her out discreetly. Nevertheless, the mere fact that she had been arrested at all for such a foolish complaint was testament to Harthill's power.

And it spoke volumes about the relative power of men and women.

Judith was mature and accomplished enough that she no longer had to hide behind a man to get clients. And yet it was still possible for a commanding male, like Harthill, to overwhelm her and push her around. He quite literally had the wherewithal to threaten her entire career.

Harthill's petty vengeance knew no bounds. He took the beanbag incident all the way to a courtroom. But it boomeranged on him. Listening to the testimony and the hair-raising stories of Harthill's behavior, the judge issued a restraining order against him. And just like that it was over. Harthill complied, and his constant threats were finally ended.

But Zouck was never really free of him. She was so utterly traumatized by the experience that many years later he still haunted her thoughts. That was true even after he had passed away. "One of my biggest fears," she said, "is that when I die, I am going to have to meet him again."

This brilliant and blemished doctor, this wild man, was the person to whom Buddy Delp turned for help on the biggest day and in the most desperate situation of his life.

There was only one little problem.

Harthill's ban from Belmont Park meant that it wouldn't be easy to get him to the Bid's stall. It would require a little skullduggery. Harthill was stuffed into the trunk of a car and smuggled to his patient like a Greek outfoxing the Trojans. He emerged from his dark and inglorious hiding place only when he was safely beside the Bid's barn.

Harthill examined the horse and treated him as only he could. But what he did for Spectacular Bid was known only to himself and God. He told no one else.

One former jockey who knew everybody in Spectacular Bid's circle well had a hypothesis. "Look," the jockey said, "nobody in racing will want to say that the horse was shot with painkillers, but Harthill was more than just a great vet; the guy was a fucking chemist."

Nobody knew Harthill better or disliked him more than Zouck did, but she denounced that theory as strenuously as she could. "Alex wouldn't do that," Judith said. "Alex would treat the horse with respect. I saw the good and the bad in Harthill, but he loved horses. He was a brilliant veterinarian. And never, ever, would he jeopardize a horse's health over something like that." But Judith knew better than anyone that Harthill sometimes hurt the things he loved.

And his own words suggested that his love of horses could be overstated. Once, speaking to a respected journalist about a trainer who was an old buddy, Harthill revealed where his real loyalties were. "[We] went way back," Harthill said. "If [he] had asked me to give [his horse] strychnine, I would have."

Harthill may have been exaggerating, but his point was crystal clear. There was absolutely nothing the good doctor wouldn't do to help out an old friend.

14 *A Fearful Ride*

Jacinto Vasquez and Buddy Delp sat together in the warmth of the morning light. It was Belmont day, and they watched the early races together, side by side, and chatted like the old friends that they were.

Amiable Jacinto had ridden for Buddy many times, going all the way back to the 1960s. They had the intimacy of two veterans who had heard and seen it all in the racing business, and they had no qualms about speaking to each other frankly. But what Buddy said to Jacinto that morning astonished the Panamanian. "Today," Buddy said, "I'm going to break Secretariat's record."

It was an absurd statement. Secretariat had won the Belmont by a staggering thirty-one lengths to set the track record. It was a performance that was unequaled in history.

Buddy's prediction was ridiculous but nevertheless fascinating. He was actually revealing his strategy, right there. In effect he was telling Jacinto precisely what his horse would do. He intended to have the Bid charge right out of the gate to the lead and then sprint the lengthy mile-and-a-half track in order to show that his horse was even faster than Secretariat.

Jacinto, who thought only of winning, couldn't wrap his mind around why Buddy would risk losing only to chase the ghost of a horse from the past. But Buddy had different considerations than mere victory, and ego and money were chief among them.

Winning the Triple Crown, and beating Secretariat's record, would enrich Buddy. The trainer was tied into Spectacular Bid's next business venture as a high-class horse gigolo. It was a forgone conclusion that Spectacular Bid would win the Triple Crown and make a great deal of money in syndication. But besting Secretariat was another matter. It would cement the Bid's reputation as the greatest racehorse of all time and take the price tag on his syndication to stratospheric levels.

Jacinto didn't care about any of that. He was all about sound racing strategies, and he knew a bad idea when he heard one. "Mr. Delp, listen," he said. "The day Secretariat raced and broke the [Belmont Stakes] record, the track was two, three seconds faster than it is today." Jacinto looked Buddy right in the eye and laid it on the line for him.

"You trying to do the same thing Secretariat did?" he said. "You never going to win the race."

"I'm going to win," Buddy repeated, "and I'm going to beat Secretariat."

"Bullshit!" Jacinto shot back. "They gonna catch your ass the last part of the race."

Jacinto knew what he was talking about. He was one of the few riders who had ever beat Secretariat, and he had done it on an undistinguished animal named Onion. Buddy, of course, did not heed the words.

And so that was how the day began, with a braggart boasting that he would torch the century's fastest racehorse with an animal that had just been Scotch-taped together by Dr. Harthill.

Meanwhile, Ronnie Franklin, the young man who was under tremendous pressure to actually ride that horse to victory, had a difficult day ahead of him. Besides the Belmont Stakes, Buddy had him scheduled to ride in the sixth race. Like the Belmont, the sixth was a one-and-a-half-mile race, so Buddy believed that riding in it would familiarize Ronnie with the track and especially its brutally long distance.

But Ronnie wouldn't be riding alone in the sixth race; his old tormentors from the Florida Derby, Angel Cordero and Georgie Velasquez, were scheduled to ride too. And it had been only three days since Angel had thumped Ronnie with his horse out on the same track. It was the Puerto Rican's retaliation for their war of words that had spun out of control. Cordero was still seething, and no one could say for sure what he might do.

Ronnie's mount, Seethreepeo, had been purchased at the same Kentucky yearling sale that had produced Spectacular Bid. He was named for the effete, gold-plated robot in *Star Wars*, but he was in a talent galaxy far, far away from the Bid. Nevertheless, he was a fine horse that had finished in the money in his last twelve straight races.

The sixth race was anything but easy for Franklin. He was bumped by both Cordero and Velasquez, and he was in no mood to take it. When the running was over, he confronted Cordero back in the relative privacy of the jockeys' room, and they almost came to blows again—this time, only a few moments before the Belmont Stakes.

The two riders got face to face in an aggressive posture. They shouted loud obscenities at each other as the other riders and the valets watched them express their blistering rage and mutual contempt. The unwitting audience looked on as the two riders thundered at each other, raining spittle, and becoming more aggressive. Finally, they were separated.

As they all appeared for the post parade, Spectacular Bid was a prohibitive favorite, but it would be no cakewalk. Instead of the paltry five-horse posse that Franklin and the Bid had faced at Pimlico for the Preakness, the Belmont featured ten hearty horses and riders. Flying Paster was gone, a victim of failed expectations. But a new challenger was there to take his place, a talented and well-rested horse named Coastal.

Coastal's owners and trainers had been indecisive. They took their time before deciding whether they would even enter him in the Belmont. Buddy Delp watched their deliberations with a great deal of interest. Although Buddy was a true believer in his own baloney about the Bid's being the greatest horse in the world, he also knew what Coastal could do. "Obviously this horse can run," Buddy said. "I wish he'd stay in the barn."

The highly regarded Coastal wasn't going to sneak up on anyone, yet his owners had much to consider before forking over the $20,000 entrance fee. First of all, like everyone else, he'd already lost to Spectacular Bid. At the World's Playground Stakes he'd finished seventeen and a half lengths behind the Bid.

But that was back when both horses were still only two-year-olds, and a lot had changed since then. For one thing, Coastal's 1979 schedule was leisurely. He'd had but three races for the entire year so far, and all were victories. One of them was the prestigious Peter Pan Stakes, also at Belmont Park, where Coastal had smoked a well-regarded field by thirteen lengths.

Even with his relatively breezy schedule Coastal had his bruises. His massive, almond-shaped right eye was ulcerated and had required surgery. After the operation he wore a special cup to shield the eye from further damage. It had only recently been discarded.

The Bid was surely as exhausted as Coastal was rested. Buddy had worked his star horse hard in 1979—some felt too hard. He was on a streak of twelve straight stakes victories. In the last year he had run sixteen races on twelve different tracks—a brutal pace.

The previous three weeks, in particular, had been torrid. Bid traveled to three different states—Kentucky, Maryland, and New York—to face the most formidable competition in the nation. In addition to the strain of the Triple Crown races, Buddy's training regimen included "blowouts," running his horse full speed during exercise to simulate racing conditions, something he did only days before both the Preakness and the Belmont Stakes.

In both blowouts the Bid had registered blistering speeds. These exercise sessions proved the health and vitality of the horse, but they took a lot out of the animal and should have required a period of recovery. For brutal Buddy, however, running hard was simply what a racehorse did. He saw no need for accommodation.

Despite Coastal's advantages, his team members were not at all confident that he could beat the Bid. They didn't make the final decision to enter their horse and pay the remainder of the supplemental fee until race day. Perhaps they should have felt a little better about their chances. After all, Coastal had a few things in common with Spectacular Bid. He, too, was Kentucky-bred with noble bloodlines. And like the Bid, he had an excellent trainer with Maryland roots.

Coastal's tutor was David Whiteley, the son of Frank Whiteley Jr., the difficult trainer who had once given Jacinto Vasquez so much grief about his Latin heritage. David wasn't considered to be as talented a trainer as his father, but he was a much calmer, more decent and polished man.

In high school, David had been a distinguished, even brilliant, student. He stood out at the prestigious McDonough School in North Baltimore, giving his father hopes that his son would pursue a more lucrative and less manic career than his own. He wanted David to study veterinary medicine. But David was adamant that he wanted to follow in the footsteps of his hero-father and train horses.

Frank continued to push his son toward college, but David held his ground and insisted that his father teach him the skills of a trainer. It was a father-son standoff that ended only when Frank pretended to give in. He agreed to take David on as an apprentice trainer but held a secret and ugly plan to get his kid back to school. "Dumb little son of a bitch," Frank told an old friend. "I'll work his ass to death."

Knowing how anxious his son was to please him, Frank kept him hopping all day long in the broiling summer sun. The work pace was so brutal that David finally collapsed one day near the exercise track in a pool of his own perspiration. The young man was rushed to the hospital, where he was diagnosed with exhaustion and dehydration. His dangerous situation had been created by his own father's secret agenda and misapplied love.

However harmful Frank's plan was, it worked. When David finally got well, he did indeed agree to go to college. He enrolled at the University of Maryland and studied alongside his boyhood friend, Jimmy Stewart.

Stewart's father, like Frank Whiteley, was a horse trainer, and Stewart was on track to be a veterinarian. The two boys had a lot in common—so much so that Jimmy couldn't help but compare himself to David and found himself wanting. "I had good grades," Stewart remembered, "but David had a 4.0. I took regular math, but David took math for engineers. I took French, but David took Russian. And he gets the 4.0."

In short, David easily had the intellectual ability for veterinary school or any other significant profession. But he went back to his dad and told him he wanted to quit school and resume his lessons in horse training.

Frank would still not relent. He sent David back to school, this time to George Washington University, which he perceived to be more challenging than Maryland. David got all A's there too, but he was done. At the end of the semester he asserted control over his own life, left school for good, and began his training career in earnest.

Because Frank Whiteley had such a singular and difficult personality and a legendary career, David was naturally compared to him. One jockey who rode for both father and son observed their striking differences. "I knew Frank; he was really, really a tough guy," Ruben Hernandez said. "He was the type of guy you sometimes hesitate to talk to because of the way he come about. He didn't lose his temper, but he always cuss a lot and he always talks tough. Sometimes, I like to approach him and ask him a question, but I hesitate to do it because I don't know what his reaction is going to be."

Ruben did not find David to be nearly as intimidating. "David Whiteley was a different guy, one of those very quiet guys," Ruben said. "He don't fool around. . . . It was black and white for him. He tell you the way he thinks, tell you what he wants, tell you the way things [are] supposed to be done. He know his business."

Hernandez appreciated David's straightforward approach, and David felt a rapport with Ruben. Perhaps that connection was why David chose Hernandez for Coastal, his prize colt, though he might have selected any one of the other, more celebrated, New York jockeys that he knew. David stuck with Hernandez, and the decision was a wise one since much of the horse's later success was attributed to the rider.

Ruben Hernandez was a gentle, genial, and likable man who had started on the path of a professional athlete in Panama City when he was only thirteen years old. One of his uncles, also a rider, saw his potential and enrolled him in a school for jockeys.

But before Ruben learned to ride, he was taught to be humble. He started out by working in the stables as a groom and a hot walker. "I did everything you're supposed to do in the backstretch," he said.

From there he followed a methodical path to becoming a full-fledged jockey. At age sixteen, he moved up to galloping and breezing horses. By eighteen, he was 5 feet tall and one hundred pounds, the ideal size for a rider. And he already had experience. With his perfect build and impeccable training, Hernandez appeared at the gate of Hippodromo

Presidente Remón, Panama's only race track, and obtained his professional license.

Hernandez led Panama's jockey standings for two and a half years. After four years, he already had more than four hundred professional victories. His early success amplified his talent and put him on the radar of others in the business. He was quickly approached by an American agent who urged him to ride in the States.

Hernandez saw the opportunity and agreed. He started out in Puerto Rico, but nothing there went his way. The week he arrived in San Juan, there was a jockeys' strike at El Comandante Race Track. The regular jockeys had stopped working because they were disgusted with men like Ruben who were coming in from the outside and taking the better mounts. So after two weeks without races, or paychecks, Ruben went right back to Panama. It would take him another year before he worked up the courage to leave home again.

In 1973 Ruben Hernandez arrived at Hialeah. He found Florida, with its large Latin populations, welcoming and comfortable. But as a young rider, he ran right into the same difficulties with the veterans that later plagued Ronnie Franklin. "The jockeys there began shutting me off all the time and keeping me from winning," Hernandez said.

Again, much like Ronnie, the veteran riders made it impossible for Ruben to ride on the inside. "I try to get through the holes," he said, "but they close up on me." His solution for opening up those closed holes lay in his fists. He was suspended again and again for fighting.

Not all the jockeys he met in the United States were hostile to him. That winter Hernandez was introduced to Angel Cordero and Georgie Velasquez. He would forge close, life-long friendships with both of them. That was especially true of Cordero. He had a vastly different opinion of the intense and high-strung Angel than others did. "[Angel] was a happy go lucky guy," Ruben said. "A very nice guy, very nice to me. He was funny, liked to joke around, all the good stuff."

Hernandez idolized Cordero and marveled at his skill but also appreciated his cerebral approach to riding. "Angel knew everything in riding horses from A to Z," Hernandez said. "He take the maximum ride of the horse. It doesn't matter if he ride a favorite or a 10–1 shot, you would see him riding with the same enthusiasm."

Ruben was a fine rider, too, and a winner in both Florida and New York. But he never grabbed the national spotlight like Cordero or Jacinto had. That was true even when Ruben was the leading stakes rider in New York. Instead, he was content to enjoy the reputation of a nice guy and the respect of those who knew him best. When he was instructed to list his hobbies for a questionnaire given to him by the track publicity department, he put but one item on his list: "My family."

And indeed, Ruben had one thing going for him at the Belmont that even Spectacular Bid's rider did not have, and that was a home-field advantage. No one knew Belmont better than he did. When the cold winds blew in off the Hudson River, guys like Cordero and Velasquez flew out to Florida. But Ruben was no snowbird. He spent his winters in the same place he spent his summers, and that was New York.

While Ronnie had his fitful night of sleep at the Plaza, Ruben was in his own bed next to his beautiful wife, Maria Isabella. In the morning, when he rose from that bed, Hernandez was well rested, comfortable, and happy. He didn't have any sorts of dreams or visions the night before. And for that matter, he was under no false illusions.

Hernandez arrived at Belmont Park much like everyone else, with the firm belief that Spectacular Bid would win the race and capture the Triple Crown. And he was fine with it. "Everybody thought that [Spectacular Bid] was tough to beat or unbeatable that day," Ruben said. "My feeling was that we were going to see another Triple Crown; I just wanted to be there to be a part of history."

Hernandez said he "didn't have any premonitions," but Maria Isabella was so confident of his victory that she lectured her husband, instructed him, to go slowly to the winner's circle. She planned to watch the race from the fourth floor, she told him, to get the best view of the action, so she reminded him that she would have a lengthy walk to meet him after it was over. "I want to be in that winner's circle photograph with you," she said.

Now all Ruben had to do to fulfill his wife's expectations was go out and pull off the biggest upset in modern racing history.

Ronnie's pressures and problems were a far cry from Ruben's domestic bliss. He went to the gates like one might go to the gallows. Cordero was out to get him; that was clear from their crash-car horses earlier in the week and even their jousting and aggressive arguing earlier that day. Angel had already demonstrated that he feared neither bodily risk nor authority. If he wanted to use his animal as a weapon and take a crack at Ronnie, he would do it right there in the Belmont Stakes. He had no qualms about destroying the Bid, putting Ronnie in danger, or, if necessary, risking his own neck. It was that simple.

Ronnie got a leg up into the irons knowing that the world was watching his every move. Expectations from the press and the fans were sky high. "I knew that the pressure was with him," Ruben said.

And then there was Buddy.

This was Delp's moment, his chance to sanctify his life and career. He'd literally emerged from the flames to arrive here. He had persevered through setbacks and tragedies that would have sidelined many lesser men. And now here he was, in this position and on this day, about to realize one of the hardest achievements in professional sports. If he succeeded, it would be a once-in-a-lifetime payday and respect. It always came back to respect.

But it all depended on Ronnie's ride, his ability to avoid trouble and coax victory from his hurting horse. Buddy often publicly disparaged Franklin's intelligence, and his view was that Franklin couldn't do much to win the race, but he could do an awful lot to lose it.

When Ronnie took the mount, Buddy Delp's dreams and aspirations went right along with the exhausted, frightened, and deeply troubled teenager draped, appropriately, in the black-and-blue silks.

All of the jockeys took their last instructions from their trainers just prior to the post parade, but Ronnie was different; he had the advice of many experts. Even Lucien Laurin, Secretariat's sainted trainer, knew just what the kid on the Bid should do. "I'd tell Franklin to put [Spectacular Bid] right on the lead and not fool around," Laurin said.

Buddy agreed, and his advice to Ronnie was elegant in its simplicity.

"Take 'em away," Buddy said, utilizing an old race track expression for running away from the pack.

Winning the Belmont meant every bit as much to Whiteley as the Triple Crown did to Buddy. He had fought his hard-bitten father for his right to be a trainer. Now he was on the biggest stage, on a tense day, with a fresh horse and a fine rider.

Whiteley was cool under fire, and his advice to Hernandez was tinged with humor. "I just want you to break good, and get a good position, and then you take it from there," Whiteley said. "I won't say anymore, because you pinheads don't listen anyway."

But pre-race, no one spoke louder than Spectacular Bid. He paraded to the post in a fashion uncustomary to him. He trotted on his toes, walked in diagonal lines, and showed copious amounts of foam at his haunches. His neck twitched so incessantly that he looked like a Tourette's patient. And he bit and chewed at the horse ponying him to the gate.

Bid was clearly in pain from his encounter with the business end of that safety pin. Whatever Dr. Harthill had done to help him, it clearly wasn't working.

"The Streets of New York" played in the background as all the other horses went calmly to the post. Except for the Bid's behavior there was little drama. The riders of note, and their horses, all loaded easily. Angel Cordero was on General Assembly, who went to gate number two. Ronnie and the Bid were loaded into gate five. The least likely horse to have a bearing on the result, Gallant Best, an 80–1 shot, went to the seventh position. Ruben Hernandez and Coastal were in number nine. And Mystic Era went to gate ten, Georgie Velasquez up.

In the split second after all the horses were loaded and before the gates opened and the powerful animals unleashed, all that could be heard in the hushed track were the Latin riders shouting to each other in Spanish at breakneck speed. And then there was the startling and satisfying sound of the steel gates opening all at once and locking into place.

Ronnie and Bid, following Buddy's orders, exploded out of the gate. Right from the get-go they were in the pack of leaders. It was a sign that Franklin's ride would be unusual, far different from his work at either the

Kentucky Derby or the Preakness. In those races he had been content to hang back a good distance and patiently wait for his moment. But here, in the longest race, where patience was rewarded unlike at any other track, Ronnie and the Bid were hot on the heels of the long shot.

Gallant Best was in the lead at the first turn and setting a blazing pace. And that was precisely what Buddy had hoped to see. Ronnie, just as he was instructed to do, stalked the leader. He hung close to Gallant Best as they galloped around the backstretch, and then he exhorted the Bid to make a decisive move. "Let's go, Big Daddy!" he said.

As the horse catapulted himself forward, the rider's black-and-blue silks blurred and streaked across the New York air, and the Bid's mane caught the breeze and stood up on the back of his neck, and it looked like jagged flames.

At first, overtaking Gallant Best was an intense pleasure, an exhilaration unlike any other. But it wasn't long before a certain hollowness set in. Ronnie had spent a lot of horse, very early in the race, chasing a competitor who had no chance to win.

The fans groaned as they could only imagine the fuel spilling from the Bid's tank. Meanwhile, Cordero was many lengths off the action but still a factor. He paid close attention to Ronnie, and when the Bid made his move, so did he. Angel whipped General Assembly and the colt perked up, came alive, and was, for a moment at least, a worthy son to Secretariat. General Assembly's reddish chestnut hue became more orange-vibrant as it glinted in the sun, and he strained to give Cordero everything that he had, which was ample.

About three-quarters of the way down the backstretch Cordero masterfully guided General Assembly to the rail, and he actually closed the gap on Spectacular Bid. Angel menaced Ronnie by coming closer and kept the pressure on him. The Bid was forced to run at his highest speed for a protracted period. And he was still a long way from the wire.

And then the Bid labored. It was as if he were carrying all of the dysfunctions of his team like lead weights. The bloat of the addictions and the moral failings were all aboard the fabulous colt just as surely as the jockey was, and it was finally too much for even the Bid to bear.

But the heaviest burden of all was the delicate psychology of the

105-pound rider. His chemical dependencies, anxieties, and stresses were weighing him down, and his body appeared limp and exhausted. Right there on that horse with Franklin was all the money he'd lost to cocaine and poker pots. Riding Franklin's back as surely as he was riding the Bid were the little baggies of pills and powder, the whores, the letters and calls form threatening lawyers, and the little boy who looked so much like him but whom he didn't even know. There was also the rage and racist taunts, Angel's death threats and pranks, the fights, Buddy's insults and expectations, and the press that printed only the half of it.

It was all too much for even the greatest horse to ever look through a bridle. And it all seemed to coalesce right there in the throbbing toothache that was the Bid's left forehoof.

Ronnie could see Cordero gaining on him like a conquistador, and he pushed the Bid harder. But as the boy and his steel gray made their way around the far turn, the finish seemed hundreds of miles away.

Ronnie believed that the Bid refused to change his leads, a consequence of the mishap in the stall, and he felt the horse labor and huff beneath him. Cordero's horse was every bit as much spent as Ronnie's, and General Assembly slowed and fell off the pace.

In the backstretch Coastal looked like a goner, dead on arrival. He was a distant fourth, and even Whiteley believed that it was over. He was simply too far behind to catch a great horse like the Bid even on his worst day.

Ruben alone kept the faith. He knew Belmont as well or better than any rider, and he knew that it was finally time to make his charge. Cordero's now plodding animal blocked Coastal's path forward, but the fierce competitor inside of Angel must have been fast asleep because he moved to the right as gently as if he were riding a lamb in a baby's dream.

Cordero gave up his own position to make a wide and comfortable inside lane for Coastal. As Ruben passed him, Cordero smiled and became a cheerleader. "*Alcánzalo!*" Angel shouted to his friend. "Go get him."

Ronnie hugged the rail with no intention of yielding an inch, but in his panic and zeal to revive the Bid he furiously whipped with his left hand, moving his horse ever so slightly to the right. And that created the small sliver of light Ruben had hoped to see. It was a tiny, danger-ous crevice, but Ruben urged Coastal to charge through it confidently.

It was his to take.

Clothed in the flaxen silks of Coastal's owners, Ruben disappeared into the black hole and then reemerged, streaking out of the darkness like yellow starlight, beams and particles bent by gravity and propelling through space.

Ruben charged right past the suddenly inconsequential Bid, gaining confidence with every stride. He actually opened a lead on the great horse, and the humiliation of that reality dazed both Franklin and his colt. From Middleburg to that moment they had never experienced anything like it, and before they could contemplate the enormity of it, it happened again. Golden Act slipped past them too, but on the right. Wily Sandy Hawley crossed the finish line a mere neck ahead of Ronnie and the great Spectacular Bid.

The sight of it, the unexpected deflation and crushing disappoint-ment, reduced Teresa Meyerhoff to tears. She buried her face in her hands and softly said, "No, no, no."

The sadness of the Meyerhoffs, the Delps, and Ronnie was a stark relief to the elation of the Whiteleys. Ruben maintained his composure. True to the promise he'd made Maria Isabella in the morning, he went to the winner's circle as slowly as he possibly could. When the outrider picked him up, he blew a puff of air and said, "Let my horse relax." All the while he was thinking about his wife, the woman who had so much confidence in him.

Like Coastal, Maria Isabella was swift enough to make it to the win-ner's circle right on time. She stood beside her husband as the shutter clicked on a moment that lasted for both only a fraction of a second and for all time.

While Ruben was praised on national television for his daring and skillful ride, Franklin dismounted and suffered the horror and humil-iation of a far different experience as he strode off in the direction of the jockeys' room. The fans and bettors beheld his small, defeated form and loudly taunted him. Their profane jeers and debris combined and rained down upon his helmeted head like a wintry mix.

Franklin used gallows humor to deflect the sting of his low moment. "Don't nobody stand too close to me," he said. "I might get plucked off."

Someone wanted to take him out all right, but not with bullets. In the jockeys' room a jubilant Angel was celebratory, even exultant. It was a peculiar posture for the most intensely competitive man in racing, considering he had just finished seventh in a field of ten on a horse that had the best blood lines in the race.

Angel enjoyed Franklin's and Spectacular Bid's disgrace as if it were his own glorious victory. His antics hogged the spotlight from both the day's winner and the devastated favorite who had lost.

Cordero seized the opportunity to train Ronnie in his sights and shoot devastating barbs right at him. Angel grabbed the microphone to the PA system and bellowed into it in thick Spanish locutions. In the guise of addressing his friend Hernandez, he took Ronnie apart like a roaster. "Ruben, Ruben, you make all the spics happy!" Angel shouted with glee. "All of the spics love you, Ruben. The spics in New York, the spics in Puerto Rico, the spics in Florida, the spics in Minnesota, the spics in California. All of them love you, Ruben!"

And then Angel turned his venom on Spectacular Bid himself. "I tole you," he shouted, "no horse is unbeatable. Every turkey has his Thanksgiving."

Back at the stalls Delp, the braggart, was subdued. Deprived of the victor's champagne, he gulped a working man's beer and spoke to the greatest of American sportswriters in a self-pitying tone. "[Ronnie] ran a perfect race," Buddy told Red Smith. "I got beat, that's all. Tomorrow's another day."

No one on the Bid's team mentioned anything about the safety pin. Not a single word. In his post-race interviews, Ronnie alluded to the fact that the horse had been unsound but never said a word about his bad hoof. "He choked, he couldn't get his breath," the young jockey told reporters, implying that there was blood in the Bid's lungs. "I noticed it as we were coming into the stretch. He wasn't right. I had a lot of horse at the beginning, but when I asked him to respond, he didn't."

It was a lie that he would later disavow.

To the outside world Ronnie was the one who had choked, chasing a huge long shot and tiring out his horse.

The real controversy didn't start until Buddy and the Bid were back in Baltimore. That's when the trainer finally told everyone about the safety pin. But in New York, Dr. Manuel Gilman, the veterinarian for the New York Racing Association, disputed everything. "The horse was checked at 8:30 a.m. Saturday," Gilman said. "He was sound then. He was sound going into the race, he was sound coming out of the race. He was sound when he left here this morning."

In fact, very few people in racing bought into Buddy's story. In Middleburg, where they knew the horse, the trainer, and the jockey all too well, everyone believed it was a lie. The backstretch workers in Baltimore thought it was a lie too. But nobody was more skeptical than the Latino riders; to a man they thought it was *mierda*, horseshit, a way of deflecting shame and robbing Ruben of the glory.

"If [Spectacular Bid] step on a nail and he sorry about it, he won't lead all the way to the sixteenth pole," Angel Cordero reasoned. "The sixteenth pole is the only time the horse remember that he step on a nail."

"He didn't step on no pin," Jacinto said. "Is a bunch of bullshit."

"Spectacular Bid's safety pin," Ruben Hernandez said more succinctly than anyone, "was Coastal."

The Meyerhoffs were devastated by the loss and blamed Cordero's intimidation tactics for their young jockey's poor ride and ultimately their horse's defeat. "[Ronnie] was scared Cordero was going to go after him," Tom Meyerhoff said. "And he responded by getting away from the field."

Ruben Hernandez saw it that way too. "Franklin got Cordero on his mind all the time," Ruben said, "and I know it."

But it was Jacinto Vasquez who knew the real reason behind the bizarre ride. He knew why the boy had chased the long shot and unwisely burned up his horse out there. "He just do what his trainer tell him to do," Jacinto said.

But fear did play a role in Ronnie's devastating loss; it just wasn't what everyone thought. Cordero could not intimidate Franklin. It simply wasn't in Ronnie's nature to fear any man in a fight. Ronnie could deal with hate, but love was another story.

Buddy Delp had come to mean everything to him. Pleasing Buddy was all cocaine and good times. Letting Buddy down meant enduring an incredible wrath and a free ticket back to Dundalk to be a nobody and a nothing.

"I wasn't afraid of Cordero," Ronnie Franklin said in a highly secret moment. "I was afraid of Buddy Delp."

15 *Moving On*

Spectacular Bid was back in Baltimore, tired and sore. His hoof ached thanks to both his mishap with the safety pin in his New York stall and the pounding the sore hoof had taken in the Belmont.

Dr. Harthill had treated Spectacular Bid before the race on Saturday, sneaking into Belmont Park in the trunk of a car because he was banned from the premises. But on Sunday he drove right through the gates of Pimlico like the eminence that he was. He'd come at Buddy Delp's request to operate on the horse's hurt foot, but his back still ached from his clandestine journey on Saturday morning. Instead of operating on the Bid himself, he oversaw Buddy Delp's talented day-to-day veterinarian, Jimmy Stewart.

Dr. Stewart was a young man, still in his thirties, but he and Harthill had known each other for many years. They had first met when Stewart was a boy. Young Jimmy had bought a pony to train and resell, but the animal developed navicular disease and was lame. As a special favor to Jimmy's father, a trainer, Harthill came to Jimmy's house and treated the ailing pony as though it was a top thoroughbred and not the prized pet of a child. Afterward Stewart's grateful mother invited the hero-veterinarian to a hot, home-cooked meal.

After dinner, while she cleared the table, Mrs. Stewart tentatively asked Harthill, "What do we owe you?" The good doctor took out his pad and pen and wrote up a bill. He tore it out and handed it to her.

"Paid in full," it said, "for services rendered to Mrs. Stewart for a wonderful dinner."

That was the Harthill that young Jimmy Stewart knew, a kindly and generous genius who would give his valuable time to a concerned child, save a horse's life, and charge nothing for it. Other people may have had their problems with Harthill, but Dr. Stewart admired him, felt affection for him, and was eager to work with him.

When Harthill arrived at Pimlico, Stewart had already taken pictures of Spectacular Bid's injured foot and had the X-rays in hand.

"What do you think?" Harthill asked before looking, a sign of deference to an "equal."

"Well, I haven't had him out of the stall yet," Stewart responded.

So the two vets took the famous horse out of his stall and jogged him on the blacktop. They observed his movements and then looked at each other. The Bid clearly appeared lame to both of them. Stewart applied pressure to the affected hoof and found a sensitivity in the specific area of the wound but still could not see any visual evidence of it.

Based on the X-rays and his own pressure test, Dr. Stewart knew where to go, and he cut a small, curved opening on the hard surface of the hoof. Harthill, nursing his aching back, looked on and supervised him. There was no liquid inside the incision. That told the two doctors that there was no abscess.

Stewart cut farther, and a millimeter or two down he saw a spot. He continued on until he could finally see the pin's distinct path. The small, sharp metal had made its way about a quarter of an inch down, all the way to the bottom of the horse's sole. Fortunately the path stopped just above the laminae, where there would have been a far greater possibility of infection and a threat to the horse's mortality. Instead, he could see that the pin had hit the coffin bone, causing it to take a sharp right turn.

Stewart cleaned out the area and prescribed the appropriate medications to ensure against the possibility of a post-operation infection. And just like that, the traumatized hoof that had changed racing history was addressed, and Spectacular Bid was on the mend.

Ronnie Franklin had injuries resulting from the pursuit of the Triple

Crown too, but his weren't so easy to see or treat. The complex young man was physically and mentally exhausted. He had been publicly criticized all over the country for his supposedly poor ride in the Belmont. But it wasn't until he went out to Southern California to participate in an all-star event and get some rest that the public got a glimpse of his biggest problems.

Taking a day off from work, Ronnie met up with California-based relatives to go to Disneyland. But instead of enjoying an idyllic and innocent day inside the park filled with innocent childhood icons, he and some of his cousins hung back in the car.

There, in the parking lot of the "Happiest Place on Earth" Ronnie took out a glass surface and a razor blade and a little baggy of white powder. He poured the powder onto the glass and used the blade to chop it up into fine particles.

The young jockey was dealing with his stress and unwinding just the way he'd learned to do it back at Buddy's house in old Laurel. But just then, a security guard happened by and saw what was happening. He knocked on the window, and just like that an era was over. Franklin was arrested on the spot, and in an instant his public image as a likable young man was irretrievably shattered.

Cocaine possession in California was serious business, a felony. But even worse than that was the onslaught of negative publicity. Newspapers from coast to coast carried the story, many accompanied by harsh commentaries that piled on the troubled kid and detailed how unpopular he was in the jockeys' room and throughout racing.

Ronnie wasn't the only coke user in Spectacular Bid's inner circle, but he was forced to stand in the harsh glare all by himself. Nobody stood up to protect him.

When the press turned to Buddy Delp for answers, the trainer's initial impulse was to disavow his protégé. He talked about how unintelligent Ronnie was and how untruthful. He told the press that Ronnie was indefinitely "suspended" from riding any of his horses. And in particular he would be replaced on Spectacular Bid. And then there was the usual Delp-blabber about the foot-in-ass corporal punishment he would mete out as soon as he and Ronnie were in the same room.

Few if any journalists pressed Delp to find out how extensive Ronnie's drug use was. Many merely accepted Buddy's explanations that he didn't know anything about the problem. In the meantime, Buddy spent twenty-four hours a day, seven days a week, with the kid. How could he not know?

No one asked that question.

Incredibly it was Delp, and not the media, who adeptly shaped the narrative of the story. Although Buddy had introduced Ronnie to cocaine and indulged in it himself, side by side with both Ronnie and his own teenage son Gerald, he feigned surprise by the arrest and claimed ignorance of the entire culture of cocaine. "I don't know about that stuff [cocaine]," Buddy said, "but Ronnie tells me it was a quarter of a gram. I don't condone fooling with it."

Buddy utilized these lies to insulate and distance himself from the drugs. He made use of his crude but effective oratorical skills to rehabilitate Ronnie's image. He called the kid "a victim of circumstance" and said that the boy was targeted only because he was a celebrity. "I don't think he would have been arrested," Buddy said, "if he weren't Ronnie Franklin. I don't think anybody would have made much of it if there had just been a bunch of teenage kids [in the car doing drugs]."

Before making any statement to the press, Ronnie conferred with Delp. When he finally spoke up, he didn't spill his guts about the world of drugs he lived in (and paid for) at Delp's house. He didn't mention the fact that he had seen Harry Meyerhoff smoking a joint. And he didn't breathe a word about the pervasive drug culture he saw in the jockeys' room at the track more generally. He merely humbly said, "I've never used the stuff before."

The media might have readily accepted these gross deceptions, but around Laurel and Pimlico's stables they knew better. Ronnie's old colleagues derisively referred to him as "the Cocaine Kid." The backstretch workers all knew that Buddy and Ronnie were vastly different than the public's sterling image of them as a fresh-faced kid and a paternalistic trainer.

In the weeks that followed, Delp created even more fiction. He said that at his direction Ronnie was living under a stringent-discipline structure. He claimed that Gerald was keeping an eye on Ronnie. He also said the jockey was subject to an early curfew that required him to go straight home after work each evening and then stay in for the night. And finally, Buddy discussed the fiscal discipline that he imposed on Ronnie. He explained that he allowed the boy only a $50 to $60 a week "allowance" while he looked after the rest of the kid's considerable earnings for safekeeping.

In all these ways Buddy created the image that he was caring for a young man too hardened and ignorant to care for himself. Ronnie's troubles, Buddy suggested, all happened when he was beyond Delp's gaze and outside the protective walls of his home. And yet the truth was more or less the opposite of that.

Buddy's house was the place where Ronnie had been introduced to cocaine and where its use was perpetuated. Fans didn't know that Gerald wasn't keeping an eye on Ronnie; he was the jockey's middleman to the illicit and provided him the pills and the coke that the two boys, and often Buddy, happily indulged in together. No one knew that Ronnie's money wasn't really protected; it was evaporating. Ronnie's paychecks were helping to fuel the good-times engine—the coke, the booze, and the pills enjoyed by everyone in the house.

Removing Ronnie from Spectacular Bid and replacing him with the unassailable Willie Shoemaker was another measure taken, supposedly in the boy's best interest. Ostensibly it relieved Franklin of the pressures that had caused the drug use, though the official story was that Ronnie didn't use drugs. But it wasn't really Buddy who removed Ronnie from the Bid, and it wasn't for Ronnie's benefit. In fact, behind the scenes, Delp lobbied Harry Meyerhoff to keep Franklin on the famous horse.

It was Harry Meyerhoff who was adamant that Ronnie be replaced on the Bid. The owner was the one who decided it was time to move on from the teenage jockey.

Harry wasn't protecting Ronnie in any sense. By making the change, he was looking after the best interests of his prize horse, his huge investment in his racing operation, and his own image.

Meyerhoff blamed Ronnie for the loss at the Belmont, believing that it was the boy's fear of Cordero that had blown the race. But mostly he didn't want to be associated with the kid's drug use. He and Teresa were recreational drug users too, and the last thing they needed was any scrutiny applied to themselves.

As usual Harry's instincts were right on the money. Ronnie's removal from the Bid was a public relations stroke for the owners, who appeared concerned and compassionate, and it reduced their exposure should Ronnie's problems flare up again and erupt into the public sphere. Even in a competitive sense, it was a net gain. Though Spectacular Bid had run exceptionally well for Ronnie, with Shoemaker aboard the horse would be in the most capable hands in racing.

Ronnie's parents might have stepped in at this point, but they were at a loss as to what to do. As they considered what was in the best interests of their son, they saw nothing but bad options in front of them. Ronnie wasn't easy to manage even when he was living right under their roof. By this point, however, he was utterly emancipated. He hadn't lived with his mother and father on a full-time basis for years, since he was fifteen. And now he was a national celebrity, making a lot more money than they were. It wasn't plausible to think that they could simply order him home and that he would comply. They also had to consider what Ronnie's life would look like without Buddy's patronage. He'd probably be back in his parents' basement and putting on his old Roy Rogers uniform.

It simply wasn't going to happen.

The Franklins might have considered confronting Buddy directly, but what good would that have done their son? Rocking that boat only meant alienating Ronnie's best hope for a career and a future. Buddy might have been the source of his problems, but he was also Ronnie's fount of opportunity.

Anyway, it wasn't the Franklins' nature to question authority. At root they were Dundalkians, and like their steelworker neighbors, who were utterly devoted to the plant that killed a thousand of them, the Franklins understood a workplace to be a dangerous and toxic environment by its very nature. They believed in the redemptive quality of hard work and in the chain of command. "I never had no dreams of being nothing until I came to a race track," Ronnie said. And that's the way his parents saw it, too.

As the memory of the Disneyland episode faded, Ronnie went back to work for Buddy, riding many of the trainer's other horses, but nothing was the same. Ronnie was no longer a big star, and his many remarkable accomplishments were now viewed skeptically, through the lens of his fishy loss at the Belmont, his drug arrest, and his many lesser scandals.

Teenager Stevie Cauthen's daring rides on Affirmed made him a media darling and pitch man for American Express. Ronnie was quickly becoming an untouchable, a pariah.

Despite Buddy's best efforts to paint Franklin as wiser, chastened, and more mature, the kid was in fact descending into a devastating addiction. Getting high, using cocaine, drinking to excess, and gulping pills were all a regular part of his life, and worse than that, the drugs had become a necessity that he could no longer do without.

But if insobriety was Buddy Delp's negative legacy to Ronnie, it wasn't the only one. Buddy (and especially Barbara Graham) had made Ronnie a jockey, and a damn good one. But working so closely with Delp, Ronnie picked up his mentor's swaggering arrogance. It was, to say the least, off-putting to the other trainers the kid hoped to court as clients.

Mark Reid was one of them. He was initially excited to have the famous young jockey ride horses for his up-and-coming stable, but that feeling quickly wore off. After one race that didn't go particularly well, Ronnie came back to the paddock and complained about the colt. "This horse ain't much," Ronnie sputtered. "He stinks."

Reid was put off by the unwanted feedback. "He sounded like a little carbon copy of Buddy Delp," the trainer said.

It wasn't a compliment.

"I didn't like [Buddy]," Reid said, "so why would I like [Ronnie]?" After that, Reid didn't use Ronnie very much.

While Ronnie struggled, Spectacular Bid reemerged in grand style. After an almost three-month layoff to recover and rest, he made his debut under Willie Shoemaker at Delaware Park and issued a warning that his historic run of dominance was far from over.

In an allowance race the Bid crushed the field by seventeen lengths. After it was all over, Shoemaker was almost as free with the superlatives as Buddy. "He's as great as any horse I've ever ridden," said the man who had ridden more winners than any jockey in history. After that auspicious start, Bid and Shoemaker won the Marlboro and Meadowlands Cups, defeating Coastal in both races. For some, those victories had only proven Ronnie's ineptitude and reinforced the notion that a "competent" rider like Shoemaker on Spectacular Bid would have more expertly negotiated the demanding Belmont track and won the Triple Crown with ease.

That theory would get its real test in October, when the Bid returned to Belmont Park for the Jockey Gold Cup. The one-and-a-half-mile contest had the feel of a match race. It pitted Spectacular Bid against Affirmed, though the four-horse race also included Gallant Best, whom no one took seriously as a challenger, and Coastal.

The Jockey Gold Cup was a highly prestigious race, all the more so since it would almost certainly determine if Affirmed or Spectacular Bid was the "Horse of the Year." That title was, in a sense, meaningless since it was decided by committee and not on the track, but it also carried serious financial repercussions. The "Horse of the Year" designation would certainly command top breeding fees for the winning horse's owners and trainer.

This race crackled with historical import, and though there were four horses in it instead of two, it was reminiscent of Seabiscuit versus War Admiral in the Pimlico Special. Both the Bid and Affirmed were healthy and at the peak of their athletic greatness. They both had elite riders aboard, Laffit Pincay, a future Hall of Famer, on Affirmed, and Shoemaker, the all-time earnings leader and widely acclaimed as the greatest rider of all time, on Spectacular Bid.

Affirmed was trained by Laz Barrera. A Cuban American then in his early sixties, Laz had the feel of a much older man with his leathery, sun-beaten face and a long, zipper-like trail on his chest, a battle scar and badge of honor for having survived major heart surgery.

Barrera was born in Havana in 1924, one of twelve children of a jockey and his French-missionary wife. Laz was the ninth child and one of four boys who all grew up to be horse trainers.

Laz showed a great deal of intelligence and maturity, not to mention skill, at an early age. He started his career at Cuba's Oriental Park, when he was only sixteen years old. Looking for more lucrative markets, he soon moved on to Mexico and won his first five races there. Nevertheless, he was suspended when officials realized he was still under twenty-one, below the minimum age for a licensed trainer in Mexico.

Barrera came to the United States in 1948, but success didn't come easy. He soldiered on in obscurity for many years in the country, training claimers and lesser-known horses for decades. Finally, in the 1970s, he met a man who changed his life. Barrera was hired by Louis Wolfson, an enormously successful, though questionable, financier. Wolfson had made a fortune but had done so by pioneering hostile corporate takeovers, and he eventually spent time in jail for his business practices.

But to Laz Barrera, Wolfson was a deliverer, and the two proved a great combination.

Working for Wolfson, Barrera finally had access to a better class of horses, and he made up for lost time. With Wolfson's stock, Laz's skills finally became evident to the wider world. He won the Eclipse Award for outstanding American trainer, a career achievement for most others, but he won it four years in a row, from 1976 to 1979. From 1977 to 1986 he was America's leading money winner five times. Over the course of his long career Laz would ultimately train 128 different stakes winners.

Affirmed, of course, was the greatest achievement of the Barrera-Wolfson partnership. Not only had the horse won the Triple Crown, proving his great worth, but he had demonstrated the qualities of a pugilist with a granite jaw in his hotly contested series with Alydar.

Anticipation for the Jockey Gold Cup was enhanced by the contrasting styles of the two protagonists. The race featured Affirmed's will to win versus Spectacular Bid's record-breaking speed. Though it had only been a few months since Coastal had whipped the Bid on the very same Belmont track, that was regarded as a rare misstep, an anomaly in Spectacular Bid's otherwise almost flawless career. No one seriously considered the possibility that either Affirmed or the Bid would not win the cup.

The parade to the post reinforced that notion. Bid looked well rested, calm, and confident under Shoemaker; there was no sign of his lathery and manic jig to the starter's gate back in June before his ill-fated Belmont ride. Affirmed, of course, with his rich red coloring, high haunches, and calm demeanor, looked like a king.

Shoemaker would start the race with one advantage. Angel Cordero and Georgie Velasquez were in attendance, but they weren't on the track. They were safely tucked in to the broadcast booth, where they could do no mischief. So unlike Franklin, Shoemaker would have it relatively easy; he'd have *only* the great Affirmed to deal with and not the malignant, coordinated attentions of Cordero and Velasquez.

All four horses loaded with ease, but they didn't all break that way. When the gates opened, Affirmed asserted himself. He took the lead from his very first step. The Bid, on the other hand, emerged tentatively, maybe even stumbling slightly. In the run to the first turn everyone was packed tightly together, though Affirmed led all the horses while Bid was in third. They got to the first quarter in twenty-five seconds. When the pack rounded the first turn, Affirmed was still setting the pace, but Gallant Best, the long shot, was behind him by only a neck.

Shoemaker, interestingly, took a very different approach than Ronnie Franklin had. Ronnie made it his business to find the outside. He'd gotten into trouble riding in the interior spaces, and he believed that the Bid didn't like to run inside. In any event, Franklin's reasoning was that the Bid crushed the best horses in the country and didn't need to save fractions of seconds.

Shoemaker, on the other hand, clung to the inside, not hugging the rail exactly, but not fighting his way out either. This left him boxed in. Two horses were directly in front of him, one was to his right, and to his left was the rail. He appeared as he always did: cool and unconcerned, in command. He looked as though he was biding his time until his opportunity appeared.

Affirmed, still the leader, reached the half-mile in forty-nine seconds, a slow pace. No one was pushing him, so he enjoyed the lead, and at the same time he didn't have to expend too much of himself to maintain it.

The four great animals went into the heart of the backstretch still running as a pack. When Shoemaker finally found his opening, he moved to the outside. Ruben Hernandez, looking like a canary in his feathery yellow silks, carefully watched Shoemaker, and when the Bid moved, he exhorted Coastal to also make his move.

For a long while Affirmed showed the fight for which he was famous. Spectacular Bid pushed him from the outside, but Pincay kept his horse moving at a lively pace, and he stayed in front, his lead never diminishing to less than a neck.

Meanwhile, Ruben and Coastal may have been overlooked, but they were about to prove that they were still relevant. With Ruben's coaxing, Coastal moved inside, hugged the rail, and made a determined charge. It seemed like a good gambit, the right move at the right time. Coastal's strides were long and fluid, and he gobbled up the gap between himself and the leaders.

As the race neared the second turn, Coastal and Ruben crashed the party. The white streak that looked like it had been painted with a broad brush down Coastal's long face emerged right between Affirmed and the Bid. At first, it was a mere flash of white, peeking out, but then horse and rider impudently pushed their way in front of the two favorites who had, foolishly, been concerned only with each other.

This bold move had forced Coastal into the conversation, but Ruben had clearly expended too much horse, too early, and the burst for the lead was an impressive but unsustainable business model. Even worse, Coastal's gunning for the lead only awakened his ferocious competitors. Only a few strides into the homestretch Spectacular Bid and Affirmed quickened their heels.

Despite his dissipations, Coastal gamely hung in far down the stretch and remained within striking distance. He kept it a three-horse race that was as unexpected as it was thrilling. But eventually Affirmed and Spectacular Bid came to their senses and restored order by picking up the pace to a point that poor, proud Coastal had no choice but to fade.

Everyone had come to Belmont Park to see the duel between the two superhorses, and there it was in the homestretch, stride for stride and neck and neck. But it was Affirmed who maintained a slight lead.

Typically, leading too early at Belmont was considered a poor strategy, as it had been in Franklin's disaster. Yet in this race the pace was so slow that Affirmed was still sprightly heading to the finish. Meanwhile,

Spectacular Bid had the burden of making up ground. He simply couldn't do it. In the last electrifying moments Affirmed pulled away ever so slightly and won by less than a length.

It had been an incredibly suspenseful race, filled with dramatic twists and tension.

After it was over, Buddy had the temerity to criticize Shoemaker's ride. "Anytime *you let* Affirmed go . . . a half mile in forty-nine seconds there's no horse in the world that's going to beat him," Buddy said.

Delp also proved, once again, that he was a poor loser when he refused the victors their due. "The best horse finished second," Buddy said.

Perhaps Delp genuinely saw the flaws in Shoemaker's ride, but it might well have been frustration and disappointment doing the talking. The loss, as close and exciting as it was, cost him dearly. Affirmed won "Horse of the Year," not Spectacular Bid. And Laz Barrera was named Trainer of the Year, not Delp.

All of those negative consequences were due only to a thin-margin loss at the Jockey Gold Cup. In fact, Bid's year had not only been historic; it had also been epic. Besides the broken track records and the Kentucky Derby and Preakness victories, his streak of twelve straight stakes victories (all but two with Ronnie Franklin aboard) was an accomplishment matched only by Citation and Man o' War. In addition to all of that, the Bid had won almost $1.3 million in purse money, more than any horse ever had for a single year.

Buddy might have been a braggart, but he had a hell of a case for much of what he claimed. If the voters for "Horse of the Year" couldn't see it, the public certainly could. When Affirmed retired, rather than risk injury or tarnish on his record, Spectacular Bid was left as the marquee name in horse racing. And he was in high demand everywhere high-profile horse races were run.

Buddy Delp wasn't an oil millionaire, but like Jed Clampett before him, he decided that California was the place he ought to be. It wasn't Buddy's way to load up some junker and go; he went to Beverly Hills decked out in a chartered DC-8 at a cost of nearly $70,000. That plane carried Buddy, twenty-four horses, Gerald and Dougie, Ronnie Franklin, exercise rider R. A. Smith, Charlie Bettis (an assistant trainer), a domestic worker who cooked and cleaned, and the family dog, Champ, to Los Angeles.

Something else snuck its way onto that private flight, something that Buddy was probably hoping to leave back in Baltimore: Ronnie and Gerald's problems were all aboard too. Both boys had moved far beyond casual drug-user status and were showing the serious signs of addiction.

Removing Ronnie from Spectacular Bid and taking him out west might have relieved pressure on him, as Buddy would suggest, but it also allowed the kid a shadow in which to operate. Without the media scrutiny or even his parents close by, his worst impulses were given free rein.

Buddy rented a home in Arcadia, California, that was the western version of the Delp house back in Laurel. Gerald and Ronnie shared a room, just as they did in Maryland, and they continued to live like libertines. "On the weekends we'd get some dates and we'd get some blow," Gerald said.

By this time Ronnie and Gerald had little if anything to do with Spectacular Bid, and yet their behavior distracted Buddy and threatened the horse's success.

Gerald was only sixteen years old, but he often passed for a full-grown man. He was tall and thin with a thick head of brown hair. He also dressed above his years. Gerald didn't wear athletic garb like most of the boys his age. He looked like a successful-but-relaxed businessman in dress shirts and shoes, nice slacks, and sport jackets. The illusion of his maturity was more than skin deep. Despite his bad grammar, Gerald spoke knowledgeably about adult subjects and had an expert's understanding of everything that happened at the track or in the barns. He knew all the players in the racing business—at least in and around Maryland—and he was already in training to be a jockey's agent. And he had plenty of money to splash around.

There was a lot of benefit in all of this for Gerald. He walked into any bar he wanted without being "carded" and romanced women far older than he was. But for Buddy the boys' growing independence and experimentation was a complication, a distraction from his burgeoning career.

Buddy's work was becoming more demanding and complex at the

same time the boys' issues were begging for his attention. Meanwhile, Delp was in the midst of his window of opportunity. This collision of fatherhood and work responsibility came into sharp focus for Buddy the evening before the Santa Anita Handicap. It was Bid's first high-profile West Coast race. It included a rematch with Flying Paster, and it was projected to be on an extraordinarily wet and sloppy track.

None of those details stopped either boy from going out the night before the race and finding enough trouble to drive the indulgent Buddy to his breaking point.

Ronnie hopped behind the wheel of a rented car and picked up a girl. But by the end of the night he was driving alone and drunk when he hit something and blew out one of his front tires. He stopped on the side of the road to try and repair the damage. A police officer pulled over to assist him.

Two things immediately grabbed the lawman's notice. Number one: Ronnie was visibly inebriated. And number two: the boy had already had an earlier accident in which he had blown out the other front tire. He told the cop that he had been so intoxicated he hadn't even noticed the first accident.

Needless to say, Buddy was called down to the police station to bail out his contract jockey. And he wasn't thrilled about it. Meanwhile, he had no idea where his son was. Gerald had gone out, but understanding what a big day was ahead the next day, he vowed to be home by 10 p.m. That didn't happen. He was out with one of the female grooms, a girl much older than Gerald. She had a boyfriend, but that didn't stop her from driving up into the secluded hills with Gerald, where they smoked a little dope and had sex in the front seat.

When Buddy got back from the police station with Ronnie, he was already in a foul mood, but he boiled over when he realized that Gerald still wasn't back. By the time his son finally pulled up, hours after his promised return time, Buddy was waiting to bushwhack him. He sat in the dark until he heard Gerald's key in the lock. Once his son walked through the front door, Buddy flipped on the lights and then flipped out. "Where the fuck you been!" Buddy thundered. "You were supposed to be back at 10."

Gerald stumbled to respond. Delp could see how wasted his son was and he could smell the stench of booze and pot smoke wafting off the kid's clothes and breath. "You got blew eyes," Buddy derisively told him. "One blew that way, and the other blew that way."

And then, bam! Buddy laid him out with half a fist, knocking Gerald clean off his feet.

Gerald was surprised by the violent attack but not sobered. Still in the bag and still on the ground, he baited his enraged father. "Hit me again, baldy," Gerald said. "I deserve it."

But Buddy had had enough violence for one night. He left Gerald alone to slink up the stairs.

When Gerald got to his room he was rumpled and red faced and his roommate, Ronnie, could see it.

"How are you, Doc?" Ronnie sympathetically asked him.

"How the fuck do you think I am?" Gerald replied.

"Well, look at me," Ronnie said, and then he showed off his own lumps and scrapes and bruises and red blotches. He'd tangled with Buddy too, just a few moments before Gerald had gotten home.

Ronnie told Gerald all about it: the chick, the drunk driving, the accidents, and the cop. Gerald listened patiently to the whole twisted story and then shook his foggy head and uttered the only levelheaded sentence of the long night. "Well," he said to Ronnie about the beatings they'd taken, "we both fucking deserved it."

Gerald stripped off his clothes and left them on the floor. The two boys went to sleep with the sweet, sickly smell of dope wafting up from the discarded garments and swirling around the room.

The next morning, with the exhausted Delps and Ronnie watching from the stands, Spectacular Bid and Willie Shoemaker strode out into the soaking-wet bog of a track and effortlessly beat the field by three lengths.

16 *Saying Goodbye*

According to legend, William Lee Shoemaker was born in West Texas on August 19, 1931. He was expelled from the womb prematurely, as if he was in a hurry to get to the finish line. When he emerged, he was nothing more than a breathing zygote, weighing less than forty ounces and measuring only ten and a half inches long. His grandmother, it was said, put him in a shoe box and gently warmed him in the oven all night long so that he would not die.

Living through that night was only the first of many miraculous things Shoemaker would do in his life.

His parents divorced when he was four, and he was sent to live on his grandfather's farm in Abilene, Texas. He rode his first pony there when he was seven years old.

Three years later, Shoemaker moved to Southern California to be with his father. Despite his tiny stature, he displayed obvious athletic ability. His first sport was not the oval of the race track but the squared circle of boxing. He won a Golden Gloves championship in the 95–105 pound weight class, though he was technically still less than ninety-five pounds on the scales.

At age eighteen, Shoe, as he was already called, still wasn't 5 feet or a hundred pounds, but that was the year he started his professional riding career. It took him a month to win his first race, and it earned him the princely sum of $10.

In 1950 Shoe participated in his first full year of racing, and all he did was win 388 races to tie as the top rider in the country.

Many felt that the secret to his success went beyond his ideal size. He had great hands, which were noted for both their vice-like strength and also a feathery touch. Unlike the coming generation of magnificent Hispanic riders who stood out for their command over a horse, their ability to demand and get from an animal, Shoe was distinguished for letting a horse find his own way.

Whatever Shoe did, however he did it, it worked exceptionally well. Every single year from 1958 to 1964 he was racing's biggest money winner. He rode six winners in a single day, six different times. Over the course of his long career he'd won multiple Kentucky Derbies, Preaknesses, and Belmont Stakes.

By 1970, with more than twenty years still left in his career, Shoemaker had won more races than any other rider in history. So for two long decades, every single time he hit the winner's circle, he broke his own record.

Shoemaker's career had its low moments as well as its triumphs. In the 1957 Kentucky Derby, he was on the back of Gallant Man, the favorite, and made a far more embarrassing mistake than anything Ronnie Franklin ever did on Spectacular Bid. Shoe had the race in the bag when he mistook a furlong post for the finish line and stood up in the irons to soak in the glory. While he celebrated, Iron Liege zoomed past him to the real wire and won the race. It was a mortifying moment, on racing's biggest stage, and it was something that he never entirely lived down despite all of his many subsequent accomplishments.

Shoemaker was a mostly lucky guy who avoided major accidents on the track, but when he finally had them, they came in quick succession and they were brutal. In 1968 he was thrown off his horse and broke his leg so severely that he required a pin to repair his bone. The only problem was there was no pin his size available in the operating room. While he waited on the table, hospital workers had to scour the building to finally locate one that fit his bone. The issue was solved only when one of the ER nurses thought to look in the children's ward.

Very soon after returning to work, Willie was hurt again. As he entered the track, his horse was spooked and flipped over, landing on top of the tiny rider. Fortunately for Shoemaker, a friend of his, a doctor, happened to be at the race and ran to his aid. "Doc," Shoemaker said, "I'm hurt, I'm hurt real bad."

Indeed he was. Shoe had broken his pelvis, injured his bladder, and damaged the nerves in his leg.

Like Ronnie Franklin, Shoemaker's problems went far beyond the track. Shoe also had a tumultuous personal life with multiple divorces and substance abuse issues. Though less well known and flamboyant than Ronnie's problems, Shoe's love for the bottle would eventually be his undoing.

By 1980 Shoemaker was in the homestretch of his distinguished career. He was considered by Buddy Delp and many others in racing to be the perfect rider for Spectacular Bid. While many viewed Shoemaker as the tonic for Franklin's fitful tenure, the truth was Ronnie was a successful and winning rider on Spectacular Bid, and filling his boots wouldn't be easy, not even for a Shoemaker.

Georgie Velasquez's short tenure on the horse had been successful; he had won both races that he rode, but the horse clearly did not respond as well for him as he did for Franklin. But Shoemaker had a lighter touch on the reins and, perhaps more important than that, a better chemistry with Buddy.

Under Ronnie, the Bid had broken speed records and won huge races, including two-thirds of the Triple Crown. The horse had also brought home an Eclipse Award in each of his two racing seasons so far, even though he had faced virtually every great horse of his generation.

And yet, under Shoemaker, the best was still to come.

In 1980 Shoe was in the irons for every race the Bid ran. That included nine races, on two coasts, in four different states—California, Illinois, New Jersey, and New York. He ran on wet racetracks and dry. He ran with different weight allowances and at different lengths. And he ran against the very best competition available, ducking no one.

The Bid started the year in style. On January 5 he kicked off "the Strub Series," a three-race string all held at Santa Anita. The first of these prestigious and lucrative competitions was the Malibu Stakes. The Bid started the four-horse race slowly and in last place. After the far turn, however, he rumbled all the way to first place and crossed the wire five lengths ahead of his old rival, Flying Paster, who finished second.

Despite the slow start, Bid finished the seven-furlong race in only 1:20 and set a new Santa Anita record, eclipsing the old mark, which went all the way back to 1954. Besides that, he was only a fifth of a second off the world record.

Two weeks later, in the San Fernando Stakes, the Bid had a much more challenging race. He was about ten lengths behind on the backstretch before kicking into another gear and closing the huge gap with an inevitability that was stunning in its ease. When he sidled up next to the leader, Relaunch, a thrilling sequence unfolded.

For a long stretch the two horses battled with a ferocious perfection and equality, and Relaunch showed no craven qualities or signs that he was intimidated. He went stride for stride with his more famous opponent. But after a protracted battle, the Bid finally inched his head and neck in front, and it was as if a seal had been broken. A moment later the white horse that had shown so much game was suddenly a spec in the distance, far behind Spectacular Bid.

Breaking out into the open was almost always a joyful moment for the Bid, a time when he alone was in the eyes of the fans and the cheers were all for him. But this time, he could not enjoy his hard-won lead. Flying Paster, finally demonstrating the rapidity that his trainer and jockey had sworn he had within him, stunned the Bid and approached his neck around the far turn. To Spectacular Bid, Paster was the most unexpected of visitors, like someone knocking on the exterior door of a 747 in midflight.

For a moment it appeared that the burst that had blown the Bid far past Relaunch may have also taken too much out of him. The momentum, it seemed, was clearly with the Paster; Even Shoemaker thought so. "It really gave me a scare," the great Shoe said. "I thought [Paster] might have us."

But Spectacular Bid had no such fear or loss of confidence. He showed his heart and neither gave in nor relinquished the lead. He dueled Flying Paster all the way to the wire. The Bid won, but only by a little more than a length. The margin was incredibly small considering that it was one of the most impressive races of one of history's fastest horses.

The gap between the Bid and Paster and the other two horses was truly impressive. Flying Paster finished fifteen lengths ahead of Relaunch, who finished in third place and a whopping forty-eight lengths ahead of last place Timbo.

The Bid's winning time was a minute and forty-eight seconds.

The race had been vigorously contested and was exhausting, but Spectacular Bid had only two weeks to recover. A mere fourteen days later he appeared at Santa Anita yet again, for the prestigious Charles H. Strub Stakes, a big money race that would pay the winner about double what Bid had earned just two weeks earlier.

By now, racing world enthusiasts had grown accustomed to Spectacular Bid's remarkable performances. But nothing they'd seen thus far could compare with what they were about to see at the Strub.

If one believed in preternatural signs, they were all there. Bold Bidder, Spectacular Bid's sire, had established an earlier Strub record by finishing the race in the blinding speed of 1:59 ⅗ in 1966. His rider that day had been none other than Willie Shoemaker. The record they established was so secure that it stood for more than a decade.

Buddy Delp could read the omens as well as the evidence. "Bid is better now than he has ever been in his life," he said. "The track is fast, the other horses are good, and if they force things you'll see a track record."

There was one thing that Buddy did not mention. In the San Fernando Stakes, Bid and Paster had carried equal weight. In the Strub Stakes, Bid would carry five more pounds than Flying Paster, 126 pounds to Paster's 121.

Almost fifty-eight thousand people packed Santa Anita on a perfect day, hoping to find out if Buddy was a true prophet whose predictions would come to pass or if it was a new day in which the weight allowance would bring a different result.

Relaunch was certainly prepared for a rematch. Right out of the gate he showed yet again that he had magnificent speed, if only in short bursts. As was his wont, he asserted himself early and quickly sprinted to a six-length lead. Spectacular Bid was again content to be in last place, with Valdez and Flying Paster both ahead of him too.

The Bid seemed unconcerned with his place in the pecking order as he galloped beside the rail. Relaunch kept the lead for most of the backstretch and did so at a blazing pace.

But then Shoemaker emboldened the Bid. The gray colt quickened and expanded his flawless stride. Within seconds he easily closed the large gap between himself and Relaunch. But he picked up a companion on the journey. Valdez strode right alongside Bid, and before long all three horses raced side by side with the Bid in the middle.

But the far turn was like a slingshot for Spectacular Bid. He went into it with his competitors but was flung out of it with great thrust and propulsion. He flew down the homestretch with so much sheer speed that he might have caused a sonic boom. He crossed the wire after traveling one and a quarter miles in only 1:57 ⅘.

It was a new Santa Anita, American, and world record for a dirt race.

The superlatives came in as fast as the horse. Even Paster's rider, Don Pierce, wouldn't dispute it. He had been supremely confident of his horse before the Kentucky Derby the year before, but now he was dejected. "Maybe we just can't beat [Spectacular Bid]," he glumly admitted. Had Paster been born in a different year, who knows what he might have achieved? He clearly had both the speed and the heart of a Triple Crown winner and a "Horse of the Year." Instead, he had the misfortune of emerging into the world the same year as Spectacular Bid. Because of that, he'd never forge his own path to racing immortality; he was merely destined to be a footnote in Spectacular Bid's story. Paster faced the Bid five times in his career, and he lost to Bid all five times.

The Strub Stakes was the high point of the Bid's glorious career, but coming in early February, it was hardly his ending. The rest of his four-year-old season still awaited. After one more race at Santa Anita, a victory by five lengths, Spectacular Bid moved on to Hollywood Park and won two more races by wide margins. After that, it was on to Chicago, where he won the Washington Park Handicap by ten lengths.

Finally, in August the Bid came back east. On a streak of eight straight victories, most of them dominating, he went to Monmouth Park, on the Jersey shore, for the Haskell Handicap. There, he raced against a field of lesser competition that included four undistinguished males and a filly with the melodic name of Glorious Song. She was his most formidable competition.

The Bid carried 132 pounds in the race, the most of his career. And with that to her advantage, Glorious Song put up a fight. She and the Bid were right beside each other going into the far turn. Treating her with complete equality, Bid pulled away from Glorious Song in the homestretch, as he had done against so many male competitors. But he beat her by only a length and three quarters.

It was noted by reporters, however, that Shoemaker had barely applied the whip. Nobody believed that the superhorse had run his hardest. The relaxed ride, despite the filly's spirited competition, was a sign that Delp and Shoemaker were taking measures to avoid the handicappers' assigning them an even higher weight for the upcoming Woodward Stakes at Belmont Park. Had the Bid smoked the field at Monmouth while carrying 132 pounds, he might have been looking at an assignment of 137 pounds or more in New York.

The Meyerhoffs and Delp already felt that there was a great deal of thinly veiled disdain for them by officials at the New York Racing Association (NYRA). They based their foreboding hunch on the many fiascos that had surrounded their ill-fated participation in the last Belmont Stakes. And clearly they had a point.

NYRA racing secretary and handicapper Lenny Hale, the man who decided the weight assignments at Belmont Park, took the opportunity to taunt Meyerhoff and Delp. "The mark of the truly great horse, the horse remembered for decades, is the one that carries the weight and beats quality horses," Hale sniffed. "So far Spectacular Bid has beaten precious little."

It was a ludicrous statement, but Hale persisted. He compared Bid to Forego, the sainted New York–based thoroughbred who had won eight Eclipse Awards and who had won the Marlboro Cup in 1976 with Shoemaker aboard and carrying 137 pounds.

Hale assigned only 136 pounds to Spectacular Bid's broad back, prompting a question from Forego's owner, Martha Gerry, that any reasonable fan might've asked.

"If Forego carried 137 [pounds]," she queried, "why can't Spectacular Bid?"

"Because Spectacular Bid is not as good as Forego," Hale told the shocked Mrs. Gerry.

In fact, giving Spectacular Bid 136 pounds was a brilliant piece of revenge. It was still a very high weight allowance, but at one pound less than Forego had carried, it was impossible for the Bid to equal that legendary horse's accomplishments. For Bid's team, it was a no-win situation.

Delp, understandably, was livid. In his mind the question wasn't why Hale was asking the Bid to carry one pound less than Forego had, but why he was being asked to carry twelve more pounds than Secretariat had for the same race. It was also eight more pounds than Seattle Slew had toted just two years earlier.

Affirmed had carried more than 130 pounds only twice in his career. Spectacular Bid had done it more than five times and had won all five races handily, and yet Hale questioned his greatness.

Meyerhoff and Delp were sure that the real reason for the high allowance and cutting words was that Hale was taking advantage of them. Hale's comparison of Spectacular Bid to Forego was bogus in their book. Forego was a gelding; his owners had no future breeding earnings to worry about if Hale's weight assignment proved too much. If Forego had broken down on the track and died a gruesome death due to the excessive weight he was asked to carry, that would have been tragic, but it would not have been a business disaster.

To ask the Bid, who still had all the manly equipment he should have, to carry almost the same weight that Forego had done simply didn't make sense. If the Bid broke down, tens of millions of dollars for the Meyerhoffs, and a tidy sum to Delp too, were all at stake.

It is not surprising that Meyerhoff and Delp made the business decision to withhold Spectacular Bid from the Marlboro. They might have looked like babies, but only one year before Laz Barrera had made the same decision for Affirmed.

Harry and Buddy could opt out if they wanted to; there was nothing to compel them to race. But in making that decision, they showed up

Hale, a powerful man in racing, and in effect they made him look like a vindictive and petty ass.

In fact, Hale was applauded by the other owners for his stance. They saw no point in racing the Bid under equal circumstances, but racing fans had a different point of view. They believed Hale's antics had only prevented them from seeing the best horse in the nation for the second straight year.

Buddy Delp and his team also took some heat. No less an authority than Red Smith taunted Buddy and Harry in his column when he noted that by refusing Hale's weight assignment for Spectacular Bid, they had in essence "chickened out."

Smith explained that there were expectations, even obligations, that went along with owning and managing an exceptional thoroughbred. "When a horseman dreams of a truly great horse," Smith wrote, "he pictures one that wins the futurities as a 2-year-old, adds the Triple Crown at 3, then goes on to the handicaps where he gives weight and still wins."

Smith believed Bid had fulfilled most of the menu, but he nevertheless had yet to prove his place in history. The fault, he implied, was all Delp's and Harry's for complaining and taking their horse home.

Showing up Lenny Hale was undoubtedly satisfying, but it proved a short-term pleasure. Just a few weeks later the Bid came back to Hale's domain, Belmont Park, for the Woodward Stakes. A small slate of good horses was scheduled to oppose him, including Dr. Patches, Temperence Hill, and the talented Winter's Tale.

One by one they all made their excuses and withdrew from the race. Dr. Patches and Temperence Hill simply decided that they had no chance, after all, and gave up without any real reason stated. Winter's Tale was the most likely challenger, but he scratched too when his handlers claimed he had a chipped bone in one of his forelegs.

In a racing rarity called a "walkover," the Bid went out on the track and ran all by himself. Although it almost never happened, a walkover was the highest demonstration of respect, like intentionally walking a baseball batter with the bases loaded.

In fact, Bid's walkover was the first one in the United States in more than thirty years. It was believed that in all of U.S. racing history there had been only about thirty-two walkovers, and seven of those had been run by steeplechasers. The last one, coincidentally, had occurred at the old Havre de Grace race track just a few minutes from Buddy Delp's childhood home.

Despite the lack of competition, Shoemaker and the Bid put on a memorable show for the fans. The horse smoked his way around the track and finished the one and a quarter miles in only 2:02 ⅖. The track record, set by Triple Crown winner Seattle Slew only two years earlier, was two minutes flat.

The walkover might have been unplanned and unusual, but it gave the Bid another unique feature for his resume. It recalled the legendary Citation's walkover at the Pimlico Special in 1948 with Eddie Arcaro aboard. Citation crossed the wire at 1:59 ⅘, a considerably faster time than he had clocked in the Preakness Stakes with top-level competition to push him. His time in that one (though on a bad track) had been 2:02 ⅖.

Buddy Delp was initially thrilled with the walkover. The reluctance of fine horses and respected handlers to compete against the Bid provided credence to Buddy's relentless crowing about possessing the greatest horse in the world. It was hard to disagree with him when no one dared challenge him.

And yet the fact that nobody stepped up to race the Bid was peculiar. After all, there was no particular disgrace in losing to him, regardless of the gap, and a lot of easy money was to be made for merely running and finishing either second or third.

The first clue why they all refused to race against the Bid presented itself the moment the walkover ended. That's when Harry Meyerhoff collected his check for $73,300, or about half of what he had expected as the winner. Harry wasn't aware of the condition book that spelled out the reduced fee in the case of a walkover.

In that context, there were rumors that NYRA had bullied the other owners into scratching from the race with the intent of paying out less money and thus saving about $85,000 by not paying the Bid's full fee as the winner and also not paying the rest of the field at all.

Harry was livid of course. He had gone to great pains to do his part for both the race and racing. He had paid his team to go to New York, and he had incurred all of the associated expenses. More than that, his horse was clearly the star attraction, not only of that day but also perhaps of the entire decade. It was Harry and his team who had drawn the spectators and no one else.

But for all that effort, Harry felt stiffed. He conceded that Hale and NYRA had the right to pay out less, per the condition book, but he felt that it was, all things considered, the wrong thing to do.

Teresa, who'd grown up in upstate New York in a community where everyone was more or less like her, couldn't fathom how or why she and her husband would be treated so unfairly. "Why would they do this to us?" she asked Harry.

Meyerhoff shrugged his shoulders. "Anti-Semitism," he said.

Perhaps paranoia was getting the better of Harry. Although he had confronted anti-Semitism on the racing circuit, it is unlikely his problems in New York had anything to do with his exotic ancestry.

The officials' behavior was probably just another shot across the bow in the war of words that had escalated between the Bid's team and NYRA since Angel Cordero had plowed his horse into Ronnie Franklin's colt in the days before the Belmont Stakes. That time, New York officials had basically looked the other way. The reduced fee could have also been payback for the Bid's rancorous departure from the Marlboro field just a couple of weeks earlier, when both sides looked like they were trying to one-up the other.

Regardless of how Harry privately felt about the slight and the snobby northeastern elites who he felt looked down on him, in public he maintained his usual cool. Anyway, the money was inconsequential to him. The Bid had already won almost $3 million over the course of his short-but-brilliant career. And Harry had recently finalized the horse's record $22 million in syndication fees. So Meyerhoff and his family investors could absorb the loss while feeling no pain.

The ugly gesture, if indeed that's what it was, was an empty one. And everyone, including Harry, simply moved on. Anyway, the next race, the Jockey Gold Cup, also at Belmont Park, featured a purse worth more than half a million dollars. It was, in fact, the richest race in the history of the United States.

The Bid, of course, was the bankable attraction. He was ginning up interest and driving up purse money. But, as with so many of his other races, his presence came with a shroud of mystery, an element of conflict and controversy, and a surprise ending.

By now race officials, journalists, and fans were all used to the melodrama that Buddy unpacked wherever he went. Even so, his behavior at the Gold Cup was downright bizarre. In a weird incident that echoed the Bid's Belmont Stakes experience, Buddy seemed to harbor some secret information about the health of his horse.

First, rumors of unknown origin swirled that Spectacular Bid was unsound. But at 8:30 a.m. on race day, Harry Meyerhoff did everything he could to dispute the notion. Standing in front of the barn swigging a breakfast beer as though he didn't have a care in the world, he casually kibitzed with reporters and gently bragged that his horse could beat anyone in the field. He also told them that he wanted the huge Gold Cup purse in order to put the Bid over the $3 million mark in career earnings, which would make him the only horse in history to do so.

Harry's happy-go-lucky demeanor in no way indicated that he was the owner of a valuable commodity that was in any danger. Buddy, too, attempted to reinforce the notion that the Bid was sound and prepared to compete, but he couldn't resist stirring the pot. "I have heard all the rumors about my horse not running in the Gold Cup," he said, "but the rumors aren't true. [Spectacular Bid] went out on the race track this morning and galloped perfectly. I would say he was even money to start."

If the rumors weren't true and the Bid had galloped "perfectly," why was he only "even money" to race?

Buddy didn't say.

At 9:00 a.m. the mystery went even deeper. The track veterinarian, Manny Gilman, went to examine the Bid and certify that he was sound. That was an expected, even ordinary, procedure, but when he got there, the celebrated horse was standing in a tub of ice water and unavailable. The doctor left, unhappily, growling that he would be back to complete his duty.

But when Dr. Gilman returned an hour later, the Bid's handlers still refused him access to the horse. At this unusual display of disrespect, Gilman stalked off and vowed to report the strange behavior to the higher authorities. "I'll go to the stewards and tell them that I tried to do my job twice and was refused," the good doctor said.

This time there was no Dr. Harthill to sneak in and secretly treat Spectacular Bid. There was only a kind of candor, though it was tardy in coming. At 4:00 p.m., Buddy finally made an announcement. "It's over now," Buddy said, "but it was a great ride with Bid."

He'd just told the crowd that his magnificent horse had retired and would not race in that day's event or ever again.

"The problem is with his left front ankle," Buddy said. "He has had a problem with the ankle since he was a two-year-old. I would say he's 98 percent of himself right now, and Bid at 98 percent could beat the field that's entered for the Gold Cup with no problems. But he's not 100 percent, and I'm not going to send him out on the racetrack when he's not 100 percent. It's as simple as that. The decision to scratch him was mine."

As he spoke, Buddy was cascaded with boos by the angry fans. And why not? He'd basically just told them that he had known his horse would not run since that morning. But in an attempt to frustrate NYRA officials he'd kept the decision to scratch all to himself for the entire day. In trying to annoy them, he had toyed with the fans and made them suffer.

The fans were the ones who were excited to see his horse race; they were the ones who left work to be there; drove through traffic; and plunked their money down on food, useless bets, and other incidentals— all under the impression that they would enjoy a memorable night in the presence of greatness. Instead, Buddy had played with their emotions and thwarted them from seeing the horse. All of this in an attempt to make the officials look bad.

But it all boomeranged back on him.

The Bid should have retired to great cheers and the good wishes of everyone. After all, he was an anomaly of nature, an ideal, a once-in-a-lifetime creation of God that hinted at the possibility of perfection. He should have moved on like Secretariat had, with the awe and adulation of the racing world, the press, and the fans. Instead, Buddy made Spectacular Bid's exit ridiculous, a carnival of anger and an unpleasant memory for all who were there.

Even Buddy's infuriating antics couldn't diminish the horse's profound accomplishments. Spectacular Bid had won twenty-six of his thirty lifetime races and retired with a higher winning percentage than Secretariat or any other horse who had earned more than $1 million.

The Bid had won on both coasts and in between. Racing against the very best horses of his generation, he had managed long winning streaks, one of twelve in a row, and another of nine. In 1980 he had won every single race in which he ran and became the first horse in almost thirty years to go undefeated in his handicap campaign.

The Bid was even greater than the public knew because he had accomplished all of these things with a team that was as dysfunctional and chaotic as it was talented. Meyerhoff and Buddy were brilliant men. They had the unusual accomplishment of not only choosing and training the great horse but also, simultaneously, his young jockey. And in an incredibly short period they had raised both horse and rider to extraordinary levels of accomplishment.

But along the path, ego and secrecy stepped in. The owner and trainer also hid their own fragilities and weaknesses. They weren't really up for the task of caring for teenage boys. They didn't quite possess the proper qualities or fully accept all of the responsibilities. That's what had led to the manic performance at the Florida Derby, the mysterious loss at the Belmont Stakes, and, far more seriously, Ronnie and Gerald's budding addictions and spiraling lives.

Their horse might have been the fastest thing on four legs, but undeniably he was defined as much by his stunning losses as his brilliant performances—more so, in fact. That would be the burden they would all bear forever more.

Angel Cordero Jr., the charismatic, brilliant, and ruthless rider who had once coveted the horse and then did everything in his power to defeat him, summed up Spectacular Bid as no one else could. Asked if the Bid was the greatest horse he'd ever seen, he scoffed at the notion. "Not to me," he said.

Cordero discounted the blazing speed and rendered the eye-popping numbers meaningless. It all meant nothing, he said, in comparison to the embarrassing failure at the Belmont Stakes. "I don't care about time," he said with firm conviction. "Time only counts when it comes to jail and hookers. . . . Winning is the only thing I care about."

17 *Crossing the Wire*

Buddy Delp's influence as a father and a father figure was never more evident than in the spring of 1982, when Ronnie Franklin and Gerald Delp were living in a motel room in Kentucky. The boys were out on their own and utilizing the skills that Buddy had provided them to make a living. Despite his past problems, Ronnie was riding well. He'd just won seventy races at the winter meeting at the Fair Grounds in New Orleans.

Twenty-year-old Gerald was Ronnie's agent. In addition to representing the former Kentucky Derby and Preakness winner, he had also had the prescience to recognize the talent in a young female rider named Julie Krone. With those two fine jockeys under his auspice he was already gaining wealth and respectability.

It was thanks to Buddy's interest and intervention in their lives that both boys were enjoying self-sufficiency and material success. Unfortunately, Buddy had another legacy, and it was about to bring them down.

The boys wanted to get high, but they had no trusted connections in Kentucky from whom to acquire a bag. So Gerald dialed up a contact in Louisiana and got that pusher to send them some cocaine via Federal Express. Everything would have been fine—that is to say they would have received their drugs without any trouble—except they were so needy for a taste that they couldn't control themselves and picked up the phone. One or the other of them called the couriers, over and over.

"Hey, have you seen our package yet?"

"Is our package there?"

"Do you know when our package is going to be here?"

Federal Express managers had seen and heard it before. They recognized that kind of impatience as the prototypical signs of jumpy addicts yearning for something illicit to arrive. When the package finally turned up at the distribution center, men with badges were there waiting for it. They opened it up and found the coke.

After Ronnie and Gerald received the package they had so eagerly awaited, they were immediately arrested.

Once again Buddy distanced himself from the issue by persuading gullible reporters that he was shocked and angry. He assured everyone that he was attending to the problem like an old-school, hard-ass disciplinarian. He had left the boys to rot in jail overnight, he said, without any bail money from him. It was a punitive measure for their stupidity.

Buddy never mentioned if his ire was provoked by the fact that the boys were using coke or merely because they had been stupid enough to get caught. But it was no joke; Ronnie and Gerald were facing felony charges in Kentucky. Ultimately, through the magic of celebrity and adept legal assistance, they bargained their way down to a misdemeanor. Most of their sentence was suspended, but they were nevertheless assigned sixty days of incarceration.

So they arrived in a place that could only be described as the exact opposite of the winner's circle: the Fayette County House of Detention. The boys, who had been roommates for so many years, were now cellmates.

Meanwhile, the man who had given them their first taste of cocaine and who had snorted it right alongside of them on many occasions was far away, insulated from their issues. No police detective, FBI agent, or curious reporter questioned Buddy Delp about his own connection to cocaine. No one asked him if he had ever bought it or used it himself. No one bothered to ask if he had ever seen it around his house or workplace.

These questions never came up, though Ronnie was now spiraling into a pattern of incidents, and Gerald, Buddy's own young son, was incarcerated too. The boys were in deep trouble, legally and emotionally, yet no one drew the thin, white, powdery line between Buddy and the coke. To the media of the day it was all merely a matter of "boys will be boys," like Babe Ruth's much lionized drinking and womanizing.

At the detention facility it didn't take long for the other inmates to notice them. Gerald was immature but more than 6 feet tall and by appearances formidable. Ronnie, small and boyish, had an admirer.

One day, early in their sentences, the jockey sat in the common room and watched television when he was approached by another inmate. The thug turned off the TV set and then loomed over Franklin in his chair. "I want you to get in that shower," the convict told him, pointing in the direction of the spigots. Ronnie looked up at the larger man and didn't say a word. Instead, he stood up and calmly walked over to the television, and he turned it back on. Then he walked back and stood directly in front of the other convict, face to face. Ronnie clenched his fists and said, "I ain't going anywhere."

They were about to square off when an old, raspy voice came from the side of the room. An aged man sitting at a table had watched the incident unfold. "You leave them two boys alone," he snapped.

The assailant looked at the old man and then did as he was told and immediately backed off. He walked away and never bothered Ronnie or Gerald again in the two months of their incarceration. "We assumed the old man was some sort of gangster," Gerald said. "We didn't know, but if he told someone to do something, they did it."

After their sentences ended, Ronnie and Gerald reemerged from jail, supposedly chastened. Franklin spoke to reporters with a contrite tone. He said, "[Jail is a place] I never want to go back to. I don't think I'll be getting into any more trouble. It's not worth it."

He also revealed that he'd found God in jail. "Jesus came and got me when I was in the gutter," Ronnie said.

Whatever deal Ronnie made with the almighty, it worked. Though he seemed to be in big trouble with racing officials, he was back on the track, riding competitively again, far more quickly than expected. He had one problem, however, that was even bigger than getting busted for the coke.

While Ronnie was in jail, his weight had ballooned up to nearly 130 pounds—far beyond any acceptable limit for a jockey. He was filling out and maturing, at least physically. In order to ride again he needed to bring himself back to 112 pounds. He ultimately did it, but he could no longer take natural perfection for granted. From that point on, he would feel the pressure of weight management.

Ronnie went back to riding for Buddy, but their relationship waxed and waned, creating stressful career issues. That was especially true when Ronnie met Tyann, an attractive young mother from New Orleans.

Franklin fell in love quickly. When he told Buddy that he wanted to marry Tyann, his father figure didn't approve. Buddy was afraid that she and her two children would be too much of a distraction and that Ronnie wouldn't put the same focus and effort into his work. Buddy insisted that Ronnie move on from Tyann, so of course Ronnie proposed to her.

At that moment both his friendship and business relationship with Delp fractured badly, and that created a severe financial hardship for Ronnie at the very same moment he was in his greatest financial need.

Franklin was free, of course, to ride for other trainers. He was, after all, a celebrity rider with an outstanding winning percentage and victories at the highest levels of the sport. But he was hampered by the negative publicity associated with his drug arrests. The truth was that without Buddy's patronage he couldn't earn nearly as much as he could with it.

Financial hardship and the vagabond lifestyle of a professional athlete did not agree with Tyann. After only a year and half the marriage was intolerable to her, and it was all coming to a swift and volatile end.

Needless to say, Ronnie was low on cash and desperate to hear from Buddy again.

Finally, after a long absence, the Delps reentered his life. Buddy's brother Dick, now in charge of his own stable, called with a riding job. And Buddy left word with Dick for Ronnie to call him too because he had an excellent horse, Aspro, who needed a rider for a lucrative race at Keeneland.

But Ronnie never made it to Dick's barn, so he never got the message to call Buddy. Instead, he was waylaid on his way into work by police. They detained him for questioning, though in this case Franklin hadn't done anything wrong.

The cops were at the track to investigate a different jockey who they believed was in possession of drugs. They rifled through his car looking for the contraband, but they were frustrated when none turned up. In hopes that the day wouldn't be a total loss, they grabbed Ronnie, a known drug user with a rap sheet, and grilled him with a long list of questions. Mostly they wanted him to give up the names of horse people who sold or used.

While Ronnie was detained, he missed his opportunity with both Delp brothers. Dick got a different rider for that day, and Buddy found someone for the weekend. The lost opportunity with Buddy was especially painful. Aspro won his race and pulled in 10 percent of the winner's share of $34,000 for the jockey. Franklin lost that hefty payday and a chance to mend important fences for no other reason than that he had a bad reputation with law enforcement.

The turmoil in Ronnie's career echoed his tumultuous personal life. His marriage to Tayann ended acrimoniously, just as Buddy had feared it would. Ronnie was too young and immature for the responsibility of an instant family and too strapped financially to make it work. Tyann was Mrs. Ronald Franklin for eighteen months, and for that she walked away with most of what he had, including his mobile home, his car, and some land holdings.

Ronnie wasn't left with much, but at least he got his freedom back.

Gerald's problems with drugs were less well known to the public than Ronnie's, but in a sense they were much worse. While Ronnie could abstain and find extended periods of sobriety, Gerald suffered from a near constant addiction. At one point, living in Louisiana all by himself, Gerald did nothing but get stoned. Eventually Delp employees in New Orleans called Buddy to say that no one had seen or heard from Gerald in a long time; they didn't know what had happened to him.

Buddy tried calling but couldn't get Gerald on the phone either. So he dropped everything and immediately caught a flight to New Orleans to find his son. When he arrived at Gerald's apartment, he opened the door to the sight of his boy unconscious on the sofa, lying in a quagmire of his own vomit, urine, and feces. Buddy was relieved Gerald was still breathing. He wrapped up his poor son in a blanket, lifted him up, and gently carried him out of the apartment like a swaddling baby.

After that near-death incident Buddy sent Gerald to Kentucky, ostensibly to lead his operation there. The real reason, however, was to get his son away from the drug dealers and users back home who had fueled his addiction.

While out in bluegrass country, Gerald did little more than attend a drug rehab program and work. Buddy provided an additional layer of protection by seeing to it that his son was under the watchful eye of Dr. Harthill. Buddy's friend and veterinarian made sure Gerald didn't fall off the wagon or get into any other trouble.

In Kentucky, Gerald lived a simple, low-stress life. He rented an affordable apartment across the street from the race track so that he could walk to work. His primary job responsibility was to oversee only eight horses. All of these elements allowed Gerald to earn enough money to stay alive without applying the type of pressure that might have driven him back to the drugs.

When Gerald felt better, he joined his father's operation in a more meaningful capacity. He worked his way up to become Buddy's assistant trainer, the same second-in-command position that Dick Delp had once held.

But working for Buddy wasn't easy. There was a lot of tension between father and son. Gerald found Buddy abrupt, rude, and especially negative. If Buddy exasperated him too much, Gerald might tell him to "fuck off" and then hop in his car and speed away for a few hours. Even worse than Buddy's constant criticism was his complete indifference to good work. "Thank you" apparently wasn't in his vocabulary.

"You know," a frustrated Gerald finally told his father, "you just always say fucking bad things."

"I pay you to do a good job," Buddy shot back. "You are *supposed* to do a good job."

"Okay, mutherfucker," Gerald muttered under his breath.

Whatever problems they had, they were still father and son. Gerald loved and respected Buddy and chose to emphasize the old man's decency and especially his fatherly care for him. It was Buddy's paternal tenderness, not his negative traits, that Gerald saw in his dad.

But there was no denying the other side of Buddy's care: the utter indifference to education, the overemphasis of money, and especially the introduction of early-age alcohol and drug consumption that had led to Gerald's life-threatening addictions.

All told, it was a clinic in atrocious parenting.

Gerald sublimated all that, pushed it so far back that he actually believed that he owed his dad his back-breaking labor, his unstinting loyalty, and amends for "everything I'd put him through."

When Gerald tried to tell his father how sorry he was for all the trouble his addictions had caused, Buddy waved him off. "Stop right there," Buddy said. "You just keep doing what you're doing and that's all the amends I need."

Gerald accepted that as yet another generous gift from his father, a sign of his deathless love. But Gerald never even considered the possibility that the equation was all wrong. Perhaps it was Buddy who should have begged Gerald for forgiveness. After all, it was the father who had engineered the son's metamorphosis from child to addict.

In light of so many complex and conflicting emotions and corruptions, their partnership soured. Whatever Buddy's inner turmoil or deep-seated unhappiness, it surfaced in the form of heavy drinking. And not surprising, he was a mean drunk. It got to the point where Gerald, who arrived for work at 5:00 a.m. every day, dreaded his father's stumbling appearance at eight or nine because the old man was already reeking of booze and paranoia.

"You're trying to steal my owners!" Buddy shouted at his own son.

"You're bat-shit crazy, Dad," was all Gerald could say in return, shaking his head in amazement that his father could make such outrageous accusations against him. Gerald tried not to be offended; he knew it was the liquor talking.

It was only when necessity stepped in that their partnership finally came crumbling apart. Gerald's wife, Annette, was pregnant with the couple's first child. Feeling, as most men would, a sense of responsibility to his burgeoning young family, Gerald summoned the courage to discuss his changing financial situation with his father. He strode into Buddy's office, shut the door behind him, and laid it on the line.

"Listen, Dad," he said. "Annette's pregnant and she won't be going back to work. I need to make a little more money."

"I see," Buddy said.

"And If I can't make more with you, I'm going to have to go out there and try it on my own."

Buddy leaned back in his chair and clapped his hands; he took his glasses off and rubbed his eyes.

"Welp," Buddy said, "when are you leaving?"

The callousness of the response was reminiscent of Buddy's stepfather, Raymond Archer, who had said more or less the same thing to Buddy many years ago. Like Buddy, Gerald had no choice but to blaze his own path. He accepted his father's decision, but he was deeply hurt and more than a little resentful. "I busted my dick for him," Gerald said. "I didn't want to leave, and I was surprised by how cold he was. I had wanted him to prepare me to take over the business. I knew what I was doing. I had good relationships with all the owners. And I wanted to help him."

Gerald's good intentions, dreams, and disappointments meant nothing to Buddy. They parted amicably, though Gerald left with but two horses with which to start. If there was a silver lining in his banishment, it was only this: at least he wouldn't have to watch his father slowly drink himself to death anymore.

But in the end, Gerald was just like all of the other promising young men who'd come to Buddy for their opportunity in racing. The initial excitement of the experience wore off and was quickly replaced by frustration. Getting a leg up with Buddy was unfulfilling—if not debilitating.

Ronnie knew it to be so, but like Gerald and the others, whatever negative feelings he felt for Buddy were not for public consumption. Years into the future, even with close friends with whom he might have confided his disappointments, Franklin referred to Buddy respectfully as "Mr. Delp." He never uttered a word to anyone in the press about the coke, the poker and other gambling losses, or even the poor riding advice in the Belmont.

Ronnie confessed these things out loud only to his young nephew, Tony Cullum. The two had become brother-close as Ronnie's beloved father lay dying, wasting away in an east Baltimore hospital from colon cancer.

Ronnie was Tony's hero. The young, athletic boy idolized his uncle and hoped to follow in his footsteps as a jockey. And Ronnie felt a kindred spirit in Tony. He saw in his nephew someone who understood exactly where he had come from. On their trips to the hospital, he opened up and told Tony Cullum things he didn't confess to anyone else: the truth about where his life was going, his career, the terrible things that had been done to him, and some of his own sins.

Ronnie, like Gerald, was deeply conflicted about Buddy. He loved "Mr. Delp" for the opportunities the old man had provided him and the apparent kindness he had shown. But Ronnie swung back and forth between blaming himself or Buddy for one thing or another, especially for the disastrous ride in the Belmont Stakes. Ronnie told Tony about the horse's injury and the clandestine appearance of Dr. Harthill. He told Tony that it was Buddy who had instructed him to get the Bid out in front as quickly as possible and "take 'em away."

And yet Ronnie never got over his own performance in the Belmont. He replayed it in his mind again and again, for years, chastising and blaming himself for having chased the long shot and "spending" the horse too soon. He condemned himself in his own harsh thoughts even though, intellectually, he knew he had merely followed Buddy's instructions and run the race precisely as the trainer had told him to do it.

But the truth was that the Belmont instructions were the least of Buddy's sins. In Ronnie he had possession of an eager boy with a great deal of talent. With that clay, the trainer might have molded a new Shoemaker. Ronnie had everything needed: the native ability and early start, a perfect build, and Barbara Graham's impeccable training. Under the right circumstances he could have racked up the big victories and raked in the wealth for decades to come.

There was no doubt that Buddy had done great things for Ronnie, but he was also the one who had taught him to use coke. And the horses and cocaine, in one form or another, were a part of Ronnie for the rest of his life. He was preoccupied with both and subordinated everything else in his life to those two things.

In 1986, after years of problems with drugs, authorities, the IRS, and others, a small act of kindness by Ronnie for a young woman led to the single greatest possibility for salvation that he would ever be given. Going to the post one cold, rainy day at Laurel, he was led to the gates by Jane Rettaliata. Jane was a trainer and sometimes exercise rider or fill-in pony girl. Ronnie noticed her discomfort in the wet and chilly weather and sent his valet back to the jockeys' room to fetch his personal rain jacket for her. She was touched by his small act of kindness and attracted to his boyish face. She, of course, knew who he was and knew all about his troubled past, but when he asked her out, she readily agreed.

Both outwardly and beneath the surface Jane and Ronnie were an interesting study in contrasts. Jane was tall and striking, and at 5 feet 9 inches, she towered well above him by 7 inches. She had a hearty Italian look, with long brown hair and angular features, and she exuded a long-limbed vibrancy.

Jane was as buttoned up as Ronnie was tattered. Horse racing was her childhood dream too, but after galloping horses, training them, breaking them, and convalescing them, all she could envision was a bleak future of long hours, exhausting work, and low pay. She decided she needed a better plan and went to nursing school.

Although there were many differences between Ronnie and Jane, the most important one was sobriety, something that was apparent on their first date. She was swept away by Ronnie that night, captivated by his good looks and charm. But at the end of the evening things took a surprising turn. While they were still in the car, Ronnie took out a little baggie of white powder.

"Do you want some?" he casually asked her.

"No," she said. "I don't do that."

Undeterred, Ronnie emptied the baggie on a surface, cut a few lines, and snorted them right there in front of her. It was the last time he ever got high in her presence.

Although Jane never personally saw it again, she knew he continued to use. When he asked her to marry him, she demanded sobriety as a condition of her agreement to be his wife. He reluctantly complied. But the week of their wedding Ronnie disappeared. He simply was gone for several days. Jane had no idea where he was but knew that the stress of the moment had been too much for him and that he was off on a cocaine bender somewhere. He came back in time for the wedding, and everything went off without a hitch, but it was a sign of what she was in for: a husband who was capable of giving her great love and excitement, but also a fragile man who might lose his bearings at any moment.

Jane came to know Ronnie so well that she could tell in only a glance whether he was under the influence. When Ronnie was high, his upper lip stuck out in an unusual way, and his skin took on a distinct pallor. When Ronnie was sober, Jane considered him an excellent man and a fine husband. She invested large amounts of her own time assisting him to repair his life. She cheered him on when he went to community college to get his GED. She stood by him while he pursued his racing license after he had been ruled off for a failed drug test. And she helped him work on becoming current with the IRS. Most important, she encouraged him to make time for his son, Chris.

Jane's supply of compassion and understanding seemed endless. For years she carried the belief that Ronnie would beat his addictions, but it never quite happened. She had a great deal of hope when he checked into two different high-end rehabilitation facilities, but she was horrified when she believed they had used him for his celebrity without really helping him. "They wanted him because he was famous," she said, "so they took him on for free. Sounds nice, but he wasn't treated like everyone else. And because he never felt the sting of paying the high price for the treatment, he didn't take it seriously."

Their marriage finally came crashing down when she noticed a strange odor in her house. Cleaning the first-floor powder room, she realized that there was the faint whiff of something that she couldn't quite identify. Eventually it dawned on her that the reek she detected was the residue of crack cocaine, which Ronnie had been smoking in there.

At last she understood that their marriage would never work. Something irreparable had set in. Crack was inexpensive, obtainable for even a broke guy like Ronnie, and more addictive than the coke. In her heart, Jane finally had to admit that she was licked. Even with all of her love and help, he would never successfully quit the drugs.

And that was the moment that she gave up.

The most important thing that Jane helped Ronnie accomplish was to assume his role as father. First, she allowed him to play stepfather to her daughter from a previous relationship. He was pleasant and caring to that young girl. But Jane also facilitated the reconciliation of Ronnie with his own son.

With Jane's encouragement, Ronnie had his best moments as a father. He showed his son real love and attention. He picked Chris up for visits in his new home, and the boy spent nights and sometimes weekends with Ronnie and Jane, and for the first time they were like a real family. Ronnie and Jane took Chris out to dinner, and Ronnie took Chris to Dundalk to visit with the boy's grandmother.

In those moments, Ronnie was both friendly and fatherly. When Chris demonstrated that he didn't know how to use a knife and fork properly, Ronnie gently showed him how. These simple and ordinary moments, which most children would take for granted between themselves and their fathers, were cherished by Chris. They stuck with him for many decades, cutting through the shadows of childhood memory and lasting deeply into his middle age, because those simple actions were the biggest moments Chris Campbell would ever share with his father.

When Ronnie's marriage to Jane ended, so did his relationship with Chris. Ronnie disappeared from his son's life, just as suddenly as he had come back into it. As far as Chris could see, Ronnie galloped off into oblivion like a ghost on a horse. Franklin rationalized what he did. He told himself that vanishing was for Chris's own good and that it allowed the kid's stepfather to have the last word in raising the child. But Ronnie never considered the bewilderment and emptiness, the blame, that his son would feel for decades to come.

When Ronnie would finally reappear in Chris's life, the boy was seventeen years old. Ronnie was a down-and-outer by then, ruled off the track and hawking gasoline cards door to door.

This time it was Chris's sister, Jamie, who arranged for Franklin's reunion visit with Chris. She loved her brother and hoped that it would spark a renewed relationship between the father and son. Ronnie and Chris spent the day together as door-to-door salesmen. It was a happy memory for Chris, but the last one with his father; he never saw Ronnie again.

From the time he was a baby, Chris was raised by his mother's husband, Joe Jacobs, a kind and loving man who was, as far as Chris was concerned, indistinguishable from a biological father. Joe modeled many of the right things for Chris. He demonstrated a sterling work ethic and a flair for good parenting. He was a carpenter by trade who labored out on the job site all day. Sometimes he took Chris along with him to work, making the little boy clean up the work area and teaching him how to be a responsible laborer.

After work Jacobs usually took Chris to a small farm where they attended to a handful of thoroughbreds. Owning and training horses was Jacobs's hobby. It was Joe, not Ronnie the Kentucky Derby winner, who taught young Chris how to ride a pony.

Most of all, Jacobs taught Chris joy. He designated every Sunday "Funday" in his family, and he set aside time in his busy schedule to take the kids to some amusement park or on some new adventure.

Despite Joe Jacobs's sincere efforts at being a true father, Chris's mother and sister worried about Chris and feared that his childhood was painful and that he was growing up with a certain fragility due to his lack of a relationship with his real father.

But Chris was attached to Joe, and he felt whole in that.

Chris did experience real pain and loss, in high school, when his mother and Jacobs separated and divorced. After the papers were signed and the arrangements finalized, Joe Jacobs disappeared just like Ronnie had. Chris rarely ever saw his stepdad again. With Jacobs gone, Chris's mother fell into addiction, and she was largely absent from the house too. Shirley spent her afternoons and evenings providing for the family by working as a bartender. Without her, the house became chaotic and filled with teenagers every day after school. The Campbell house became a perpetual party venue for the underaged, who were free to do anything they wanted.

Many of the same temptations that had been so alluring to Ronnie many years earlier—pot, booze, and other drugs—were all there for Chris too.

Chris flirted with that lifestyle but ultimately rejected it. Instead he found fulfillment in exactly the way Joe Jacobs had taught him: Chris buried himself in hard work. After high school, he took a job at a local grocery store stocking shelves. It was intended to be only a first job, but he was diligent and hard working, and he quickly climbed the ladder. Eventually Chris was promoted to manager, leaving him in charge of a store with about ninety employees and about $20 million in annual sales.

It is interesting that when Chris became a father, he was something more than just a good one. He was present emotionally and financially for all of the children, including one who wasn't even technically his. That child, a daughter, was conceived in an extramarital affair by his wife. Yet for the first five years of her life the little girl was raised entirely by Chris while her mother was long gone. Chris not only raised the child as his own, but he also did it by himself while working a highly demanding job.

In short, Chris grew up to lead the life Ronnie might have had if he'd never met Buddy Delp. Chris's work ethic and talent, his expansive care for his family, offered a glimpse of who Ronnie might've been had Tony Franklin remained his primary influence instead of Buddy. There was a lot of Tony Franklin in Chris Campbell, though they never really knew each other.

When Chris Campbell was born, Ronnie Franklin was barely nineteen, and he was wriggling under the thumb of a man who terrified and controlled him. By then, Ronnie had already been using highly addictive drugs for at least a year, and Chris's mother was a stranger to him. What chance did Ronnie have to be an adequate father? He was already well down the road to addiction, financial ruin, and public ridicule when his son was still in diapers.

Unfortunately, most of those things were still true almost four decades later. Ronnie's years after racing were marred by his battles with drugs and his struggles to find himself. He went to community college and studied business. He worked a variety of blue-collar jobs. And he turned, at times, to religion. Despite it all, Ronnie's stubborn drug issues persisted, and he was derailed at every turn. After he had been ruled off enough and he was no longer a viable rider, he and Buddy Delp drifted apart. He didn't see much of Gerald either since they were both told to avoid old drug associations.

As Ronnie aged, the rakish good looks that were the hallmarks of his youth were replaced by a more distinguished appearance. His body had expanded so that he was thick around the chest and torso. Thanks to Mother Nature and a razor, his head no longer featured the waving, caramel-colored hair he had enjoyed in his youth.

Ronnie eventually found love again. Many years after his marriage to Jane had ended, he came into contact with Cia Carter, a racing fan who had followed his career from the very beginning. Cia first saw him ride in his earliest races at Laurel, Bowie, and Pimlico. She was only a young girl then, a fan who came to the track with her camera. After a while she realized that she had stopped showing up for the horses and was coming out just to see Franklin. She took many priceless snapshots of his early career, capturing him when he was a glorious and happy young pup as yet untouched by worry and care.

In the many years after that, Cia never stopped thinking of Ronnie. She followed his rise to the top and was still following him well into his endless descent. Long after his career had crashed and burned, she sent him long, deeply expressive fan letters. "You seem to want to do everything on your own," she wrote to him, "but I am here if you need me. You have never let me down. I won't let you down, either."

Cia cared so much for Ronnie, and he was so hard to pin down, that she went to the expense of having a letter delivered to him by hand courier all the way at the track in New Orleans. Ronnie was so touched by it that he showed it to one of his friends around the barn who told him, "Marry that girl!"

He picked up the phone and called Cia to officially reconnect with her, and thereafter she became the most important female presence in his life. She had a radiant smile that had retained its luster into maturity and a kind of genius for kindness and empathy. She was an intelligent and educated woman with complex thoughts and an artistic flair. Her voice was soft and soothing. There was a luxurious comfort to her presence.

Cia also happened to be African American. Ronnie had grown up in an era and in a neighborhood where interracial dating was taboo. But his affection for her underscored that his rough journey through life had changed and softened him. He was once well known, even infamous, for the mean-spirited racial slurs he had slung at Angel Cordero. But Ronnie's relationship with Cia, in its many redemptions, showed that he had moved on from that kind of thinking.

In return for all that Cia gave him, Ronnie gave her a little dignity. She had put on weight as the years had passed, and before she agreed to meet him in person, she wondered aloud if he might have some discomfort with her appearance.

"I want to lose some weight first, before I see you," she told him.

"No," he said. "I don't care about that."

"He was the first man in my life," Cia remembered, "who liked me just the way I was."

Ronnie showed Cia a side of himself that few others knew or recognized. He was kind and gentle with her, soothing in his words and generous in his actions. He showered her with all the few modest gifts he had left to give. Ronnie presented Cia with the winner's circle photographs from his career, one of the few trophies he had not sold for drugs, and a diamond heart pendant that he'd scratched the money together to buy for her.

Occasionally in his later years, Ronnie was invited to racing events, such as a dinner for Kentucky Derby winners, or autograph shows. These nostalgic gatherings offered him the opportunity to relive his days as one of the most improbable kings of the sporting universe. At one event Joe Namath recognized him, and the two smiled and chatted such as two colleagues might.

Mostly, though, Ronnie worked hard to subsist. He performed lower-profile work, the type he had done when he had first broken into racing as a fifteen-year-old. He mucked stalls and walked and rubbed horses. The people who hired him for these jobs liked his personality and appreciated his work ethic.

But drugs always intervened to scuttle any progress his good works might've created.

One of Ronnie's old friends, a trainer named John Bosley, had hired him to ride. The two became so close during this business arrangement that Ronnie actually briefly lived with Bosley's mother.

Bosley not only employed Ronnie, but he also often drove him to work. It was during one of those morning rides that both the long-standing friendship and the partnership hit a rough spot. Ronnie asked the trainer to pull over at a house along the path. He asked the trainer to wait in the car while he ducked into the place for a brief visit. This started to become a regular feature of their morning drive.

Each time, Ronnie exited the car, disappeared into the front door, and then reemerged a short time later. After that they proceeded to work. Curiosity finally got the best of Bosley.

"What do you do in there?" he asked Franklin.

"There's a bookie in there," Ronnie said. "I lay down football bets."

Bosley found out in the most painful way possible that Ronnie had been lying to him. That became apparent in the middle of a race. Riding one of Bosley's horses, Ronnie behaved erratically out on the track, standing up in the irons and sitting back down again for no apparent reason. That was usually a sign that a jockey was no longer riding hard. Ronnie did it several times.

Bosley was enraged. He was so mad that he didn't want to speak to Franklin after the race, though he had the responsibility of driving him back home. As soon as they got into the car, Bosley couldn't contain his anger and he confronted Franklin. "What in the hell were you doing out there!" he shouted. "That was one of the most pathetic things I ever saw.'"

Ronnie didn't even attempt an answer, and they drove home in bitter silence. But the next day, when Bosley picked up Ronnie at 5 a.m. for work, the jockey was finally contrite and ready to explain himself. "John, I'm going to come clean with you," Ronnie said. "You know when I was telling you I was betting on the football games? I was really going in and picking up [cocaine]."

Bosley believed that Ronnie had been high on the track, but Franklin insisted that it wasn't true. Ronnie admitted to using the drugs but said that it was the night before, when he had gotten high long into the evening, like he used to do with Gerald. He hadn't gotten high before the race, he said; he was merely exhausted and out of shape, and that was why he stood up.

That episode ended Ronnie and Bosley's relationship but only for a while. The two track veterans were good friends and shared a mutual respect. Bosley could talk to Ronnie about anything horse-racing related and get feedback from a man who had lived it all at the highest levels.

Eventually Bosley and his client, horse owner Don Pistorio, gave Ronnie another chance. Ronnie worked around Pistorio's stalls and even lived in his barn for a while, sleeping on a blow up mattress. But again, the allure of the drugs was just too much and the effects too obvious. "He was moody," Pistorio said. "Some days he would sleep half the day."

Pistorio was a kindly sort of man, and although he worried about the danger of having a guy like Ronnie around his horses and property, he was more worried about the kid. "Ron, you really need to get some help," Pistorio told him.

Instead Ronnie shoved off from Pistorio's job.

Franklin landed on his feet. He eventually ended up at the Fair Hill Training Center, a heavenly slice of the Eastern Shore of Maryland in Cecil County. It was a racing-training complex reminiscent of Middleburg, only bigger and more vibrant.

At Fair Hill, Ronnie got the best break he'd had in many years. A novice horse owner whom Ronnie had met at a card show made it known that he needed a trainer for his talented young colt. Star-struck by Ronnie's celebrity, the owner rashly hired Franklin to handle his horse. The only thing was, Ronnie had never been a trainer before, and he didn't even have a license to do it. Given his past history with drugs and his having been ruled off so many times, it was unclear if he could even obtain one. "Everyone told us, warned us off him," the owner said. "But we really liked him."

The owner committed to Ronnie and then went all in. He ferried Franklin around to convene with more experienced trainers and get their advice. More than that, he signed a lease for an apartment for Ronnie and directly paid the rent. He also provided Franklin with a car and bought and paid for his groceries.

Despite these advantages and kindnesses, despite the opportunity to start over with a new career, Ronnie's addiction issues still loomed. "I tried to be careful and pay his bills directly instead of handing him money," the owner said. "But he found a way around that."

Ronnie would go to the feed store to purchase needed tools and supplies. Afterward he would show the owner his receipts to confirm that he'd spent the money for its intended purposes. But then he'd turn around and sell the same implements he'd just bought to get the cash back and use it for drugs.

After a while, Ronnie asked his patron for a loan. He offered his Preakness trophy as collateral. "I knew he'd sold it a long time ago," the horse owner said.

On another occasion Ronnie went into the tack room of another trainer to offer her a "business opportunity." "Would you like to buy a bottle of clenbuterol?" Ronnie asked her.

Clenbuterol is a bronchial dilator that is used to help horses that are considered "bleeders." Veterinarians typically distribute it by prescription only and only in acute episodes. Prolonged use can make the animal resistant to it. It is also a drug used for cheating since it is believed to have a steroidal effect.

"Where did you get that bottle?" she asked him.

"Somebody was supposed to pay me to ride, but they gave me the bottle instead," Ronnie said.

The trainer knew about Franklin's reputation with drug abuse. Taking that into consideration, she decided that the bottle was likely stolen and the money he'd make by selling it would be used to get high. She didn't want any piece of it or him. "No thank you," she said, "but thanks for coming by."

More than forty years after Ronnie started using drugs with Buddy Delp, he was still an addict, reduced to grifting and hustling. Sensing he had to do something to save his own life, Ronnie quit his training job and moved to Southern California, where he checked himself into a Salvation Army rehabilitation clinic. One of his old friends correctly called it "a Betty Ford clinic for the indigent."

For a full year, Ronnie was an inpatient living on the campus. He was learning to control his desire to get high and also picking up menial job skills. He received a certificate of achievement for completing a class in janitorial work. He communicated with Cia from California and told her his goal was to finally kick the drug habit and leave racing behind forever. He wanted to start over with a new career.

Racing was a part of his uncomfortable past, and despite his talent and accomplishments, there were too many negative memories associated with that life. His new ambition was to be a drug counselor and help others beat the addiction issues that had swallowed his life and career.

As Ronnie prepared to finish his program and leave the Salvation Army, however, he picked up a little cold. After a while it worsened to flu-like symptoms, and he was fatigued and slept longer than usual. It didn't appear to be anything serious. But his symptoms were stubborn and refused to go away, so the Salvation Army personnel sent him to see a doctor. After a round of testing the medical staff knew for sure that he didn't have a cold or a flu. He was diagnosed with inoperable lung cancer.

After everything he had been through, after all that he had suffered and overcome, he was now living under a death sentence.

Franklin returned to Maryland and moved in with his sister in her suburban Baltimore townhouse. He was a hit with her friends, winning them over with his sense of humor and colorful personality. But with each passing month he was reminded of the seriousness of his condition. He got weaker and weaker.

As he approached the end, the pain was excruciating. He didn't want to take the highly addictive pills prescribed for him by his doctor; they made him nauseous and provided him no relief. So he returned to what he knew. Though his addictions had been under control for about a year, he found cocaine again, and for once, without regret, remorse, or fear, he used it to ease his torturous suffering.

Ronnie died in Baltimore with his family around him, still a few years removed from his sixtieth birthday. At his request, he was cremated and his ashes were scattered on his father's grave, reuniting their molecules and restoring the paternal line that had been severed so long ago when he had been far too young to leave.

There was no chance to fix anything anymore; there was not time left to make anything right. Ronnie had crossed the wire.

It was hard to believe that a boy who had once been so vividly alive, who had captivated an entire nation with his talent and audacity, was now merely buoyant dust floating on the wind and not riding it.

Afterword

It was a testament to just how ugly and hidden this story was that the list of people who would not return my calls or speak to me was almost as long and prominent as the list of those who did.

One retired journalist from Spectacular Bid's era, now working in racing instead of covering it, not only turned down my interview request, but he also sent me on a wild goose chase to waste my time. Another ex-journalist who had covered the story back in the 1970s refused to answer my questions unless I provided them to him in advance. Prominent Hall of Fame jockeys who were friends or business associates of Buddy Delp ducked me, undoubtedly not wanting to be connected to the behaviors I would dredge up. Some of Buddy Delp's family members ignored me too.

But the people who spoke to me left an indelible image on me. Without fail, they were candid, honest, and even courageous. Three of these happened to be most connected to the center of the story.

The first one was Tony Cullum. I met him at his aunt's house just days after Franklin had succumbed to cancer. It was the same house where Ronnie spent his last days before moving on to a hospice. Tony was the first one to speak up to me and tell me about Buddy Delp's role in Ronnie Franklin's drug use and demise.

Cullum said that Delp had "humiliated" Franklin early on and "set him up" to "take the fall" if and when the Bid lost or failed to achieve his potential. More troubling than that, Cullum claimed that "Bud Delp did more cocaine than Ronald did." He said that Buddy used cocaine side by side with Franklin and his own teenage son, Gerald. "Ronald lived in that house with the Delps," Tony said, "and it was a 24-7 party."

Frankly, it was hard to believe Tony. Buddy was a revered figure in Baltimore. He had a huge reputation. Not only that, but he also worked for Harry Meyerhoff, one of the richest and most respected men in the state. It was awfully difficult to imagine Delp and Meyerhoff leading an operation that turned a fifteen-year-old child into a coke addict. It simply didn't seem plausible.

Nevertheless, I decided to look into Tony Cullum's allegations and see if I could substantiate some of what he said, but candidly I didn't expect to find any corroborating evidence. My feeling was that Tony was still angry and in shock at having lost Ronnie, his uncle, a man he loved and looked up to. I thought perhaps that he was merely lashing out.

With a little investigation I found Gerald Delp. He was living in a rented house north of Philadelphia. I wrote him a text message and asked him if I could talk to him about the Bid. I didn't explain everything I wanted to know, but I didn't expect to hear back from him. But he almost immediately answered me, and sight unseen he invited me to his modest home for a visit.

I accepted, but I was a little apprehensive too. I had to ask Gerald some very uncomfortable questions about his father, a man he probably loved and looked up to. I thought there was a better chance that he would haul off and slug me then tell me anything useful.

I needn't have worried. When I got there, Gerald was shuffling along in bed clothes, severely weakened from advanced lung disease. He had to have the assistance of an external oxygen tank and a plastic tube forcing air into his nose just so that he could breathe. But more than that, Gerald was a kind and gentle guy. He welcomed me in, offered me a seat at his table, and got me a cold drink.

When we got down to business, I went through my questions, beginning with a few that were noncontroversial. He answered each one pleasantly and thoroughly. If I asked a follow-up, he went into more detail. He never complained or evaded.

I enjoyed talking to Gerald, and I liked him. But the most important thing was I could see that he knew just about everything there was to know about his father, Ronnie, and Spectacular Bid. He was a witness to it all and a confidante to everyone. But I still had not asked him the big questions. In fact, my heart pounded in my chest as I worked up to them.

"Some people in Ronnie's family are still bitter," I began.

"I understand that," he replied, biting off my preamble in his haste.

"They said there was a lot of cocaine in the house," I said.

"There was," he quickly replied.

"They also said that your father was a coke user."

This time he looked at me long and hard with his sad, weary, and watery eyes. And then the real conversation began.

Gerald, that day and over a series of many interviews, was candid, lucid, and even eager for the truth to be told. He didn't look good in his own stories, and neither did his father, but he believed in the redemption of confession, and he told me about everything that he personally had witnessed, which was just about everything.

The next important person I met was Cathy Rosenberger. Cathy had seen me interviewed on television, talking about Spectacular Bid, and then sent me an email. We spoke by phone later, and Cathy told me all about her role in Buddy Delp's organization and in Ronnie's development as a rider. Cathy filled many roles for me, including technical adviser, proofreader, and editor. Her personal story is one of the few in the book that ends happily. After racing, she moved on to a career in residential real estate, where her natural talents for being friendly, ruthlessly organized, and level-headed led to a highly successful life. She lived in Columbia, Maryland, in a suburban home, not far from Laurel Race Track. She was living an affectionate and fulfilling life with her longtime companion, Ed, taking care of Ed's business. A highly intelligent and engaging woman, Cathy also was working on researching and writing books of her own. Over the years she had lost much of her eyesight but still had keen insights on just about everything related to racing.

The most fascinating interviews I did for this book were with the trio of Hispanic riders: Angel Cordero Jr., Jacinto Vasquez, and Ruben Hernandez.

When I first called Angel Cordero, I told him I wanted to talk to him about Spectacular Bid, and he briefly put me off. "Call me back in forty-five minutes," Angel said. But when I called back, he let it ring a while before he answered. When he finally picked up, he wasn't so sure he wanted to talk.

"Look," he said. "I never rode Spectacular Bid, and I never had anything to do with that horse. I think you got the wrong guy."

"This is Angel Cordero Jr.?"

"Yes," he said. "But I'm not too crazy about doing an interview on a horse that I never rode or anything. There's not much I could tell you about it."

"Mr. Cordero," I said, "you are one of the most interesting horsemen, one of the most interesting men, of the twentieth century. I would like to include you in my story."

"I never even rode a horse that could compare with him," Angel said.

We went back and forth that way for a little while before Cordero admitted he was worried about his "bad side" showing up in the story. "Everyone has a bad side, Mr. Cordero," I said. "Me included. It's what makes us interesting as human beings."

After that, we agreed to talk, and we had a rather lengthy interview. I found Cordero to be smart, charming, articulate, and very intimidating. He was guarded but honest. In retrospect, he was wise to be concerned about how he would appear in the story because forty years later he knew and remembered what had happened and how he had behaved. And it wasn't good.

In many, if not most, situations Cordero's crazy-aggressive tactics, his dangerous movements, could be written off as almost positive, the traits of a man dedicated and obsessed with victory and willing to pay any price to achieve it. In Ronnie Franklin's story, however, his work habits, even his brilliance, took on a more sinister quality as they stood in relief to the immolation of a promising young rider who was not yet twenty years old.

When I first spoke to Jacinto Vasquez on the phone, he also claimed to not want to speak to me but for vastly different reasons.

"You are a writer?" he asked.

"Yes," I said.

"So," he shot back, "are you a Communist or a socialist?"

I imagined he was sitting back in his easy chair in his Florida retirement, watching quite a bit of Fox News. He railed for a few minutes about "AOC," the congresswoman from New York, Alexandria Ocasio-Cortes, and also against Jewish voters.

"What's the matter with the Jews?" he asked me.

"I don't know," I said.

And then he answered his own rhetorical question: "They voted for that fucking Obama, and he screwed them," he said, cracking up laughing at his own answer.

Like Cordero, Vasquez was a fascinating and competitive man, a legendary rider also willing to do questionable things to win. But there was no shame or regret in his voice, only humor and an inherent decency. Rare among the characters in this story, he was forgiving and one of the few figures from either the racing or journalism worlds who understood that Franklin was still essentially a child in 1979 and in need of dispensation.

Vasquez was the bluntest, and profanest, person I spoke to, though he dropped his expletives with perfect comedic timing. I asked him about the infamous Preakness race in 1980 in which he rode the Kentucky Derby–winning filly Genuine Risk against Cordero and his horse, Codex. Cordero won by four and three-quarter lengths but only after riding Vasquez out to the parking lot.

After the race, Jacinto claimed foul and said that Cordero had interfered with his horse by whipping her in the face with his crop. The stewards upheld Cordero's victory, but the case went to court anyway. Cordero's brilliant Baltimore lawyer, Arnold Weiner, widely hailed as one of the very best barristers in the country, successfully argued from photographic evidence that Angel was too far away from Genuine Risk to have impeded her in any way. Weiner won the case, and Codex's victory was assured.

I had to ask Jacinto anyway: "Did Cordero whip your horse?"

"Did he whip her? You're goddamned right he whipped her; he whipped the living fuck out of her," Vasquez said.

"Do you still hold a grudge against Angel?"

"Nah," Jacinto said. "A few years earlier, I barbecued him. I ran him into the hedges in Atlantic City. I knew he'd get me back sooner or later; it just happened to be at the Preakness."

Ruben Hernandez, the jockey who defeated Spectacular Bid in 1979 to win the Belmont Stakes, was temperamentally as different as he could be from Cordero and Vasquez. Hernandez was a calm man, with a good sense of humor, and analytical.

It is interesting that one of the first things he told me was, "I am happy with my career." My sense was that he assumed that I or others might have regarded him as a mediocrity. But how could a rider who beat the fastest horse in the world and pulled off the biggest upset in history on one of the most highly anticipated racing days ever be average or undistinguished? The thing about Hernandez that stuck out for me was his love for his wife and the role she played in inspiring him.

I spoke to one other jockey of consequence to this story, and that was Stevie Cauthen. I dialed him up soon after Franklin died. He was clearly sad and moved by the circumstances of Franklin's early death and troubled life.

Cauthen interested me because he provided almost a mirror on Franklin. They were in an exclusive club of teenagers who rode in and won Triple Crown races. They were almost the same age; had grown up in the same era; and had experienced the same unique pleasures, pressures, and opportunities. Very few other people in the world experienced life like either one of them.

But Cauthen's experience was a far happier one from start to finish. He won the Triple Crown and then became the only jockey to ever be named "Sportsman of the Year." He beat out Muhammad Ali and Reggie Jackson for the distinction. What's more, he enjoyed unprecedented financial opportunities outside of the track. He married happily and has so far lived a healthy life.

Cauthen, who never had a whiff of scandal about him, knew all about the temptations and pressures. "When you have a lot of success, people expect you to do man-size things," he said. "If you have been successful in the past, they expect you to continue to be successful."

The difference between Franklin and himself, Cauthen said, was his parents' experience in the racing industry. Ronnie's mother and father didn't really know anything about the business of horse racing. So they had to put their trust in Buddy Delp.

"Many young jockeys find bumps in the road," Cauthen said. "When you're young, you're so dumb that sometimes you don't even know when you're in a bad situation; you think everything is great."

And that was exactly how Ronnie felt with Buddy Delp.

I also looked in on the Meyerhoff family, starting with Tom. He was kind enough to invite me to his modest but nice Manhattan apartment, where he still had Spectacular Bid's mementos, including the Preakness trophy, and a striking painting of the great horse.

Tom was still much like he had been in the late 1970s, a nice-looking man and in good shape, but no longer young. He was more than sixty years old and a new grandfather when we met, a good bit older than his dad had been the year the Bid ran for the Triple Crown.

Obviously an articulate and intelligent man, Tom was as insightful and candid as he could be, although I asked him to recount some stories that must have been painful for him, including the dissolution of his parents' marriage, the things that went wrong with Spectacular Bid, and his father's alcohol and drug use.

Tom said that the Meyerhoffs' view of Buddy Delp was simple and succinct. "Buddy was family," he said. Their affection for Buddy was based on his professional skills. "Buddy had a great eye," Tom said. Their belief in his character came from their observation that Delp "always put the horses first." But Tom also said that the Meyerhoffs knew nothing of the inner workings of Buddy's relationship with their jockey. And as things went south with Ronnie, they had no sense of how much Buddy might have had to do with the kid's issues. They simply didn't ask.

A few years after the Bid's magical run, Harry Meyerhoff purchased a historic building and property in one of the United States' most picturesque small towns, St. Michaels, Maryland. He used his skills as a developer to reimagine the ancient site as a hotel, bar, and restaurant that he called the Inn at Perry Cabin.

Although Harry was an adept and polished man, aspects of his private life sometimes came spilling out in embarrassing ways for others to see. One of his employees at the inn, a young college-age man, accused Harry of using the bar to traffic drugs. In a letter to Harry the young man asked for "tuition money" from Harry to keep his mouth shut about the alleged trafficking. Instead of paying the ransom, Harry immediately alerted the police, who arrested the young man. They found no merit to his claims, but the incident spoke to the larger truth of Harry's addiction issues. When it was all over, Harry continued his life as a functioning alcoholic and a regular marijuana smoker.

Harry and Teresa's storybook love affair eventually fell apart too. Although they had been visibly and deeply in love for much of their marriage, they began to fight and did so loudly, regardless of who was around to hear it. Eventually Teresa met another man on the Eastern Shore, and she left Harry to be with him.

When Teresa and Harry divorced, the loss was devastating to Harry, who enjoyed her affection so much that he had once risked everything for it. Because he had loved her, she walked away with a generous settlement. They were two halves of a glamorous and highly successful partnership, something that would always connect them in the eyes of the public, but they both moved on, and eventually they married other people.

Teresa settled down to a happy life in New England with her new husband. After a long and successful third marriage Harry died of complications due to a stroke in 2016. He was still living at Hawksworth Farm at the time of his death.

When I spoke to Teresa, it was at the height of the pandemic, and I did so by Zoom platform. She was in the neighborhood of seventy but still an attractive woman and a highly cheerful person. She was generally mistrustful of reporters but agreed to speak to me and did so in the spirit of the request. She was quite candid and even revealed to me her own brief flirtation with cocaine. She also corroborated what Tom had said about the Meyerhoffs knowing literally nothing about the inefficacies in Buddy's relationship with Ronnie. She asked me to tell her what I knew, and when I ticked off the drug stories and financial issues, she broke down and sobbed and ended the interview. "You have to believe me," Teresa said. "Had I known about these things then, I would have done everything in my power to stop it."

I did believe her. But in all candor, I felt that she and her husband and stepson all might've taken a more active interest in a teenager who was clearly and visibly imploding under their watch.

A few years after he rode Spectacular Bid, the horse's "other jockey," Willie Shoemaker, retired from racing with virtually every record in the books. It was a fitting end to his prodigious and historic career. When he was done riding, he enjoyed a successful second career as a trainer.

Shoe's life was changed forever, however, by something as simple as a long day of golfing capped by a few beers. Somewhere along the way home, he reached for his phone, lost control of his vehicle, and rolled it over an embankment. It was a single-car accident, but he was paralyzed from the neck down, and he never walked again.

Shoemaker's wife left him soon after that tragedy, but as always, he emerged triumphant. He guided his horses and riders to ninety victories and almost $4 million in earnings, all from his wheelchair. He died in 2003.

Angel Cordero Jr. continued on his torrid pace as one of the most skilled, respected, fearless, and—especially—feared riders in racing history. He never admitted any untoward behavior in regard to Ronnie Franklin or Spectacular Bid in 1979.

Cordero said he didn't collude with Georgie Velasquez in the Florida Derby. He didn't ride Ronnie out to the parking lot in the Preakness. And he didn't intentionally ram Franklin in the days leading up to the Belmont Stakes. But he recalled with particular vehemence Franklin's statements to the press, the physical altercations they had, and also the writers' portrayals of him.

As far as Angel was concerned, whatever happened, happened. And the things people said about him were irrelevant. "They wrote so much shit about me," Cordero said, "but I never worry about me. I know what I can do. I know what I was. And I know who I am. I didn't become a jockey to sleep with anybody. I became a jockey to make a living."

And a hard living it was.

In 1986 Cordero was riding High Falutin when the horse went down.

Cordero sustained catastrophic injuries, tearing his liver into seven pieces; puncturing his lung; and fracturing his ankle, tibia, and elbow.

In 1990, he went down again. This time, riding Gray Tailwind in a simple claiming race, he was part of a five-horse accident. Again, he tore his liver into seven pieces, ruptured his spleen, broke four ribs, punctured his lung, and fractured his arm and elbow.

It was all the byproduct of a style that was either daring or ruthless, depending on how one viewed him. No one, it seemed, who witnessed his brilliant and controversial career was indifferent to him. The thin line between love and hate, for Cordero, was respect.

Without regard for affection, everyone had to agree that Angel Cordero Jr. was one tough hombre and a great rider.

Buddy Delp remarried and started a new family with his wife, Regina. They had a daughter, Pajeen, and a son, Cleve, both of whom loved horses and worked at the track. After Spectacular Bid, Buddy sold his house in Laurel and expanded his operations in New Orleans, California, and Chicago. He remained a successful trainer.

Buddy was inducted into the horse racing Hall of Fame at Saratoga, New York, in 2002. His record was unassailable. His 3,674 wins were good enough to put him in the top ten all time, and he had won $41 million in purses.

About ten years after Buddy's magical ride with the Bid ended at the Belmont Stakes, he was once again asked by a reporter about that fateful day. In 1979 he had put responsibility on his own shoulders and also invoked the catastrophic safety pin. In 1989 it was a whole different story. "There's no doubt in my mind that Shoemaker would have won on Spectacular Bid that day, with or without the pin," Buddy said. "It was a mile-and-a-half race, and after about half a mile, Ronnie was running past an 80–1 shot, taking the lead with a mile to run. Had he just laid back there and relaxed the colt, I still believe he would've won the race."

Buddy summed up a lot of conventional thinking in that statement, but he never mentioned his desire, as stated to Jacinto Vasquez, to beat Secretariat's record time that day or his unwise Belmont instructions to Ronnie. He was the one who demanded that the young jockey "take 'em away"—that is, take an early lead—but ten years later, with Ronnie's reputation in tatters, that detail slipped Buddy's memory.

Delp's "expert opinion" was nothing more than a few lies and a massive betrayal of his protégé.

As the years went by, Buddy would do much more harm to Ronnie Franklin's reputation, often speaking "frankly" to journalists about Ronnie and his problems. "[Franklin] could've been as good as anyone in the sport," Buddy told the great broadcaster Jim McKay, who included Buddy and Ronnie in his memoirs. Buddy misled McKay, leading him to believe that Franklin's demise was in trying "cocaine . . . at the suggestion of friends."

In a sense, that was a true statement. But Buddy himself was the "friend" who suggested those first lines of coke to Ronnie. He was the one who led Ronnie and Gerald into addiction with his full knowledge, blessing, and participation.

Buddy died of cancer in 2006. In his lifetime he was never publicly connected to Ronnie's or Gerald's substance abuse issues.

Gerald's life was complicated by addiction issues, in one way or another, for many more decades. He suffered two divorces, the loss of his wealth, and crippling health issues. By 2019 he was living in suburban Philadelphia, near the Parx Race Track, in a small white rented home with a front door that was practically on the highway.

For many months Gerald walked around in a near-death state, connected by tubes to a large oxygen tank. He passed his days waiting for the phone to ring, hoping to hear someone tell him that they had new lungs for him. That call finally came, and he underwent a successful transplant operation in 2019, though he almost died due to complications from his life-saving surgery. After that he suffered cardiac issues and eventually required yet another set of lungs.

As this book was being written, Buddy's brother and one-time assistant trainer, Dick Delp, died. A mere few days after that, Buddy's daughter, Pajeen, died from a cardiac issue. A few months earlier she had refused to go to the hospital after a cardiac event because she lacked health insurance. On the day she died, Pajeen was still a few years shy of her fortieth birthday.

Nor was Spectacular Bid immune from problems in the ensuing years. Although he lured a king's ransom in breeding fees, he wasn't much of a sire. He sired forty-seven stakes winners but not a single champion.

After years of trying but producing little, the Bid left Kentucky's prestigious Claiborne Farm, where he lived in a barn near Secretariat's, and moved to a secluded pastoral locale in upstate New York. He continued to breed up there but was no longer under the same expectations.

The great horse had a heart attack and died on June 9, 2003, exactly twenty-four years to the day since his mysterious defeat in the Belmont Stakes. His caretakers asked the Meyerhoffs if they wanted his remains shipped back to them at Hawksworth Farm. They declined. The Bid might have been the greatest horse of the twentieth century, and he was certainly the most sensational horse to ever come out of Maryland after centuries of racing there.

But Spectacular Bid was laid to rest in New York state, forever an exile who couldn't quite make it back home.

Acknowledgments

Any expression of gratitude connected to the creation of this book must begin with my triumvirate of sources—Tony Cullum, Gerald Delp, and Cathy Rosenberger. I admired and respected all three of them for their courage and their willingness to speak up and tell their uncomfortable truths to me.

No one on this planet knew Ronnie Franklin better than Tony did. He was Ronnie's nephew, though he was raised in the same house with him like a brother. Tony was Ronnie's confidant, and he was able to pass on many of the facts and feelings that Franklin knew and experienced. Most of all, Tony was the first one to tell me how different the real story was from the one that had been reported for so many years. He is a living monument to why a writer must go to the primary sources, the living, breathing people, and ask them over and over: "What really happened here?" I found out only thanks to Tony. Everything he ever told me was corroborated by others who were also in a position to know.

Gerald was not only Buddy Delp's son but also his workmate. He was also Ronnie's agent and, for most of their lives, Ronnie's best friend. Gerald was always available to me and helped me fill in many gaps. He was utterly courageous in admitting many details about his own life and his father's that most other people would have buried. When I met him, he had already been through addiction recovery and was staring death in the face. He had a desire to set the record straight and get the details right.

I worked more closely on this book with Cathy Rosenberger than any other individual. She worked in Buddy Delp's organization for a number of years and described its inner workings, strengths, and failures to me. But she was much more than a source. Cathy also read my work as I wrote it and scrutinized it to make sure it would pass muster with track insiders, who demand that racing's customs, nomenclature, and facts are presented properly. Cathy is an extraordinarily bright person who can tackle any difficult task and become proficient if not excellent in performing it. She has an extremely lively mind and a talent for organization. She also introduced me to many key sources in this book. And she helped edit the book as well. I cannot stress enough how generous she was to me or how essential she was to the finished product.

I also wanted to thank the jockeys who took their time to speak to me and share their information: Steve Cauthen, Angel Cordero Jr., Richard Duncan, Ruben Hernandez, and Jacinto Vasquez. All of them were candid and illuminating.

No one was ever backed up by a better agent or editor than the ones I have had. Rob Taylor, my acquisitions editor at the University of Nebraska Press for both of my books, embraces my work like no other publishing professional. I admire him for many reasons. I also want to thank Sara Springsteen for her tireless work and Bojana Ristich, the extraordinarily excellent copyeditor and proofreader.

Emily Williamson, of the Williamson Literary Agency, has been a zealous representative and a tireless and tolerant listener of outrageous profanity and invective.

I would have fallen to pieces over the course of the project without the support of my family and friends. Gerry Frank and Margie Valin mean the world to me and provide me a great deal of emotional support in everything I do and go through. Evan and Alexis Davis literally kept me moving. Evan has been my best teammate, best friend, business partner, and adviser. Alexis, his beautiful wife, treats me like I was her own brother.

My sister, Juliet Gilden, a talented artist achieving great things in the creative world, gave me a standard of excellence to which to aspire and daily creative advice. My cousin Rina Kaplan has been my biggest cheerleader for my entire life.

I also want to thank the friends who have supported me: Steve Belkowitz, one of the best professional photographers in the country; Larry Lichtenauer, the go-to public relations professional in the Baltimore-Washington area; Chris Hamby, an honest-to-god lumberjack and an old high school buddy who helped me procure an important early interview; Amir Kahn, Dave Scherr, and Darlene Yeager, at K&S Auto, who kept my car running so I could write.

Two sets of brothers also deserve my thanks. The Layugs (Joe, John, and Tom) and the Zissimos boys (Rob and Pete). Pete Zissimos and I were high school football teammates and favorite friends to each other. He died while I was writing this manuscript. I am still heartbroken about that and will be for the rest of my life. He was the friendliest and funniest guy I ever knew.

I also want to mention some of my Washington College friends who supported me in various ways: Skip Middleton, Sheaffer Reese, Peter Shafer, Richard Bagby, Travis Aldous, and David Hilliard.

Also a special thanks to a few more Washington College people: Claire Ricci, a librarian who believed in my work, and Beth Keyser, the best assistant, indexer, and marketing adviser an author ever had. Tim Gray and his wife, Christine Franek Gray, helped me a lot, and so did Tommy Moore and his wife, Diane.

Barry Gogel was always there to save me in a multitude of ways.

I want to thank my teachers and coaches from Owings Mills High School: Keith Taylor, Ken "Speedie" Johnson, Kathy Freeman, Ann Kenney, Elizabeth Sherman, James Bradley, and Sharon Dorsey. From Washington College, I thank Richard Gillin. Every single one was an extraordinary mentor who shaped my thinking and kept my life going in the right direction.

From the journalism world, Michael Olesker, my personal hero, and John Eisenberg, an accomplished author, have always been there for me when I needed them. Mark Kram Jr. has the bloodlines of a thoroughbred writer—his father was a legendary boxing writer—and Mark is a great prose stylist too. He exhorted me to work harder and improve my work. He also introduced me to other writers who were valuable interviews and gave me great advice.

I also want to thank Dean Smith, a terrific poet, a publishing professional, and a friend to anyone who loves Baltimore and appreciates great writing.

In Middleburg, Virginia, Vicky Moon and Len Shapiro, two writers who are married to each other, treated me like a friend and also provided valuable information and advice. Sharon Maloney and Kristin Dillon Johnson were also very helpful in Middleburg and gave me my best glimpses of Barbara Graham and her magnificent operation there. They also connected me with others who understood Barbara and her world, especially Junie Marlow.

I was aided greatly in my work by the dynamic sister duo of horse trainer Sherene Bracho and her assistant trainer, Su Chung. These two have an incredible work ethic and a great sense of humor. They each have their own lives but are dedicated to each other too. Sherene helped me find many of the most important interviews in this book, especially the jockeys. Georgia Andreadakis, another horse trainer and a friend of Ronnie Franklin's, also helped me find important sources.

Roxy Roman, a good friend of mine, helped me understand Latin American culture. And Dika Seltzer discussed many different aspects of this project with me.

Donna Delovich has been one of my best friends for many years. Her friendship has been one of the most meaningful I have ever had.

Mary Jo Cranmore is an intelligent, good-hearted, and highly generous person. She really helped me. A special thanks to her.

Selected Bibliography

The research for this book was mostly conducted through personal interviews. That was essential since much of what had been written in the past was simply inaccurate. Nevertheless, I also did a great deal of secondary research to understand how events were viewed contemporaneously to their occurrences.

Grisel, Judith. *Never Enough: The Neuroscience and Experience of Addiction.* New York: First Anchor Books, 2019.

Mitchell, Derek. *Steve Cauthen.* London: Partridge Press, 2007.

Obama, Barack. *Dreams from My Father.* New York: Three Rivers Press, 1995.

Phillips, Mackenzie, with Hilary Liftin. *High on Arrival: A Memoir.* New York: Gallery Books, 2009.

Pietila, Antero. *Not in My Neighborhood: How Bigotry Shaped A Great American City.* Chicago: Ivan R. Dee, 2010.

Rogers, Marian Elizabeth. *Mencken: The American Iconoclast, the Life and Times of the Bad Boy of Baltimore.* New York: Oxford University Press, 2005.

Sahadi, Lou. *Affirmed: The Last Triple Crown Winner.* New York: Thomas Dunne Books, 2011.

Michael Anderson
Georgia Andreadakis
Carl Jackson Beckner
John Bosley
Sherene Bracho
William "Willie" Brown
Chris Campbell
Bruce Carter
Cia Carter
Steve Cauthen
Su Chung
Angel Cordero
Tony Cullum
Gerald Delp
Nancy Graham Dillon
Judith DiNatale
Richard Duncan
Janet Elliot
Alan Foreman
Carolyn Franklin
Marian Franklin
Anthony Grigsby
Judith Grisel
Alexis Harthill
Ruben Hernandez

Shirley Holthaus
Joanne Houle
Donna Hunter
Dick Jerardi
Kristin Dillon Johnson
Theodore Madfis
Sharon Maloney
Horace "Junie" Marlow Jr.
Greg McCarron
Tom Meyerhoff
Nancy Cusimano Morris
Paula Parsons
Teresa Meyerhoff Pete
Don Pistorio
Scott Regan
Mark Reid
Cathy Rosenberger
Deborah Rudacille
Jane Scuto
Bonnie Smajda
Dr. James Stewart
John Dale "J. D." Thomas
Jacinto Vasquez
Alix White

Index

Pistorio, Don, 287
Pitts, Clinton, Jr., 205
Playboy, 172
poker, 106, 133, 175, 235, 277
Polinger, Milton, 27
Pope, Edwin, 193
Pope, George, 168
Port Ebony, 128
Povich, Shirley, 175
Preakness Stakes, 31, 46, 57, 123, 192–
    93, 200, 264
Puerto Ricans, 117–20, 136–37, 139,
    185, 201, 209, 225
Puerto Rico, 136, 139, 230, 237

racism, 53–54, 73, 117, 121, 158, 169
Reed, Billy, 193
Regan, Scott, 104–5
Reid, Mark, 36, 105, 218, 246
Relaunch, 258–60
Rettaliata, Jane, 279
Rettele, Loren, 180
Rickey, Branch, 9
Ridder, Bernard "Ben," 166
Rodgers, Marian Elizabeth, 67
Rosenberger, Cathy, 24, 34, 42–44, 58–
    59, 106, 134, 156, 162, 293
Rouse, James W., 69–71
Rouse Company, 70–72, 188
Rudacille, Deborah, 10–11
Ruffian, 120
Ruth, Babe, 4, 46, 94, 272

Salvation Army Rehabilitation Clinic,
    288–89
San Felipe Handicap, 167
San Fernando Stakes, 258–59
Santa Anita Derby, 167
Santa Anita Handicap, 253
Saturday Night Fever, 159

Scanlan's Monthly, 172
Schaefer, William Donald, 75, 189
Schapiro, John D., 20
Screen King, 178, 180, 184, 198–99
Seabiscuit, 50, 56, 126, 247
Seattle Slew, 57, 128, 169, 180, 262, 264
Secretariat: and Belmont Stakes, 224–
    25, 234, 300; and Kentucky Derby,
    169, 180–81, 183–84; and Laurel
    Futurity, 130–31, 136; and Lucien
    Laurin, 180, 232; and Preakness
    Stakes, 200; retirement of, 108, 302;
    and Ron Turcotte, 212; and Spec-
    tacular Bid, 262, 267–68; and Stevie
    Cauthen, 130, 136; and Triple
    Crown, 31, 57
Seethreepeo, 179, 226
Segal, Henry, 60
Seven No Trump, 64
Shoemaker, Willie, 124–25, 148, 168,
    174, 244–49, 254–61, 263, 278,
    299–300
Silberman, James, 172
Sir Ivor Again, 143–44
Ski Pants, 208
Small, "Dicky," 63
Smith, R. A., 251
Smith, Red, 237, 263
Spectacular Bid, 2–3, 6, 91; and Bel-
    mont Stakes, 214, 225–27, 233, 247,
    265–66, 269, 295; and Buddy Delp,
    131–32; career of, 258, 260, 268;
    death of, 302; and Eclipse Award,
    132; and Georgie Velasquez, 127–29;
    and Gerald Delp, 101; and Harry
    Meyerhoff, 64, 131, 164, 244; injury
    of, 214–16, 240; and Jockey Gold
    Cup, 265–67; and Kentucky Derby,
    184; and Preakness Stakes, 200;
    retirement of, 267–68; and Ronnie